GROWING UP ITALIAN

To Linda De Mike, + Brian,
with all good wishes.
Linda Brandi Cateura

1988

PREVIOUS WORK BY LINDA BRANDI CATEURA

Oil Painting Secrets from a Master

GROWING UP ◇ ITALIAN

◇

Linda Brandi Cateura

How being brought
up as an Italian-American
helped shape the characters,
lives, and fortunes of
twenty-four celebrated
Americans

William Morrow and Company, Inc.
New York

Library of Congress Cataloging-in-Publication Data

Cateura, Linda Brandi.
Growing up Italian.

1. Italian Americans—Biography. I. Title.
E184.I8C37   920'.009251073   86-18078
ISBN 0-688-06090-0

Printed in the United States of America

4 5 6 7 8 9 10

BOOK DESIGN BY RICHARD ORIOLO

To
Patty Cateura and Frances Rickett
for their interest and encouragement

PREFACE

These twenty-four memoirs were taken from person-to-person interviews (with one exception) between the subject and the author during the years from 1984 to 1986. For ease in reading, the author's questions have been winnowed out.

Contrary to popular belief, first-generation Americans are people who actually settle in the United States. Second-generation Americans are the children who are born here. Each group is so designated on these pages.

One last point: This book is about Italian-Americans who were born *in the United States*. No one interviewed on these pages is an Italian born in Italy. There is a world of differences between the two. Italian-Americans are a species with qualities that combine two very opposite cultures—the Italian and the Anglo-Saxon—and thus vary greatly from their forebears.

ACKNOWLEDGMENTS

The author wishes to express her appreciation to the Italian-Americans who took time from their super-active lives to talk about their childhoods and summon up the memories and recollections that are the essence of this book.

And she gives special thanks to Harvey Ginsberg of William Morrow, who first saw the possibilities, and Paul Lerner, who, along with Harvey, helped to give the book its shape.

CONTENTS

GROWING UP ITALIAN

The Cuomo store, with proprietors Andrea and Immaculata Cuomo, and son Mario clutching a toy. The two men at right are unidentified.

Mario Cuomo
Papa Mio!

◇

A charismatic personality, Mario Cuomo burst on the American scene when he ran for mayor of New York City in the late 1970s. In fewer than ten years, he achieved national prominence, and he is now being mentioned as a possible candidate for the presidency in 1988 on the Democratic ticket. Belonging to no school of politics but his own, he has wrought an image of personal integrity and strength that has lit the American mind.

Today, as governor of New York, he keeps a tight schedule. This interview took place in New York City one afternoon, as he was being driven uptown to host a call-in radio show. Later, he continued the interview, again on wheels, as he was driven to a Sons-of-Italy dinner in Rockefeller Center.

Did I have a happy childhood? Yes, I think so, but not in the traditional sense of many celebrations together and visits to different parts of the country and Sunday picnics in the park.

I had always assumed that my father was born in Nocera Inferiore in the province of Salerno in Italy. There is no question that *his* father was born in Nocera Inferiore and that my father was raised in Nocera Inferiore.

He was born at Atlantic Avenue and Hicks Street in Brooklyn, on the site of what is now the Long Island College Hospital. Now let me tell you how ironic that is. As a lawyer, I spent a whole professional career practically trying to build that hospital. Margaret, my daughter, was working there as an intern at the time my father died. And we discovered in his papers an old naturalization certificate that described that my grandfather and grandmother had once come to Brooklyn and that my father was born at Atlantic and Hicks. Then they took him back to Nocera Inferiore as an infant. And then he came back. I never knew that.

My mother is from the town of Tramonti in the same province. I have never visited their families or the towns where they were born. I've spoken to them via television three times, most recently on the NBC morning show devoted to Italy. Matilda, my wife, is headed over to Italy soon and I'm sure she'll stop at her family's birthplace in Sicily and my family's in Salerno.

My childhood was extraordinary because my mother and father had a grocery store in which they had to work all the time. For a while, it was open twenty-four hours a day. It was never open for less than eighteen hours a day. It didn't give us a chance to sit down and have meals together or to have that kind of relationship.

Nevertheless, we were a close family. We worked together in the store, and mostly the impact on the family was the example my mother and father set. They didn't make a lot of speeches. They didn't communicate a lot with us in the traditional way. They communicated by example. We saw them working for us, we saw them giving up their whole lives and denying themselves even the simplest kind of enjoyment. I never saw my mother and father go out together. After a while, they went to the movies with us on Sunday mornings.

My father went to a dinner once in his life at the request of an Armour salesman. He never went to a ballgame. He never did anything but work for the kids. And we understood that, even though we were very young. We didn't talk about it, but we understood it. And we watched as he would relate to my mother. They treated one another with this quiet respect.

In my community there were blacks, but mostly there were Italians, Irish, Jews, and Poles. The Italians usually were family-oriented, but so were most of the other ethnic groups. I don't think you can compare childhoods by ethnic background. We have to compare them in terms of economic problems. There have always been the poor, the rich, and the people in-between. I think that people in each of these classes, regardless of background, have more in common than the different ethnicities do.

If there is respect for family among the poor, as there was in my home, it's at least partly because members of poor families need one another. In the same way, many of the poor believe in hard work. For my father, hard work was the answer to all his problems. He had nothing else to see him through.

So by watching him and my mother, I learned respect for family—for one's elders, especially—and belief in the efficacy of work. The overriding sense was of the importance of meeting one's obligations.

Incidentally, I don't ever remember meeting anyone from my family- and work-oriented neighborhood who needed a psychiatrist.

Did I have a happy childhood? Yes, I think so, but not in the traditional sense of many celebrations together and visits to different parts of the country and Sunday picnics in the park. It was a relationship confined in the earliest years to the store and even till the time I got married. You know, I got married and they were *still* in the store. As a matter of fact, the Saturday morning of my wedding, my brother Frank and I stood in the store in our tails and waited on customers. We were there just for kicks. And the store was open during the wedding. We brought some people in to run it for a few hours. My father went back in the afternoon, believe it or not.

There were three boys and one girl in the family. One of the boys died very young, and incidentally, his name was Mario. Contrary to what happens in some Italian families, my parents never gave us the sense that they preferred the boys, as bearers of the family name, to the girls. I didn't feel that my sister, Marie, was treated any differently because she was a girl.

People comment about sexism among Italians. There is a stereotype based on the belief that immigrant Italian men were all sexist males, macho types who made their wife subservient. I would say my mother was deferential to the men, but she was not obsequious, and she was not treated disrespectfully, I don't think. I never sensed a real sexism in our house. We had a specific culture pattern that assigned specific roles to women and men, and the roles were different. To the extent that the women's roles were regarded as demeaning . . .

Matilda and I tend to be very supportive of our children. It has been said that Italian parents let their kids grow up on their own to nourish their own interests and ambitions and that they are not "pals" to their kids. If there is any truth in that, and I'm sure there is, it is a truth confined to a certain generation of Italians, those who actually came over here. I think that quickly disappeared. For example, I am of the generation born here, and there is none of that in our house, I don't think. We don't deal with our children on the assumption that they should be left largely to find their own way. Sometimes we tend, almost oppressively, to give guidance and be oversupportive.

In my mother and father's case, there wasn't a lot of palship; there wasn't a lot of communication. I'm not sure what would have happened if they had had a different life. Because they were in the store all the time, they didn't have the opportunity for palship. They didn't have the opportunity for that kind of communication. So we were left pretty much to our own devices. I'm not sure what would have happened if my father had had more options.

I never felt any prejudice as a child for being Italian—not in grammar school, not in the neighborhood, not in high school, not in college, and not in law school. I felt it *after* I got out of law school, when I began to look around for a law firm. I found that even if you did well in law school, it wasn't easy to get an interview on Wall Street. And I found that at that time it wasn't just being Italian, but being Italian and from a background of non-wealth, if you will. *That* made it difficult to get into a big firm. The big firms in those days were looking for people who had economic class, and this did not include people who came from the class Italians ordinarily came from. That's when I began to feel prejudice.

And then once you get into politics, you become more sensitive to it. There have been instances of it in politics and there still are, even though it is diminishing with each generation. I don't think you had to be hypersensitive to detect some of that in the attacks made on Geraldine Ferraro when she ran for vice-president or on Al D'Amato when he ran for the Senate, in 1980.

I believe there has been discrimination against Italian-Americans. I believe there has been discrimination against Irish-Americans as well as against Jews, and there has been even more discrimination against blacks. However, I don't think that discrimination has been a substantial impediment. The principle impediment was a lack of education, a lack of wealth. As we have gathered more wealth and strength and provided our children with better and more extensive education, we've risen and that will continue to happen. It has happened with the Irish before us, and with the Jews and Italians simultaneously, and I think it will happen with the Puerto Ricans and all the groups that come after us.

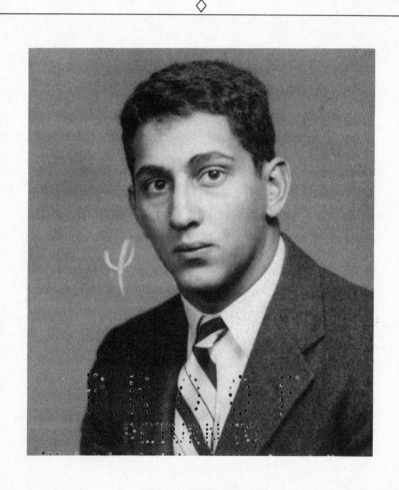

Frank Stella

FRANK STELLA
Flying the Coop

◇

Frank Stella, born in 1936 in Malden, Massachusetts, is an abstract painter whom many people consider one of the most important living artists. He has produced a tremendous and prodigiously varied body of work. Today nearly every museum of modern art has a selection of Stellas.

In his work-living quarters—a nondescript brick building in New York's Greenwich Village that from the street looks like a small factory—he maintains a studio with large pieces of equipment that help to produce his sculptural works of art. On the second floor is a warm, densely furnished living room, where he sat in his work clothes and addressed with concentrated intensity the subject of being Italian.

For my father to have a good time was taking time off to be trivial . . . and so he did it—tried to have a good time with us—out of a sense of duty.

My grandmother's maiden name was Greco. She came from Sicily and met Stella coming over on the boat, right around the turn of the century. He died on the boat. When she disembarked, she was supposedly pregnant, but who knows? She took up with a guy she met on the wharf, a stevedore, and lived with him for the rest of her life. So whether the name is Stella or not may be moot.

During the Depression she was a bootlegger. She made wine and beer. It was not a big operation, but that was how she supported herself. And she would not stop, either. Later on, when my father had the money and she did not need to, she kept on doing it. In those days, everybody was quite tolerant. Nobody bothered her or closed her down, or anything. She ran her own business and made liquor all her life without a license, which is a federal crime [laughs]. She used to serve it in the kitchen. The house was not much of a house.

My father was pretty Italian, but he had trouble with it. The Italian thing was very confused in his life. I think he wanted to get away from it all—you know, the home-and-barroom atmosphere. He did not look upon it as a heritage he really wanted to preserve. His mother's past was something he always tried to hide, and it was hard to know whether it was because she was illiterate or whether it was because her way of making a living, which was bootlegging, was illegal.

My grandmother had four children; my father was the only survivor of the four. They all died of childhood diseases. He himself was not all that healthy—he was pretty small. But he was a good student and went to the parochial school. Then, the big thing was to get out of the Italian neighborhood. Because he was good at school, the sisters did not want to send him to the Catholic high school, which he could have gone to since it was in the neighborhood, but sent him instead to the public high school, where the level of education was higher.

In those days—now they would not dare do this—they used to arbitrarily divide the students on the basis of their ability. They would tell a kid, "You're in the general class"—which meant, you do woodworking. Or, "You're in the commercial class"—which meant, you learn to type. Or, "You're in the college class"—and you studied Latin and algebra and French and the sciences. And so they assigned my father to the college class. That was it. He did not have much to say about it. He did not even know what college meant, but that was the way it was.

I think his education led him toward medicine. Medicine was a meritocracy. If you were poor, you had a better chance in medicine to make a living and have a practice and do things. In medicine, it was harder to put someone down, or to ignore ability.

But when he became a doctor, he was still tied to the old community. He worked within it as an obstetrician, and his patients were mostly the local Italian-Americans. Toward the last half of his career, he gave up obstetrics and was doing more surgery-gynecology and he was getting referrals. And so his practice changed. But for most of his life he worked in the Italian-American community. He was always pretty hard-headed and everything, but he was a real public servant and chose to work among the Italians. He always claimed that he would have had a much more successful medical career had he left greater Boston, which is very competitive. There are a lot of good doctors in Boston. And he had appointments where he could have done his residency in other parts of the country. He claims that he stayed home because of the parents. And he always regretted it. [Laughs.]

My childhood was pretty joyful, though there was a lot of strain and everything from my father. It was always going back to him. In a sense, it was always going back to a kind of working-class roots and mentality because he was a hard-core professional and so for him to have a good time was taking time off to be trivial, something that was not that pleasant to him in the first place. And so he did it—tried to have a good time with us—out of a sense of duty.

But for us kids, it was a nice life. We were pretty close to my grandparents and we used to see them every weekend. We moved out of the Italian neighborhood, but Malden is a small city, so we were still within walking distance of them. I used to spend the summer with my father's mother. She used to take me places. She never learned to speak any English at all—she spoke Sicilian. I never learned to speak any Italian, though I must have managed somehow. Maybe there is some echo there. In the house, we were very big on *not* speaking Italian. It was absolutely *out* and we were supposed to be proficient in English. My mother learned to speak a little Italian, and my father could get by in the Sicilian dialect, though he did understand Italian.

I liked the place where I grew up in Malden. Calling it a ghetto is a bit dramatic—it was not that bad. There was the North End and there was the West End. The West End was really terrible, but they tore that down. The Italian neighborhood was hardly that poor. It was a factory neighborhood and most of the people worked in the Converse Rubber Company. My mother's family had been working on the coffee plantations—they never paid their boat passage from Italy and were paying it off under a contract. The rubber company bought their contract from the coffee people, and the family came up to Waltham, Massachusetts, to work for Converse and later they moved to Malden to work in the Converse factory there. Most of the employees lived in a place called Edgeworth, which was one of the quarters in Malden. That was *all* Italian.

Life was congenial. There were lots of people around, a lot of atmosphere. We used to eat gnocchi all the time. I don't remember eating a lot of spaghetti. Actually, my mother and father lived in a remote, relatively austere way, different from that of the rest of the family. All my cousins and relatives lived a fairly normal Italian-American existence, with an emphasis on family, whereas we lived an isolated existence because we were the only Italian-Americans in a non-Italian community. We were more American than Italian. Not that we chose this—that was just the way we lived. We were not working class. We were middle class, and there was not much of a middle-class Italian community. There were a few isolated professionals like my father, but he was competitive with them. And he did not like them all that much, either.

I have not held on to customs or traditions, but I continue to see my family. We used to visit my grandparents until they died. When my father died, I stayed close to my mother. We have relatives in the North End. We still go back and visit, and they see the children and everything. We make contact, but it is very loose. It is not a sense of community.

On the other hand, I live here just off Bleecker Street, which is pure Italian. My wife is Scotch-Irish, but the Italian cooking in this house is very, very good, largely because the shopping on Bleecker Street is terrific. It is perfect—cheeses, pasta, ham, sausages. So we have Italian cuisine. We eat more pasta now than I did when I was a kid because my mother used to make it only twice a week. And we eat more Italian food now than I did at home with my mother's cooking. She used to do American cooking—baked potatoes, breaded cutlets, and stuff like that. Although my mother is a very good cook, her American cooking is terrible. [Laughs.] If you put that in the book, I will never hear the end of that.

I never thought much about prejudice. Our lives were so out in the open. Our town was divided, like Gaul, into four parts. There were the Italians, there were the white people, there were the Irish, and there were the Jews. That was it. That was the way it was. The neighborhood we were in was slightly mixed. We were in the middle, the downtown area. Our area was sort of amorphous, but actually it was nearest the Jewish quarter. The Italian quarter did not have any schools. There were only two schools you could choose, the Jewish school and the WASP school. Since I was on the borderline district, my father had me transferred from the Jewish school to the WASP school. I do not know how he rigged that, but I was only one street away.

He always felt guilty about my changing schools, though he really did not want me to go to the Jewish school. During the Depression, when he started in practice, it was the Jewish money lenders who lent him the money to start in his practice and he was eternally grateful. When the white people—the banks—would not give him the money, the Jews lent it to him because they had *faith* in doctors. That was one of the few things that people were willing to bet on in the Depression.

Catholicism was a big part of my life—which I liked, actually. But when I got to be a young man and came to New York, it started to be a burden—I guess sexually and psychologically. So I would say that my faith lapsed, as it were. Now I do not see it as such a threat and am more accommodating. But I would not say that I win any prizes. I could make going to mass, now, in a way I could not before.

The Church is a cultural leveler. It was an important part of my education—in ways I did not then realize. When I went away to fancy schools, Andover and Princeton, I found that most of the students who were supposedly better educated were totally illiterate as far as Western culture was concerned. The Church plays a big part in Western culture, and so having some familiarity with it all actually helped me in my education. I had a better way of thinking about it. It gives you a sense of history—maybe I had it anyway—which helped.

Being an Italian Catholic certainly helped me in my painting—going to Italy and seeing the great Christian paintings all over. Catholicism is rich in imagery. It is colorful. As a kid, I loved the robes the priests wore in church. I liked to look at the girls, too. They were always on parade, wearing white dresses. That was not the point of going to church, but it was the best part.

As the firstborn *and* a boy, I felt a tremendous amount of pressure.

My father wanted a worthy successor to his efforts, and everything pointed to the fact that I was a jerk. Maybe I had the ability, but I certainly was not going to do what I was supposed to do. I was too stubborn and recalcitrant and got into too much trouble. For my father, I was just a perpetual agony and anxiety. It was disappointment after disappointment. When I moved to the slums after graduating from Princeton, to him that was a kind of utter defeat. It was a bitter pill to swallow. There was no way of explaining to him. He just found it totally alien.

At Andover, everyone knew I was Italian. I was not embarrassed by my Italian name and I really did not care. I knew I was going to get it, and everything. Andover was *so* fabulous. . . . The guys who were assholes were assholes—I did not care. One of the things at being at a place like Andover is that it is at such a high level that the mere fact that you are *there* makes you equal, if not better, than the others. It does not matter that they have a lot more money or a lot more privilege—they still have to function. And it is a kind of funny reversal. They still have to function at *your* level. They have to prove they are as smart as you are. With a lot of them, it is quite a trauma: a kind of reverse . . . and they have to prove they are as tough as you are. It is not a happy experience for a lot of the privileged class to go to those places.

In the material that has been written about me, very little has been mentioned about my Italian background. Actually, I feel that is basically accurate. The Italian part of me is small and distant. Part of the thing about being independent and going off on your own—I broke with my family, I broke with the religion—is that once you break those kinds of roots, there is no going back. There is no hope that I would ever go back—not that I was much of an Italian-American to begin with—but when I set the course of my life, it was *away* from that community.

After all, the Italian-American community may have good qualities, but it has many that are terrible. All communities that help themselves are basically against other people. In any community, there is a lot of bigotry, there is a lot of stupidity, there are a lot of primitive qualities. For what is good about a community, there are just as many things that are bad.

What I did would never be acceptable to that community, so what was the point of keeping ties? I was not going to be a social servant.

I had nothing to offer them, and I had already gotten the best out of what they had to offer me. On the level that I was going to function in and the kinds of things that interested me, there just was not much there. I suppose I could have taken another tack, but it just seemed like it was over. Basically, the die was cast. I was American. The Italian part was my childhood, and you lose some connection to your childhood. I would not mind having it back, but the fact of growing up is that you lose some of it. And that was what was gone.

You know, a lot of things about Italian-Americans have not been sterling. Cuomo, for example, is something that is fairly rare in American politics. For a long time, Italians in politics were known for their brutishness rather than for their intelligence. I am thinking of Mario Procaccino and people like that.

There is no connection, as far as I can see, between my being Italian, as such, and being a painter. Perhaps there were certain things that may have led me to painting. My mother was fairly talented at art. She still makes representational paintings with a certain kind of mechanical skill. And my father was very bright and very visually oriented, very quick—very quick with his eyes and his hands. On one level painting is like a sport: Both require hand-and-eye coordination. It is a performance art. It is like dancing—you have to have the basic skills, and *they* do not count for all that much. Some kids try very hard, but if you do not have that quickness with your hands and that sort of sense of rhythm, it is hard. For example, I am not going to play the saxophone or write a sonata, because I have a tin ear. In other words, there are some sorts of basic skills that you need.

But beyond that, the really important thing is how you *think* about things. Being brought up in the shadow of a practicing physician, you learn. In that profession, the thing that my father had to do first was *look* at people. Diagnosis is real important. To understand the problem, to diagnose a malady, to see what is going on, you have *to look first* and react. And so there was always in my childhood and education a tremendous emphasis on *looking*. I think that looking, seeing, dealing with the obvious is important.

I do not believe in causes, antidiscrimination groups and that sort of thing. A few years back, there was an Italian antidefamation group, which I thought was absurd. My father was sympathetic to it, and I can understand that up to a point. But in Massachusetts, the Italians were *so* powerful by the time I grew up. One of my father's schoolmates—they went to the same public school—was John Volpe, who became [U.S.] Secretary of Transportation and, before that, governor of Massachusetts. The guy had a multibillion-dollar construction business.

The Italian power in politics was great; yet they were unhappy because they had to share it with the Irish and the few WASPs that were left that could get votes. They split the pot, and even if they were sharing it three ways, *they were getting their share.* There was no getting around it. When I wanted a summer job, for example, my father called up the councilman. And I was given work in the public-works program. They put me out on the road and told me to hide in the bushes. It was *hard* not to get a job. I do not see that they had it that bad.

After the Second World War, the Italians were pretty well set and the Puerto Ricans had not started to come in. There was very little pressure on them. They used to try to scare themselves with the blacks, but in fact, the blacks were not really competing with them. They had a big piece of the socio-economic pie to themselves in the lower, middle, and even upper classes. In Massachusetts, they all had work. Nobody was unemployed.

Consequently, I cannot be very sympathetic to their cries of discrimination. It is true that at a certain level you did not see a lot of Italian-Americans in the State Department. But there are a lot of places like that. They are not about to overwhelm the FBI, either, for example. Why Irish-Americans should be in the FBI and not Italian-Americans, I don't know. [Laughs.] Maybe that has changed now, but that was the way it was. You had to go to Fordham or Georgetown to be in the FBI. If you went to Holy Cross, you did not get in.

The way some people link every Italian to the Mafia in a half-joking way does not bother me. Actually, the Mafia has always been considered glamorous. I do not know why people find bullies that glamorous; yet it seems to be an unending source of satisfaction to Americans. But so are cowboys and Indians. Some things have reached a level of the classic. I do not think you will ever avoid it.

Among my artist and writer friends, only one is Italian—Gay Talese. We were close for a couple of years and saw each other a lot, but I have not seen him for a long time. Gay was obviously very

Italian. He seemed to make a big thing out of it, which I never did, but he liked it and enjoyed it. Then he went ahead and did that book, which actually is a terrific book, *Honor Thy Father*, about a Mafia family.

I am married to a pediatrician, Harriet McGurk. She is of Scotch-Irish blood. My father was a physician, and I married one. It may be that as I got older, I got nervous and could not stand being around the house without a doctor. But actually, they do not take care of you. We have just had a new baby son. He is an Italian, Irish, Scotch, American Catholic. If I had a genetic preference, I guess I believe in hybrid vigor. A good cross is always good.

Eleanor Cutri Smeal

ELEANOR CUTRI SMEAL
Feminist from Ashtabula

Elected for a third time in 1985 as president of the National Organization of Women, where she is known for her aggressive combat of negative attitudes about women, Eleanor Cutri Smeal brings to her position a lifetime of personal experience with discrimination. As an Italian child growing up in the Midwest in the 1940s and 1950s, she—along with members of her family—learned about bias in its many forms. Married to Charles Smeal, an engineer, who is her partner in almost everything she does, she is the mother of two children.

◇

"Work for yourselves" has been our family motto. . . . The feeling was that unless you work for yourself, you are not going to have as good a chance—because you are Italian—to become successful.

Ashtabula, Ohio, is my hometown. I am a midwestern Italian-American and I lived in Ashtabula, which is on Lake Erie, until the age of five. After that, we lived in Cleveland for five years, and then my dad moved back to Erie, Pennsylvania, his original home. The first fifteen years of my life I spent *around* Lake Erie—Ashtabula,

Cleveland, and Erie are all on the lake, in spitting distance of one another almost—and I used to say I was going to die on the lake without ever seeing anything else.

After I married, my husband and I lived in Pittsburgh for many years, which used to be called the Gateway to the Middle West. That whole area of western Pennsylvania is midwestern more than eastern. To our way of thinking, eastern is Philadelphia and New York. This [pointing to a map of western Pennsylvania and Ohio] is Middle America, where I grew up.

Each of the towns I lived in had sizable Italian populations. My dad was an insurance agent for Metropolitan Life and was sent to these towns because he was Italian and spoke the language and so was better equipped to sell insurance to the Italians. In those days, Erie was about twenty-five percent Italian. Today, it still has distinct communities of Italians, as well as Poles, Germans, and Irish. Cleveland and Ashtabula had large Little Italies, and still do. Buffalo, which lies on Lake Erie directly across from Erie, also has a large Italian population, as does the whole upstate New York area.

Moving around as my family did was not disruptive for us because in the Midwest, state boundaries don't mean very much. Midwesterners just get in their cars and move. People who live in Erie, for example, think nothing of driving to Cleveland and Buffalo, which is almost directly across the lake from Erie. Erie to Cleveland is about a two-hour drive, and Ashtabula may be about a one-and-a-half-hour drive from Erie.

There are a lot of Italians in this part of the country because immigrants entered the United States directly north from Canada. If they did not have immigration papers, which were needed to get through Ellis Island, many entered the continent by way of Canada and crossed our border and settled in the Midwest. The United States-Canadian border was not elaborately patrolled, and it was easier to filter through than at an eastern port.

As a young boy in Reggio di Calabria in Italy, my father was buried alive in an earthquake, but he survived. That was when his father, who had a farm, decided that was enough of that. They were getting out of Italy. In 1909, the family left their farm and emigrated to Erie, Pennsylvania, joining the great wave of people who came from southern Italy at that time. My grandfather found work in a forge or shop where metal was heated and wrought into iron. Erie did a lot of jobbing work, especially for automobiles, and there were many shops like that. My father was about seven or eight when he came here, and knew how to read and write Italian. Because he had to quit school at thirteen, he had only four years of American education. His father needed him in the shop to help support the family.

My mother was American-born. Her family came from Naples. The family migration started when a priest in Erie, who was assigned to that area from Italy, needed an altar boy. He sent for his nephew in the Campania, who was my great-uncle, and he, in turn, began to send for other members of the family.

In my mother's childhood in Erie, everything was off limits. She was raised as a Victorian, or so it seems to me—her upbringing sounds more Victorian than Italian. Because sports for girls were considered unladylike, she was not allowed to ride a bike or play tennis. There were taboos on dating and sex. When she married, at twenty-five, she had never dated anybody except my dad. She had not been allowed to. Once before they were married, she kissed him. As she raised me, she gave me the opportunity to do almost anything I wanted: play tennis, swim, dance, twirl a baton, ride a bike, go away to college. These were usually prohibited for Italian girls of her generation.

"You only live one life. Why should you be cheated?" she would say.

When she was eighty years old, she advised her grandchildren, particularly the girls, "Don't ever take a back seat. Don't ever think it is too late. It is never too late."

She told them that when she was sixty, her daughter (referring to me) went to graduate school. "She tried to talk *me* into going to college, while she was going to graduate school. But I was sixty years old. I felt I was too old and your grandfather was sick at the time. If I had known that I was going to live all these years, I would have taken her advice."

Her parents died when she was about ten years old, and she was raised as an orphan in a Catholic convent. She had no money. One day she quit school and left the convent forever. To apply for a job at General Electric, she walked clear across town to the east side of Erie. She got the job—I think she fibbed about her age. Later, she talked an older sister, who was married, into letting her move in with her family. At General Electric, she worked as a secretary but had to quit her job when her brother's wife became ill, and she took care of her. After her sister-in-law died, she looked after her brother's four children—someone had to take care of them. But she always wanted independence. That was important to her.

When my brothers and I were growing up, speaking Italian in our house was a hot issue. Even though she understood the language and spoke it somewhat, my mother did *not* like Italian spoken at home. My father had a fluent command of the language, as well as several dialects. He communicated with people from varying provinces and could also write in their dialects. There was no resolution; the issue caused frequent arguments. My mother used to say to him, "Speak English, so the children will understand."

During the last part of his life, he hardly spoke Italian at all—only if he was around Italians. I understand very little of the language and speak only a few words here and there. I studied Spanish at school, which I can read but can't speak. You know, the one drawback about America is there's not much chance to speak other languages.

We always lived in "American" neighborhoods, not only in Erie, but in Ashtabula and Cleveland. We never lived in an Italian section. My mother did not want to. She felt strongly that the kids should associate with people from all backgrounds. Since she felt that we should associate not only with Catholics but with Jews and Protestants, we went to public schools instead of parochial schools. We should not be only with our own kind. Incidentally, most of my parents' friends were of Italian extraction. During the last ten years of my father's life, when he had homes both in Erie and Florida, his Florida friends were more of a mixture. In the early years, the family associated mostly with Italian-Americans. The kids did not.

I have had all kinds of experience with prejudice. There was tremendous bias against Italians in Ohio, Pennsylvania, everyplace. *All* kinds. *All* the time. For people not to notice it or to say it did not exist—I can't understand that. Cutri is not a common Italian name, but everybody knew we were Italian. My family is dark, and we look Italian. I certainly do, though I am not as dark as my brothers.

My dad was a respectable professional man and president of the Italian-American business and professional group in Erie. We were members of the middle- to upper-middle class. Yet if my brother got a car, someone would be sure to say, "He got it through the numbers." In other words, if you are Italian and you make it, you must have some connection to the numbers. In Erie, the rackets were called the numbers. They sold numbers. My family never had anything to do with that, but this was the immediate assumption.

My brothers were good-looking, especially the younger one. Yet people would not date him because he was Italian. That is one thing about dealing with a mixture of people—you're close enough to know what they're thinking. Some voiced their feeling. It is not something we imagined. And my family *felt* discrimination. They *felt* it. Now, I did not meet with it as much as my parents and brothers did because I was the youngest, and by the time I was growing up, things had gotten a little better. But even so, I heard all the stories a lot of the time. When my brothers were young, my mother and father would move into a block and other people would move out. We always lived in non-Italian neighborhoods, as I said, and we were "breaking" neighborhoods. We were block-breakers, you might say. As we moved in, the neighbors would say, "My God, Italians with a large family. They have four kids." And they would move out.

But after getting to know my mother, a neighbor who stayed said to her, "We thought you kept a dirty house because you were Italian." In my mother's house, the floors were so clean you could literally eat off them. Her house was immaculate, and I think one of the reasons for this was that she wanted to prove Italians are not dirty. Slurs like this permeated the atmosphere.

Erie had a country club where no Italians were allowed. Only in recent years have Italians and Jews been accepted for membership. I can't help but think that this kind of bias was nationwide. What I know for sure is that where I was brought up, there was discrimination, and it was marked. It did not prevent Italians from doing things, though. It was simply *harder* to do things. It was harder to be in business. That was the reason the Italians formed the professional and business club—my father was president, as I mentioned —so they could band together and help one another. Today there would be no problem if Italians moved to certain residential blocks. And there was no problem when I was very young. When we moved to a certain lovely block in Erie in 1949, no one said a thing. These are stories from before that period, but they made a lasting impression on me. Even in my own childhood, I was aware of discrimination, of being treated differently.

But bias is still around, though it may be less. To say there is none is not to understand the situation. I remember an incident with my son. His name is Tod Smeal, which isn't at all Italian. When he was four years old, we were living in Upper Montclair, a suburb of Pittsburgh, and one day he came home from school crying and said, "Mommy, what is a dirty dago?"

"Why do you want to know?"

"A boy in school came up to me and shouted, *'Tod Smeal is a dirty dago,'* and I don't know what that is."

This happened in 1969.

My married name is Irish, and if it is not known that I am Italian, I frequently tell people that I am. I don't want to hear Italian jokes, and feel that people should know who they are associating with, right off. I am not bitter about discrimination. Bitterness is not part of my makeup—I am just describing the way it was.

Because Italians were not generally accepted in earlier days by the greater society, family closeness became even stronger than it was. Family was everything. To my mother, it was the beginning and the end; it was her life. She had not had many opportunities to develop herself, and so family became most important. The same was true of my dad. Although he did well in real estate, banking, and mortgaging, he was self-taught. Until my mother died—my father died much earlier—we got together for the holidays for years and years. No matter where I was living with my own family, I went home to visit with her all the time, except when traveling. During the last year of her life, when she was ill, she spent six months with us in our home outside Washington, D.C., and when she returned to Erie, my brothers took turns sleeping in her house and taking care of her. She died at eighty-four, and up until the last year, had lived her widowed years all by herself.

My mom and dad pushed education; they really pushed it. There was no question about going to college. All four of us have college degrees, and three of us have advanced degrees.

We were trained to be fighters. My father told us, "You start with nothing, and you might end with nothing. But the important thing is that you try hard. You take a chance. You take risks. If others, who may not be as qualified as you, can do it, then you can do it."

What they instilled in me more than anything else is a feeling of self-confidence. A million times or more, they said, "You can do it. Don't take a back seat. You are as good as anyone else." When I was a grown woman, my mother said to me that she never thought I would take her so literally.

Work hard. Every generation helps the next generation. The urging was constant, constant, constant. In their case, upward mobility was an understatement.

Did I resent being pushed? I loved it and always tried to excel. I was an honor student and a Phi Beta Kappa. None of my brothers had trouble academically. Perhaps *encouragement* is a more appropriate word than *pushing*. They told us we could do anything: They believed in positive reinforcement. There was never punishment. They were positive, absolutely positive. I never knew anything about negative thinking. I felt like I walked on water.

How did they do it? I wish I knew, for the sake of my own children. What was the magic that made my parents so confident, which in turn instilled confidence in us? They believed their kids could do anything, their kids were the best. God knows how they got to feel that way. It radiated from their souls.

They were both people of the modern world. Tradition did not have an iron grasp on their thinking. My father loved everything that was *now. Out there, it was great.* He never worried about just what was going on or concerned that anything was going backward. The world was going forward. Everything was progress. He was a salesperson for American democracy and loved this country and its ideals to the point where he took a vote, in democratic fashion, whenever we had to make an important family decision. Italian families are said to have an authoritarian figure, usually the father, who makes all the important decisions. Not so in our house. We argued, disagreed, and put forth our opinions about politics and other things. Your position was asked, and you debated it. If he had been a know-it-all and authoritarian chief, we would not have had a chance to discuss things.

Even though he was born in Italy, my dad never expressed any feelings of love for it. But he had great respect for his heritage, which he considered a saving grace for Italians. True, in America they lived under a cloud and were discriminated against, but they were lucky because Italians are an educated people with a history of civilization behind them. He and others like him may not have been skilled in English and lacked the American birthright, but they had a tradition of culture, which gave them the confidence and strength to accept their lot. All during his life the issue of *fairness* affected him. He was for civil rights and felt that it was not fair to compare discriminations because that against the blacks was so much more severe.

My father might have gone back to Italy to visit, but my mother was against it. His sisters returned three or four times. My mother's sister also went, and I still remember her comment: "You know, they look so much like Italians. The whole country looks Italian."

Tod and Laurie, my children, are aware of their heritage. As they were growing up, we used to go to Erie often to see my family. They did not know their grandfather, but knew my mother and loved her. The family, though, was just as much American as Italian. We did not follow traditions much, but my mother did prepare thirteen different kinds of fish on Christmas eve. Now, maybe one fish dish will be prepared.

"Work for yourselves" has been our family motto. My parents pushed this very hard. We are all small entrepreneurs—there is not one of us who works for someone else. I joined in when my husband and I began our own public-relations agency after my second term as president of NOW was over. The feeling was that unless you work for yourself, you are not going to have as good a chance— because you are Italian—to become successful. *So do your own thing. You can do it yourself.* There would be discrimination at the top. Today, that is a debatable issue. I think there still is.

Whether or not I am still a Catholic depends on how you look at it. In my family, my generation goes to church, but not regularly. Yet there is no other religion. And I intend to be buried with the rites of the Church. In my parents' time, you had the immigrant Catholic who was religious and kept close to the Church. In the next generation—my brothers' and mine—there are still a good number of strict Catholics. But among the children today, religion has lost its hold. It is much looser. There are some exceptions, of course— I have cousins who still go to church regularly. But many of the younger people do not.

Some sociologists are saying that in time ethnic life among American Catholics will disappear and what will take its place is an American Catholic life that will encompass all ethnic groups and replace individual ethnicities. I do not agree with this. For example, there is a tremendous difference between Irish Catholics and Italian Catholics that will not melt away. Tremendous—and I know, because my husband is an Irish Catholic. Historically, the role of the Catholic Church in Ireland and Italy has not been the same, and this reflects on the Catholics who live under it. In Ireland, the Church was the hero of the fight against oppression, against government. For Italians, the Church has not been the savior politically. Catholicism in Ireland defines your politics. In Italy, you may be Catholic, but politically, you could be anything. The older immigrants, the Irish, have shown discrimination against the younger immigrants, the Italians, and this has resulted in an enmity and bitterness whose effects are still visible. The Church in America has been mainly Irish, and boys of Italian extraction have been kept out of the priesthood. My dad was always commenting on how all the priests spoke with a brogue. "When are we going to get some Italian priests?" he would ask.

But *attitude* is the thing that counts here. The attitude of each group is so different. The Irish take religion in a much stricter way. The Italian view is more practical. An example of this was the recent confrontation on abortion between Governor Mario Cuomo and Geraldine Ferraro on the one hand and Cardinal John O'Connor on the other. You might say the Irish are sticklers and the Italians are liberals.

A great nostalgia for ethnicity seems to be current today. But it is not true that the melting pot has failed, as some say. America is a melting pot, and the results are positive. Outside of religion, we are bound together by an American culture, heritage, and belief system. I am in agreement with my parents, who believed that children of immigrants should be taught English and not their parents' language. If everybody emphasizes all the differences, then there is no hope for unity.

And yet there is always a little bit of difference among Americans, which is good, a little individual something—whether it be looks, a liking for certain foods and music, a religion—that says *Originally, we come from that culture*. But I think it would be terrible if we still lived in Little Italies, Germantowns, Irishtowns, and everybody spoke different languages, everybody fought—the my-dad-can-beat-your-dad sort of thing. Strong ethnicities have a danger of division. My word of caution to people who are trying to revive the ethnic aspects of American life is: *as long as they are not divisive.*

I am sure glad my parents went into those WASP-type neighborhoods to show that they were the same as everybody else. It changed my life and gave me the needed opportunities. And it provided me with the confidence to associate with anybody.

What drove my family was America itself. They *wanted* to be here, they loved being here, they believed in democracy as a better way of life. Their lifestyle was American, and they willingly gave up customs that were not a part of the American scene. They chose to go to the Cleveland Indian games and cheer for the home team.

At Duke University, I had a Spanish teacher who censured immigrant parents for not teaching their children their native language. "The trouble with Italians," he said, "is that they were ashamed of their background and would not teach their kids Italian, their own language."

A resident of the United States for more than thirty years, he still spoke with a thick Spanish accent that was almost incomprehensible. In response, I said to him, "You can afford that accent, because you are a professor and teach your own language. What would happen if you were trying to make a living competing with other Americans and wanting to succeed? Is it so bad to want your children to speak good English?"

From my father's lips, I heard the whole story of Italian civilization and the role his part of the world played in developing Western society. He respected Italy and was not ashamed of his heritage. But along with that was his determination to make it here, get along with people, and see to it that his children spoke good English.

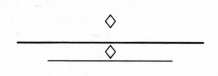

Joseph Bernardin as a child with his parents, Joseph and
Maria, and baby sister, Elaine

JOSEPH CARDINAL BERNARDIN
Growing Up in the American South

Joseph Bernardin is exceptional in that he is the first and only Italian-American cardinal of the Catholic Church in the United States. He is also unusual in that he is one of a small number of Italian-American southerners, having been born and raised in Columbia, South Carolina. As head of the archdiocese of Chicago, he oversees the second largest diocese in the nation. An opponent of the nuclear arms race, he was chairman of the Bishops' Committee that developed the pastoral letter on peace, which has received much attention from political leaders.

Remember, this was the South. As a priest in the diocese of Charleston, I had little contact with Italian-Americans because there were so few of them.

The area the Bernardins come from, which is a valley in the province of Trent in northern Italy, is called Primiero. Within this valley there are a number of little villages just a stone's throw from one another. The principal town is known as Fiera di Primiero, and the village that my family comes from is called Tonadico. So it would be known as Tonadico di Primiero, because Primiero refers to the whole valley. Both my parents were born in Tonadico.

Many of the names in that part of Italy end in a consonant rather than a vowel. Before the First World War, this was part of the Austro-Hungarian Empire, and in terms of their origin, the people often think of themselves as more Austrian than Italian. Many of their names are Germanic. In this country, some of my relatives pronounce our name Ber-NAR-din, with the accent on the second syllable, but the correct pronunciation is BER-nar-din. My mother's family name is Simion, which sounds rather French. Another family name is Zagonel. Two of my uncles married two sisters whose maiden name was Trotter, which has a Germanic ring. I checked our baptismal records in the parish church in Tonadico—the records go back for many, many years—and our name, Bernardin, has never ended in a vowel.

My father and his brothers came to the United States in the 1920s. They were in the stone business. In those days in the Primiero area, there were many people who had taken up the trade of stonecutting. We call them stonecutters, but they were more like artisans because the tombstones and other things they made were truly beautiful. They had an artistic sense that enabled them to fashion beautiful works of art out of granite and marble. When my father died, his tombstone was carved with great care by his brother. The brothers first went to Vermont and then moved to Columbia, South Carolina, because there are fine granite quarries nearby. There they set up their business. Six brothers came over originally. Three remained in Columbia, two later moved to Philadelphia, and one moved back to Italy. To choose a bride, each returned to Italy. My father went back in 1927 to marry my mother. They returned to the States, and I was born in Columbia in 1928.

My parents spoke both Italian and the dialect that is indigenous to that particular region of Italy where they were born. In Columbia, we had some very close Italian friends, some of them from southern Italy and Sicily. It is interesting that we could not understand one another's dialects. They were that different. In those early days, my parents spoke mostly their dialect at home, but later, after I grew up, my mother insisted on speaking Italian because she wanted me to learn it. But I have always understood the dialect.

It may be true that at one time northern Italians tended to keep apart from other Italians. But in the American South in those days, there were so few Italians that we all stuck together. I don't know exactly how many Italians there were, but there couldn't have been more than a dozen or fifteen families in the city of Columbia. We all knew one another. Some were in the stone business, and most of these were from northern Italy. Two families were in the seafood business, and another had a fruit store; these were from southern Italy. The point is that it was a very small community. We all knew one another, and any differences—social or otherwise—that may have existed in Italy or in the large urban areas in this country did not exist in South Carolina. Thus my experience may be totally different from that of Italians in New York, Chicago, or any of the big northern cities. At times, we would kid one another about the supposed differences, but we were all just very close friends.

My immediate family in America was small. My father died in 1934, when I was six years old and my sister was two. My mother never remarried. We were close to our aunts and uncles, and we would visit one another on holidays. But it was not a large family because most remained in Italy. By the time I came along, there were only three brothers and their families living in South Carolina. Incidentally, two of them, my father and a brother, married two sisters. Of course later, as the cousins began to marry, the family grew.

We were religious, but not overly so, not fanatic. My mother came from a very devout family. Her brother was a priest, and there were several cousins who were priests. My maternal grandfather, whom I never met, was for many years the choirmaster of the parish church in Tonadico. We went to mass every Sunday and were involved in church activities. When my sister and I began school, we first went to a nearby public school, just a block or two away. My mother had to work—my father had died—and couldn't take us to the Catholic school, which was some distance away. But as soon as I was old enough to take care of my sister and myself, we transferred to St. Peter's School. My mother's family was more committed to the faith in terms of practice than my father's. But my father was a very active Catholic, primarily because of the example of my mother.

My sister and I, and two cousins whose family lived in the same house with us, were the only Italian Catholic kids in the neighborhood. But we were very well received. I never felt discriminated against. My mother, too, was loved and respected by her neighbors.

Because there were so few Italians, however, my sister and I wanted very much to be identified with Americans. We wanted *to be Americans*. When my mother and father and aunts and uncles spoke to us in Italian, we always responded in English because we were trying to prove that we were good Americans. Since our playmates and classmates were American, we felt that this was the thing to do. I always appreciated my Italian heritage, but I thought, "I'm an American" and so I must be a good one. The situation might have been different if we had lived in an area where there were many Italians. But we didn't. As a result, we identified more with the people whom we knew and the society in which we lived.

My mother was a seamstress. After my father's death, she was our sole source of support. In the early days she worked from her home, but around 1940, when Fort Jackson was reactivated—this was just before the beginning of the Second World War—she obtained employment at the fort as a tailor. She worked with army uniforms and remained at the fort until she retired in the sixties.

Because her time was limited, Mother would prepare Italian food only on Sundays and holidays. During the week we would eat "American food," as she called it, because it was easier and quicker to prepare. Generally on Sundays, she would make various kinds of pasta, especially spaghetti. We also regularly had polenta, a dish made of cornmeal that is very popular in northern Italy. Polenta itself is rather bland, but what you serve with it makes the difference. With the polenta, she would serve a meat stew with a tasty gravy or sauerkraut with sausage, as well as different kinds of cheese. On holidays, she made cappelletti which required hours of preparation. They were a small kind of ravioli made with a filling of different meats and seasonings. The word *cappelletti* means little hats. Each one is made in such a way as to look like a little hat. She served them in chicken broth. It was always a special occasion for us children when we had cappelletti.

I still love this food. As a matter of fact, in later years—as a hobby—I learned how to prepare a number of these dishes. There's no time to do that now, except on vacation. But I *can* do it. On trips to Italy, and northern Italy in particular, I enjoy the cuisine very much.

All through my high school years I was interested in medicine. After graduation I went to the University of South Carolina with the intention of ultimately going to medical school. After one year, however, I decided to become a priest. It is difficult to know exactly what prompted that decision. To be of service to people has always been a deep concern. This was one of the reasons I wanted to be a doctor. As a priest, you are in the service of people. Probably, the immediate thing was conversations I had with some local priests, which led me to consider the priesthood seriously. When they first asked whether I was interested, my response was that I had never thought about it. They said, "Perhaps you should." I did, and that led to the decision to enter the seminary.

After a year at the University of South Carolina, I went to St. Mary's College in Kentucky. The bishop sent me there because the college specialized in Latin. In high school I had studied Spanish, and in college I chose German because German was supposed to be helpful in medicine. In a year I learned enough Latin to enter philosophy. I went to St. Mary's Seminary in Baltimore and completed my college work with a bachelor's degree in philosophy. After that, I did my theological studies at the Catholic University of America in Washington, D.C., and was ordained in 1952. While at the university, I also received a master's degree in education.

During my fourteen years as a priest in the diocese of Charleston, South Carolina, I had little contact with Italian-Americans because there were so few of them. The same was true when I was auxiliary bishop of Atlanta. In the big waves of immigration from Europe, most Italians settled in the North or the Midwest. Here in the Chicago area, for example, we have a large Italian population, probably around 220,000. Large numbers simply did not move south. In every town, in every city, you would find a few, but not the numbers that settled in other areas. That is why my experience is so different from that of Italo-Americans who grew up elsewhere.

In Cincinnati, I found more Italians but the predominant ethnic group was German. We estimated that over sixty percent of Cincinnati Catholics were of German origin. In an archdiocese of one-half million Catholics, we may have had about 15,000 or 20,000 Italians. This, of course, was more than I was accustomed to in the South. Still, they were a minority.

And yet, as an Italian-American prelate in the midst of this large German enclave, I did not feel different or isolated. I felt very much at home. It was like being, for the second time, one of the few Italian children in the neighborhood. And as I did as a child, I identified with everyone around me. Thinking of myself primarily as the archbishop of the area, I related well to everyone. Occasionally, I kidded about my Italian heritage and remember saying once, "You people are all Germans and always insist on crossing every *t* and dotting every *i*. That's the Germanic way. But I'm Italian and have a freer spirit." That always drew a laugh.

One evening, I became very "ethnic." An Italian fraternal group in Cincinnati was honoring me, and my talk was on our Italian heritage. Of course, there was intermarriage between the Germans and Italians, and many of the people present had spouses that were of German origin. After the talk, which, as befitted the occasion, was quite laudatory of my Italian heritage, with a big smile on my face I said, "Now, all of you Germans, just eat your hearts out." [Laughs.]

Nationwide, it is true that there have been relatively few Italian priests and bishops. There have been more Irish priests than any other group. And there have been more Irish bishops because to be a bishop, you must first be a priest. It's difficult to know why there have been so few Italians in the clergy. It may well be that young Irish men were encouraged to become priests more than other groups. But the situation has changed, and today the various ethnic groups are well represented in the hierarchy.

Italians are surely proud of bishops of Italian origin, as they are proud of me. It's understandable that every ethnic group is attracted to its own. But we must remember that we are all part of the whole. Here in Chicago, for example, we have many ethnic groups. Each weekend, mass is celebrated in more than twenty languages. I have six auxiliary bishops. Two are Irish, one is Hispanic, one is black, one is Polish, and one is Bohemian. It is like a League of Nations. That is good.

There are two values that must be kept in balance. One is *diversity*—the cultural diversity that exists among our people and adds a certain richness to the life of the Church. We celebrate that. We applaud it. I've done a great deal to reach out to the various ethnic groups.

The other value is *unity*. I have a great desire for unity within the Church. Even though we have varied cultures and backgrounds, we belong to *one* Church. Our basic unity, as a faith community, must be respected and supported. We cannot let the archdiocese be divided into many different little dioceses. We are one Church, one diocese, and we all have to work together. We must support one another. I spend most of my waking hours making sure that those two values are kept in balance.

How do I do it? One way is to keep *talking* about it, stressing that we are *one Church* and must work together. Also, the different ethnic groups are represented in the various structures of the archdiocese, such as the Archdiocesan Pastoral Council. In all our consultative bodies, we do our best to make sure that the various ethnic and racial groups have a voice. The archdiocese has also established specific offices that promote various ethnic ministries, such as the offices for Hispanic Ministry, Italian Ministry, Polish Ministry, Black Ministry, and so on. All these groups have their individual needs and they want to maintain their identity to some extent. As I said, that is good. But, at the same time, we are one Church, constantly trying to bring people together. We do not want them to be divided, isolated.

Together with my desire for unity within the Church is a longing for peace. I have given much attention to this issue in recent years. I served as chairman of the Bishops' Committee that developed the pastoral letter on peace, entitled, "The Challenge of Peace: God's Promise and Our Response." This document addressed various issues that we face in the nuclear age. It provided a framework within which people can make a moral analysis of those issues. This document, or pastoral letter as we call it, has received much attention. It is used now extensively in Catholic schools and other Catholic educational programs. It has also become a standard work, which is read and used in secular colleges and universities.

The Pastoral Letter on Peace has helped to sensitize people to some of the problems we face today. In the past there were so many who felt that issues of this kind should be decided *by someone else*. I think, however, that we see things differently now and realize that as citizens we *do* have responsibility for the well-being of our country and, indeed, for the well-being of society generally. What *we think and do* is very important. We may not have the burden of making the final decisions, but we are the ones who are responsible for electing our leaders, who do have that responsibility. There are so many ways in which we can, and do, affect what goes on in our country. Moreover, what happens here also impacts what happens elsewhere. I have been identified with the Pastoral Letter because I was chairman of the committee that drafted it, but I want to emphasize that it was ultimately accepted and endorsed by the full body of bishops. It is their document, not mine.

I first visited Italy in 1957, when I was twenty-nine. I had been ordained for five years. My mother had returned to Italy for the first time in 1952 to visit her mother—she hadn't been back in twenty-five years—and she promised that she would bring my sister and me to meet her. Five years later, we went.

Throughout my childhood, I had thumbed through my mother's album, which was filled with photographs of the village where she and my father grew up—pictures of all the houses of the village and the mountains that surrounded them. When I entered the village for the first time, I felt I had been there before. A strong sense of *déjà vu* overwhelmed me. While a number of new houses had been built, all the houses I remembered were still there—as well as the mountains! It was an unusual feeling. At first, I couldn't understand it. And then I remembered the photographs.

When I was named cardinal in February 1983, my relatives from northern Italy came to Rome for the consistory. It was the first time that many of them had met their American relatives, who had also come to Rome. The younger ones were complete strangers to one another. It was quite an occasion. The relatives from Primiero wanted to have a celebration in my honor, so I promised that I would return to visit them. In September of that same year, on my way to the Synod of Bishops in Rome, I spent ten days with them.

The reception on that occasion was extraordinary. I arrived on Saturday and the next day celebrated mass in the church in Tonadico where my parents had been baptized and married. The entire community met me at the entrance to the little village, and we walked in procession to the church. After mass, there was a reception, an outdoor party, for everybody. On the Sunday before I left, there was an outdoor mass to which the people of the other valley towns were invited. Several thousand were present. In between these two occasions, I confirmed the young people from the valley, celebrated mass for a group of retired people, and visited a nursing home. They also scheduled a visit to the historic city of Trento; I spent several days with the archbishop and gave a talk to young Italians in the cathedral on the War and Peace Pastoral. There were also a number of other celebrations, including a civic reception.

It may well be that because of my Italian roots—I am just one generation removed from Europe—churchmen and political leaders in Europe may feel closer to me. But I do not know how important that factor is. More important, perhaps, is one's personality, one's ability to reach out.

As a bishop, I work within the framework of the Catholic Church. I believe in church order and in the fact that we must have rules and regulations. However, I feel very *comfortable* with the Church, and I think that most Italians do. They do not see it so much as a distant bureaucratic structure as a kind of family. As a result, they are somewhat freer. For example, if you go to an Italian parish church—to some extent, this is changing now—there are many more children. They move about more; people talk more than in other churches. That is because Italians feel very much at home in church. They do not see the need for as much formality as other groups. There is a freedom of spirit. This is not to say that Italians are not serious about the Church and religion generally. Both have a significant meaning for us. Perhaps our behavior is more relaxed and down-to-earth because of the way we approach things.

Incidentally, the first naturalized American saint, Mother Francis Xavier Cabrini, was an Italian. She was born in Italy and became a naturalized U.S. citizen. She died here in Chicago at one of the hospitals she established, but her body lies in New York. Mother Seton—Elizabeth Ann Seton, who was canonized in 1975—is the first American-born woman to become a saint. St. John Neumann, the archbishop of Philadelphia, like Mother Cabrini, was also a naturalized American.

There is no question that we need some structures. In an archdiocese as large as Chicago's, there would be chaos without them. But in the final analysis, these structures exist *to help people*. We must not miss the forest for the trees. This belief may come from my Italian heritage, or it may be simple common sense: I try to give a more personal touch to my duties and to all the things that I am involved with. This personal dimension is very, very important.

Claudia DeMonte

CLAUDIA DEMONTE
The Whole World Was Italian!

Claudia DeMonte's memories of her childhood are full of fun, hysteria, funerals, weddings, saints—and heartache. She is an artist whose work has appeared in the Philadelphia Museum of Art, Queens Museum, and the Corcoran Gallery in Washington, D.C. Her art is "participatory," which draws directly on herself and her past for subject matter.

At school, the priests and nuns told us graphic stories about exorcism, about priests being beaten by spirits. . . . The lives of the saints were always gory . . .

I grew up actually thinking that my mother was Italian. I mean, the whole world was Italian to me. My family was Italian, and I had no idea my mother wasn't. She acted like the Italian relatives, she outcooked them, she adopted the whole thing. If you asked her, she would probably say she *was* Italian.

But she didn't look it and that should have clued me in. She was a huge woman, and the relatives were short. She was about five feet nine. I should have realized something was wrong since she towered above the whole community. But it wasn't until I was a teenager that I realized I was not a hundred percent Italian. She is a German from Baltimore and met my dad during World War II when he was stationed at Fort Meade in Maryland. It's hysterical—*I did not know* she was not Italian.

My father's father came from Abruzzi, and his mother from Salerno. She died during the influenza epidemic of World War I. I once asked my grandfather to tell me about her. He had been married to two other women and had outlived all three. He said, "I don't really remember."

That killed me. I mean, he did not remember my grandmother? Of course, he had been married for thirty years to someone else, and my grandmother had been dead so long. They were together about four years. When she died, he freaked out. There were three kids, ages three, four, and five—my father was the oldest. To take care of them, he brought his sisters from Italy, and he went off to Texas to find fame and fortune. But his sisters had no intention of raising children—they came because they wanted to get to America. When the children were seven, eight, and nine years old, they came home from school one day and found a note on the door:

WE HAVE MOVED TO CLEVELAND.

From then on, they lived on the streets. Occasionally, my Aunt Lucy, my grandmother's sister, took them in, but they were essentially on their own. Everything about my family is not what is thought of as typically Italian—that is, warm, loving, caring. My grandfather was a cold man, leaving his children the way he did. When anything went wrong, he got up and left. He dropped anything that did not work. And I remember when my father died suddenly of a heart attack, my mother cried and my grandfather, who was living with us, said, "Don't cry your heart out to me. Don't tell me any of your problems. I do not want to die before my time."

It was just the way he was. But he did well in America because he had a skill—ironwork—and helped build Hell's Gate Bridge in Harlem. He also did decorative ironwork. That may be where my interest in art comes from.

My father, on the other hand, was very warm. After my grandfather became a widower for the third time, he called my father from Texas and said, "My wife is dead and I am sick." My father said, "Come and live with us," even though my mother had never met him. He stayed with us for years, and at the age of ninety-six, he died in his sleep.

My family settled in an Italian neighborhood in Astoria, which is part of New York City, and still live there. Today the Greeks have moved in, and it will always be an ethnic neighborhood. The women still wear the same black stockings, the same black dresses, the whole thing. They look the same and they act the same. It's like someone waving a magic wand—just the language changes. It was Italian then, and now it is totally Greek (with one or two exceptions, of course). I feel close to the Greeks. Their being there has saved the neighborhood. God knows what would have happened to it without them.

This community of Astoria, where my father lived, was essential to his existence. It fitted him like a glove. He was born there, lived there all his life, and in 1954 became the honorary mayor. When he was small, he was an extra in the movies made in the old Astoria film studios and used to see Rudolph Valentino ride through the streets. But on the whole, his childhood was unhappy and impoverished. At his funeral, my aunt told me how as kids they never had any blankets. They used their coats as blankets. And I remembered how he would come into my room every night when I was a child to see that I was covered with blankets. My aunt told me she never had a doll and used to dress caterpillars in tiny rags, pretending they were dolls.

I cried when I heard that. My father gave my sister and me everything. The American dream, that whole dream—he believed in it. Denying themselves for us, he and my mother sent us to college, sent us to Europe. Everything was paid for. We always did the wonderful things, and they stayed home and did nothing—just so we could have it all. It was very hard for me to imagine that my dad and his sisters had nothing growing up.

By the time my father died, he was of the upper middle class. If I can achieve as much as my father did, considering that he started from nothing and I started with a graduate degree and a support system, I would be king. He became an insurance broker and started his own insurance business. He was a city councilman for one term, a member of the Constitutional Convention and the electoral college, and a delegate to all the local conventions. If he had been better educated, he probably would have done much more. Speaking Italian, though, was not one of his talents. But he understood it. He spoke some kind of American takeoff of an Italian dialect. I grew up saying the same words, "galamai" for "calamari," for example. That is how different it was from Italian.

The Catholic Church was his passion. Extremely religious, totally immersed, he was an usher in his church and he attended all the novenas and functions. If I had become a nun, he would have been very happy. He thought the greatest gift anyone could give him was a child who entered a religious order. Each year on his name day, St. Joseph's feast day on March 19, we used to send him special greeting cards and eat zeppole di San Giuseppe all day. They were special pastries made only on St. Joseph's Day. When I talk about zeppole, my husband never knows what I am saying. Non-Italians don't know about this custom.

In my work as an artist, I have used autobiographical themes. My show last year was based on my Catholic upbringing. There is no saint by the name of Claudia, and I made up a saint with that name. At Our Lady of Mt. Carmel School, where I went, the kids were always singling me out and taunting, "How come you're not named after a saint? Claudia is not a saint's name. It's against Church law not to be named after a saint."

To correct this situation, at last Claudia was added to the list of saints. I created a whole life for her and a shrine. You know those big shrines they carry through the streets of Little Italy? I made one for St. Claudia.

Another work based on my life is a calendar of important dates, which I illustrated with family pictures. [Picks up the calendar and shows a picture of her father, a handsome man with an open, direct gaze, and a picture of a family wedding of the early twenties, the type that many families kept in frames on their living-room walls. The women were all seated, wearing white satin dresses and slippers, holding large bouquets of roses, the men in tuxedos standing behind them in a row. The bride's veil fanned out in front of her and almost covered the floor.]

The bride and groom in this photograph had no money, and neither did their families. After the wedding, they sat and counted the gifts of money, paid off the wedding expenses, and had thirteen dollars left. This lady [pointing to a wedding attendant], Josie Massa, had a son who was born with two thumbs on each hand. They thought it was good luck and would not let the doctor remove the extra thumb when he was an infant. So this poor kid grew up with all these thumbs, and guess what he did for a living? He played the trumpet. But he died—he died before his parents did. [Pointing to another member of the wedding party] She had a restaurant in Astoria. She couldn't understand me at all. Her family were really lower-class Italians and they had no vision. They thought education was silly, unlike my father, who really believed in the they-can-never-take-the-degree-away-from-you-once-you've-got-it sort of thing.

When we ate in her restaurant, she would give me a double helping and say, "You're so thin. No one is ever going to marry you."

When I graduated from college, she said to me, "What are you going to do now—now that you've gone through college and still not married?"

"I am going to go to graduate school."

"Graduate school? Graduate school and so thin? You'll never find a husband."

No matter how well you do, if you are an Astoria girl and are not married in your early twenties, you are a failure. I didn't get married until I was 29, which in Astoria was like 105. Actually, my mother told me, "Don't get married until you're older." Both my parents said that; they were very good. They understood there are other things to do in life that they missed, like graduate degrees and travel. Once you settle down, it is over. And it was a mental high for me not to have that *when-are-you-going-to-marry?* pressure.

But then, on my twenty-fifth birthday, my mother called and announced, "You're older." So at twenty-nine, which is old for them, especially for the neighborhood, I got married.

Now it is something else. No matter how much I may do or accomplish as an artist or person—I can have museum shows, travel to India—*now* their concern is: *I don't have children.* It is not so much my family, but the neighbors. My mother is very good about that. But the neighbors are not quite sure.

My great-uncle, my grandfather's brother, whose ring this is [points to her finger] was the only one in the family who was educated. He came to America with an equivalent of a college degree and could speak eight languages. He fascinated me because he could speak all these languages and play the guitar. Once he made me a small set of furniture that he kept in his house for me to play with when I visited. His name was Joe; my father was named after him. My mother gave me his ring last Christmas. It means a lot to me.

My father told me horror stories about discrimination. When my grandmother died, the Irish priest started the mass before the coffin got to the church—they had horse-drawn carriages then—and everyone felt this showed a lack of respect for the Italian family. In our neighborhood, the Irish and the Italians did not speak to one another. They did not get along. The Irish considered us almost black and would call us niggers. Sometimes they called us wops. I was made aware of prejudice, but I always thought it was a result of *their* ignorance, and I never took it seriously. I thought of the Irish as stupid rather than of myself as inferior. One time, in the sixth grade, we had a teacher who was Irish and gave the Italian kids extra homework. Then the next year we had an Italian teacher who gave the Irish kids extra homework. Word must have got around. The Irish-Italian thing could be pretty bad. And yet there was a lot of intermarriage. We all lived in the same place; we all went to the same schools. I myself married an Irishman, Ed McGowin.

It takes a while for people to assimilate and become rooted and get power. In the neighborhood I grew up in, the Italians were held back because of their attitude toward education. Education just wasn't that important to many of them. In my aunt's family, her daughter quit school and it was not important to them. I think there was a fear that if the children got educated, they would leave or change, or something. The Italian kids who did go to college had unusual parents. I like to think of them as nature's aristocrats. Their life situation did not allow them to develop their own bents and interests, and they wanted their kids to get an education and do these things instead.

Before he married my mother, my dad had a little band and played the tenor sax. He was supposed to be very good, but he did not play it when I was alive, so I don't know much about it. We had a piano in the house and he could play by ear. He always listened to opera and hated that I did not know anything about it.

As we listened to music, I might ask, "What instrument is that?"

That is such and such, he would say. How could I *not* know that

that was what it was? It was important to him that I know these things. When he was young, he had heard Caruso sing; he had stood in the back row. That was part of his life, nothing unusual. It was part of his nature to be interested in culture.

There is no doubt that I am an artist today because of that underlying parental support for the arts. In a moment of practicality, I went to college with the intention of studying history, but then switched to art. Some of my friends were telling their parents that they were switching from business to the theater, or whatever, and their parents were upset. They refused to pay tuition fees unless their children studied business, and some of them complied. Thus, because their parents felt that studying the arts was impractical, they ended up with jobs in areas they didn't like. When I called my parents to tell them I was changing my major, they said that it was all right. They never asked, *How are you going to support yourself?* Maybe they should have. It has been hard.

After finishing college, I stopped going to mass, and don't practice religion anymore. But I think I am a religious person. From first grade through graduate school, I went to Catholic schools. People have looked at my resume and asked if I had been a nun, because it reads one Catholic school after another: Our Lady of Mt. Carmel School, College of Notre Dame, graduate school at Catholic University. At Notre Dame, it was very Catholic, with masses celebrated every morning, though you did not have to go.

I am resentful of the restrictions and fears that Catholicism placed on my life as a child. The priests and nuns told us graphic stories about exorcism, about priests being beaten by spirits. I never saw the movie *The Exorcist* and I never will, because of those terrible stories they told us. The lives of the saints were always gory—St. Lucy plucking out her eyes so that people would not think she was beautiful and distract her from spiritual life. And the picture of her is always with her eyes on a tray. And Maria Goretti—the nuns loved Maria Goretti, the young girl who fought off rape and was stabbed thirteen times to her death. And they always had these movies about the Crucifixion. That kind of thing scared me. I was so afraid of saints appearing to me—because they said if you were good, a saint would appear. So I used to pray, knowing I hadn't done anything wrong, "Even though I am good, please don't anybody appear to me because it would really scare me."

One night I remember waking—I was seven or so—and thought I saw the Blessed Mother on the fire escape in our apartment building, and I went and got my mother up. I said that the Blessed Mother was on the fire escape. I mean, *Right from the grotto with Bernadette to the fire escape.* I transferred it totally. But I was afraid; stories like St. Stephen with the arrows were terrifying. We were too little to be told about the gore and the blood. And another kind of fear hit me when I had to enter that little black box. I used to shake before going in to confession. I'm sure it is not like that today. It was barbaric; it was medieval.

As for s-e-x, they taught us all the basics, like the patent-leather shoes. You were never to wear patent-leather shoes because they reflected up your dress and the boys in the class would see e-v-e-r-y-t-h-i-n-g. You were only supposed to wear white underwear. It was a sign of purity. When I grew up, I think you could *only* get white underwear. And you were supposed to carry a telephone directory with you when you went on a date because if there was no room in the car, you would not want to sit right on the boy's lap. You put the telephone directory on his lap and sat on that. The nuns told us all of this. The best advice of all was that you were always to take a shower, not a bath, because the shower would steam up the mirror and you would not be tempted by the evils of your own body. That whole attitude really makes me mad. It is hard for me even to talk about it. I grew up and have a healthy sex life, but imagine what this may have done to some kids, who are still running around taking showers instead of baths, thinking that their bodies are evil.

But my falling away from the Church had more to do with the times. In the late sixties, when I was finishing college, the world was in an uproar about the Vietnam War, and our young people were rebelling against tradition and patriotism and that sort of thing. Pope John opened up church windows to let in fresh air. To top it all, I had a strange priest at college who, I presume, was gay. He had feminine characteristics and was always quoting from St. Paul that women were stupid. He made me very angry.

It just didn't seem evil for me not to go to church anymore. So I stopped going. But I do think of myself as Catholic. When I have to fill out a certificate that asks for church affiliation, I don't put *nothing* down, I write *Catholic.* John Paul II bothers me. He is such a nice person, charming and personable, but his religious beliefs are just too conservative. His views on abortion and homosexuality, for example. And I cannot understand the Church's stand on birth control in the Third World countries. It is very hard for me to accept. For the Pope to go to India and tell people not to use birth control because it is against the religion . . . what is the alternative? Starve to death?

When I die, I will be buried in Calvary, the Catholic cemetery in Queens. My father bought us a plot. My grandparents are in that cemetery, my father is there, and I'm going to be buried there. Definitely.

My husband comes from an Irish-WASP family in Mississippi, and he has never seen anything like our family's Christmas and Thanksgiving meals. In his home, if five people are there, they have five slices of ham. In my house, they'll have enough food if the entire U.S. Army came by unannounced—and there would be extra. We always have an antipasto, a pasta course, and then the turkey and trimmings. It is a combination meal, Italo-American. You end up with the American food. People laugh because they never heard of such a thing. Ed said the first time he came, he thought it was just going to be the antipasto, and when we served the pasta after that, he thought, Strange, but if that's what they eat . . . He had no idea there was a turkey and all the trimmings to come. Mother used to do all the cooking, but now my sister and I take turns.

There isn't much family anymore. Since my father died, fourteen people have died in the family. At the last Christmas dinner, there were my mother's neighbor, Gracie Esposito, who is a widow lady, my mother, my sister, Ed, and me. We pick up other people occasionally. We eat fish on Christmas Eve. The eve is almost more important than Christmas Day among the Italians. Easter used to be a big holiday, but not anymore. That has drifted away. New Year's was also a big thing, but not anymore.

I grew up thinking I was rich. When I go back now—my mother still lives in the same neighborhood—it is obvious that the houses and the area are pretty modest. But as a child, I had everything and felt totally secure, and that means a lot. I could not wait, when in college, to get back home, just to see my father open the door. Such a wonderful feeling! It still gives me strength. I thought everybody had that, everybody had parents who adored them. I miss my father a lot, because he was a source of strength. He said to me that I could do anything.

If you want to be the first woman president, you can do it.

Nothing ever made me feel, "Oh, I can't do that." I never thought, "I'm a woman. I can't do this," or "I'm from Astoria. I can't do that." I was surprised when people didn't know where Astoria was. This was a whole lot to be given. Many of my friends didn't have it. Women have been going through a big change, women's rights and all that, but that did not impress me. It never occurred to me that I could not do anything.

What has been against me, even as I was growing up, is my height. In my neighborhood, I was about two feet bigger than half of the parents. Italians are usually short, even though my father was six feet—he was the tallest one in his family. In my block, being tall was not popular. I looked ridiculous. Weren't you supposed to be short, bouncy, blond, adorable, and full-breasted? I was none of those things. A friend told me she didn't get her breasts until she was sixteen. So I waited for my sixteenth birthday and woke up, thinking they would be there. I was devastated. At thirteen, I was five feet eight. A funny thing happened in high school. One of the nuns announced—it was career day and we had to get up and say what we wanted to be when we grew up—that it was my turn and said, "Now, I don't want anyone to laugh. Claudia can't help it. She is deformed."

It was because of my height. I hated that nun for that. I hated her. I am very tall. It is a big part of my art theme.

Strange at it may seem—Italians are supposed to be so warm and friendly—half of my family does not speak to the other half. I remember when my grandfather was in the hospital, and my aunt [his daughter] was there, they did not speak to each other but spoke through me, and I had to transmit the messages. In another instance, I had not seen my uncle for eight years, and *he walked right by me on the street.* For a long while, I thought that this was peculiar to my family, but it also seems to happen elsewhere. I thought my family was crazy. They don't speak, they hold grudges *forever.* For five years now, we have not seen my father's sister—I mean a *deliberate avoidance.* I do not know why we do not see my aunt, you know what I mean? It is that bizarre. It has something to do with what happened in 1932 that I don't know about. Even my father and his brother and his sister did not speak for years.

How can this be, with the image of the warm Italian family gathered in love around the table eating those big meals? And those big meals! Someone was always getting hysterical—my aunt, usually. After an emotional outburst, she would faint and fall in the plate of spaghetti. All this kind of small-mindedness and bitchiness bothers me. In my own family, it bothers me a great deal. Certainly, we are all a bit crazy and everybody has shortcomings, but I have such a small family now that when a few people don't talk, you end up mute. And I saw this sort of thing the whole time I was growing up. And my mother, who is German, is just like the others. She does not speak to my father's sister, or rather it is my father's sister who does not speak to her. That is the better way of saying it. Being Italian is catchy. It is overemotional.

There is so much peculiarity. The talk at the dinner table is often about sickness, disease, death, details of surgery and operations, who did what to whom and when, who is not talking to whom, for how long, and so on. It all goes on with smacking of lips, clucking, and tsk-tsking. And the behavior at funerals! My father's Aunt Rose—that would be his dead mother's older sister—would take it upon herself to go to every funeral. Funerals were a major part of our social life. We went to funerals all the time. Aunt Rose would habitually go to these funeral parlors in Astoria, where there were as many as twenty rooms. She usually knew the deceased, and her visits became a kind of ritual.

In Italian, she would shriek, "Ohimè [alas, alas], I saw him [the body] take his first step. I took him to school his first day. I changed his first diaper. I stood at his wedding." And worked up over her own emotion, she would faint. One time she did this and found herself surrounded by people she did not know who were standing over her and staring. She was in the wrong room. So she got up, straightened herself out, went to the next room, and said again,

"Ohimè, I saw him take his first step . . ."

Screaming and hysteria were the norm. The women were like the Greek chorus in Euripides, commenting and wailing. The men stood in the corner.

When I got married—I was twenty-nine, with a graduate degree, marrying a man who taught at a university—my mother said to me, "You have to have one of the velvet bags at the wedding, the booster bag."

These were large satiny purses for money gifts that were usually placed on the table where the bride and groom sat.

I said, "Ma, I'm doing the wedding, and forget about the booster bag. There is no way I'm doing that."

What happened? I did not have the bag, and the Italian guests came to the wedding with envelopes for Ed and me. They placed the envelopes in front of us, and in desperation we ended up using a black plastic bag that my aunt brought her old shoes in, in case her feet hurt. At the end of the day, the bag was filled with money.

Although my lifestyle today is far removed from Astoria, I am still attached to my roots, to the food and customs. I think it is great to have lasagna for Thanksgiving and to have fish on Christmas Eve. That is a wonderful part of my life, and I hate to think it might be lost. What makes America great is that each ethnic group still loves and eats the dishes their parents and grandparents ate. If we all dropped that and ate hamburgers at McDonald's, I think it would be tragic. In Astoria, I grew up eating all the ethnic food in the world, and had no idea it was all such a delicacy until I started going to embassy parties in Washington, where I ate stuffed grape leaves and piroschki and prosciutto wrapped around melon. The guests are always impressed with what they are eating. It's no big deal, I think. I had it all in Astoria. I love Astoria for all the different foods and restaurants. You can eat better there than in some European cities.

My husband and I live in SoHo, and we came here because we needed a loft for our work. But I love SoHo because it is in the Italian section. When I get depressed, I'll sit in the butcher shop and talk to Dominic or Carmine. They'll say, "Don't buy the veal today. It's not so good."

Or I'll go to DePaolo's to buy fresh manicotti, and Mrs. DePaolo says to me, "We don't have any today that are fresh enough. But here, make them yourself. Take these shells, and you mix this much ricotta with this much . . ." They are like my family.

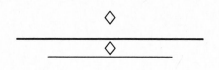

Gay Talese at twenty-two, a lieutenant on leave in Italy

GAY TALESE
The Autocrat of Maida

◇

The theme of being Italian in America is an integral part of
Gay Talese's *oeuvre*, including such works as *Honor Thy
Father*, *Fame and Obscurity*, and his upcoming book on Italian immigration. Considered by some critics as the best
nonfiction writer in America, he has introduced into current
literature a new kind of nonfiction that combines the storytelling enchantment of fiction with reality itself.

With his wife, who is editor-in-chief of a major publishing
house, and two daughters, Gay Talese lives in a Manhattan
townhouse on the Upper East Side, where this interview
took place. Mr. Talese wishes it to be emphasized that the
memoir that follows was not written by him but comprises
spoken answers to questions posed to him during the interview. For the sake of readability, the questions have been
eliminated.

*Italians are not one thing or the other—we are individualists at
the same time that we are a blend of conflicting forces.*

My family background on my mother's and father's side
begins in *one* village in southern Italy. The village is Maida, in the
province of Catanzaro. It is nestled atop mountains, midway between
the Ionian and Tyrrhenian seas. On a clear day it is possible to see
both coasts, both seas, from this small village placed at the narrowest
part of the Italian peninsula.

The village lies in the plains between mountains and is the most vulnerable part of the peninsula. This probably explains why, even before the time of the Greeks, it has been the center of invasion, with foreigners crisscrossing through the village up the mountains. From ancient times, foreign rulers conquered Italy and tried to hold on to the south and Sicily by controlling the Mediterranean from there. The toe of Italy protruding into the Mediterranean was and is, strategically, a very valuable part of the southern part of Europe. You will find different conquerors passing through this small village—French, English, German, Austrian, Spanish (be they Aragonese or Bourbon Spanish), Byzantine, Saracen—in almost every decade and every century in history.

My father, who was born in Maida in 1903, was not the first member of his family to emigrate. Some years before his own departure, his cousin went to Paris. This cousin, who was born in 1895, was, and is, a tailor. He was the fifth generation of tailors in our family. In Paris he became very successful and has for sixty-five years had a shop on the rue de la Paix, next to Cartier. His workshop has been a training ground for some of the great Italian tailors working in France.

My father was also trained as a tailor. In 1920, he left his village and went to Paris and worked briefly as an apprentice in his cousin's shop. A year later, he went from Paris to Philadelphia—an unusual route. The more common embarkation point to America would have been Naples or Palermo. The following year, he left Philadelphia because of a respiratory condition that required sea air. The doctor recommended he try Ocean City, a quiet town some twenty miles south of Atlantic City on the Atlantic coast. He liked it—the sight and the sound and the smell of it—and has been there ever since. He is now eighty-three years old.

In 1926, while attending the wedding of a cousin in Brooklyn, New York, he met the woman who would become his wife. She was the daughter of Calabrian immigrants and lived with her parents in the Park Slope section of Brooklyn, not far from Prospect Park. It is not unusual to find people from a certain area of the south of Italy who have moved to the United States, settling where there is an enclave of relatives and village friends. So in this enclave of Calabrians my mother and father met. They married in 1929, and I was born in 1932, in Ocean City. I was the firstborn; three years later, my sister was born.

It was my paternal grandfather, however, who was the first member of the family to leave Maida for the New World. In 1884 he came to Ambler, Pennsylvania, to work as a stonemason. He was fleeing from his father, with whom he had had a bitter disagreement. My great-grandfather Domenico, who has born in Maida in 1848 and lived to be almost ninety, was an autocratic, remarkably affluent person who had adopted a style of life not unlike that of the feudal lords who a century before ruled that part of Italy.

He was about twelve years old when the unification of Italy, led by Garibaldi, took away from the south the last vestiges of feudalism and replaced it with nothing. Being anticlerical, like so many of the revolutionary figures of Italy and of the French Revolution (which had a great influence in Italy), Garibaldi deprived the south, including such villages as Maida, of the structure, reinforced by the Church, that held the society together. With the unification in 1860, the emphasis shifted to the north. From then on, the future of Italy would be largely determined by the industrial and financial centers north of Rome, the areas that had been the centers of patronage and power for the founding fathers of the new nation—Garibaldi and Mazzini, Cavour, and the king, Victor Emmanuel II. Almost instantly the south lost its fabric, its structure and its capital, Naples. Naples was at one time one of the great cities of Europe, second only to Paris in size and culture. When the revolution removed power from Naples, the city gradually eroded until it became a kind of Philadelphia (in our own revolutionary era, Philadelphia was itself a capital city). In the fifteen to twenty years following the unification, there was a period of acute poverty in the Italian south, and it was then that emigration began.

There were, however, some people in the south who capitalized on this confused state. With much of the royalty almost destitute, with the land reformists largely corrupt, and with opportunists in all the levels of life—from the peasant class to the artisan class and to what passed for the upper class in this new definition of class in the 1870s and '80s—land was there to be grabbed, much in the fashion of our Old West.

One of those opportunists was Domenico Talese, my great-grandfather, who purchased for very little money what was left of a baronial estate. While he had no title or any pretense to title, he lived as if he were a baron and created a kind of feudalistic atmosphere within his sphere of influence, which included his family and his extended family, the children of his brother and his sisters. He had mills and money; in fact, he was in the business of lending money, which was not exactly considered a noble calling in the village. This caused resentment and rebellion in the family.

His oldest son, my grandfather, left Domenico's autocratic rule and went to Philadelphia in 1884. He made seven trips back to Maida between 1884 and 1914, staying sometimes for as long as two years, then going back. He worked as a stonecutter, which in those days was a seasonal job, and the season was very, very brief. My grandfather Gaetano was a stubborn man; he refused to work for anyone, and if he was not cutting stone, as in the wintertime, he would not do anything.

I sense about my grandfather Gaetano, from the photographs I have seen and what I have heard, a style, a demeanor, quite different from the tyrannical Domenico, my great-grandfather; and I also sense about him a wandering spirit, somewhat lost, certainly not well directed but directed sufficiently to know that home was not where he wanted to be. He was a man of the road—considering that he went back and forth seven times, long before airplanes or speedy vessels. He *chose* to take these long trips. He had seven children, one produced with each trip home after he married. His wife never emigrated with him. He died in 1914 at the age of forty-one, of asbestosis, I think, leaving a widow and seven children. His father, Domenico, of course, took over the family, as he had taken over everything. And in 1920, as soon as World War I ended, permitting immigration and some freedom, my own father, Joseph, at the age of seventeen, tried to go to America. But experiencing delays in obtaining a visa, he first went to his cousin in Paris, worked for a year, and then sailed for the States and settled in Philadelphia.

I physically saw three of my four grandparents. Obviously, the one who died in 1914, Gaetano Talese, I had only a sense of, although I learned a lot more about him in the last few years since I began to write a book on Italian immigration. In 1955, when I was a lieutenant stationed in Frankfurt, Germany, I took a train to Italy to visit my paternal grandmother. My two maternal grandparents in Brooklyn, I saw on many occasions. But I did not speak to them in their language because I have never learned to speak Italian.

When I was growing up, the daily life of our family was removed from what is thought of as typically Italian. For one thing, there wasn't much cooking done in our house. We would go to restaurants much of the time for our meals. When you have two parents working, often in the summertime, when there was a very active business, they would work until nine in the evening. Up to this day, I prefer a restaurant to eating at home. I will eat in restaurants on an average of five nights a week, and that has been so for thirty years. It is not that I am a gourmet seeking good food; it is the ambiance that beckons me.

My mother was always interested in clothes. After finishing high school in Brooklyn, she worked at Abraham & Straus department store as a buyer. That was something she had immediately in common with my father. Both of them cared about how they looked, how they dressed, even though my father could never succeed as a tailor in the United States because custom tailoring was a quick road to poverty in the part of the country where we lived. He moved from tailoring to women's wear, becoming a woman's tailor, and later he opened a shop that sold women's clothes. He and my mother have been in that business since 1928 and are still in it today—1986. My mother was a very compatible colleague and partner in the business. The two of them have been partners all their married life.

In dress and manner, my father acted not just like an Italian, but like a man of another world. In our seaside resort, he always wore a suit, a tie and, more often than not, a vest. He had a red moustache; otherwise, he was dark-complected and had dark hair. He dressed in a very debonair but European fashion among a group of American men who wore casual vacation clothes, or at best a Philadelphia Brooks Brothers style.

He was very proud, he kept saying—almost to the point where I doubted it—*very proud* of being an Italian. But he was filled with conflict about it because he did not like the lowly condition of Italy during all of his life. In World War I, Italy allied herself with a victorious group of nations—England, France, and the United States. But she did not triumph in any sense after the war, materialistically or in terms of glory or world prestige. Yet in the 1920s and 1930s Italy had finally risen in the international community to a position of some prominence, certainly beyond anything she had experienced immediately following World War I. Even though they would not admit it after 1943, many Italians during the late twenties and early thirties rather admired the achievements of Italy under Mussolini and the very arrogant style of Mussolini himself, who lacked humility.

Mussolini had some of the dash and swagger of the Roman Empire.

And Italians such as my father were not unimpressed with this, because they, and he, liked to identify with the grandeur that was Italy during the Renaissance—when Italy may not exactly have achieved a great egalitarian society but at least achieved greatness in art. Like most Italians, my father is very appreciative of art and sculpture, painting and, most particularly, music. The Italians are achieving but in an individualistic way. This, my father identified with. He did not identify with the nation as a collective force, one that was weak and confused. Mussolini briefly interrupted that rather impotent image of the Italians, that of a downtrodden nation that exported to American shores the impoverished, illiterate, ignorant, undirected Italians of the south.

And so Italians like my father—who came to America with a certain sense of grandeur, even though he didn't have the resources to go along with it—certainly would welcome in the 1920s, if not in the 1930s, a man representing an Italy that was above the embarrassment of the American Sacco and Vanzetti trial (however unjustified history may say it was) or above the Mafia, and most particularly above the huddled masses of which he himself was one, although he would never see himself that way.

If there were any mistakes made, I guess it was in bringing me up as a Catholic. There was a small Catholic parish in the town of Ocean City, with one church and one school. The Catholic church was very poor, and the educational level of the teachers who were nuns was even more impoverished. If the priests and the nuns did not come directly from Ireland, they were the children of people who did— the most underprivileged of the Irish, not unlike most of the Italians who came to this country. There was a strong antipathy on the part of the Irish toward the newly arrived immigrants—this is well known—and it was most acutely felt in places where the Irish Catholic was on the defensive enough, unlike places like New York or Boston, where the large masses of Irish Catholic Americans could find strength, by their sheer numbers, within their minority group. Mine was a situation where you had the Irish Catholics as an isolated minority group within a Protestant town, and within this insecure Irish group in the church and school, you had an Italian-American adolescent like myself. So I felt great prejudice directed toward me by the Irish.

As I have come to know more and more, not only about myself but about others of my generation, the sources of our aggravation and scorn are mostly the Irish. There was *such* prejudice within the Church. You see, the Church provided, as we know, the first social community that the immigrant had *other* than his family. You might be part of a village clan, and you settle within a certain town, and then, in addition, you have an affiliation with the Church. But in those days, beginning before the turn of the century and certainly continuing right through to the forties and fifties (the post-World War II period that I know something about), you had the separation between the Irish and the Italians within this one church, and of course, both groups defined Christianity, I mean Catholicism, in quite different ways. Italy has been, from time to time, very hostile toward the popes and toward the Church, whereas Ireland never was. And you have, even on the lower levels of religious life such as I experienced it within this Methodist community in southern New Jersey, this hostility on the part of the insecure majority of Catholics in this parish and the small group of Italians.

It is true that in my books I have written particularly about the father-son relationship in Italian families. The reason is that *there is where the conflict is*. There is *no* conflict within the Italian-American family home with the mother, as there is in the Jewish family. In the Jewish-American story which is so much a part of our contemporary literature, it is always the Jewish male *vs.* the Jewish female. It might be because the son must deal with the Jewish mother, who is such a force in the home; or it may be the Jewish daughter who is in conflict with the Jewish father, which is, I believe, how the American feminist movement began. The woman's movement in the beginning was largely Jewish, whether it was Steinem, Friedan, or whoever, whereas the anti-feminist movement is largely Christian women, many of them Catholic, like Phyllis Schlafly (although recently we have seen an Italian-American rise to the head of the National Organization of Women). So you have Jewish women in a very powerful role in the immigrant Jewish experience. You see this in the work of Philip Roth and Norman Mailer and Bernard Malamud.

I'm not saying Italian women are all madonnas, but they are portrayed as such in Italian culture. The Italian mother is saintly; she is never scandalous. Very few prostitutes were Italian in this country. Also, the Italian mother, the immigrant, was never a servant. It goes back to origins in southern Italy. While a family in southern Italy might have seemed impoverished, they did not want their daughter, and certainly not their mother, to work in the home of someone else as a servant woman. It was close to being a prostitute because too often it would lead to that, not to prostitution per se, but to sexual dalliance, or the appearance of sexual dalliance, with the master of the house. So in this priest-ridden part of Italy, which in the twentieth century still evokes some of the spirit of the fifteenth and sixteenth centuries, you have the mother or female figure on a pedestal, always fighting amidst the poverty and pestilence, fighting with courage, and often having an absent husband because of immigration. Through so much of the period of American immigration—certainly among the first generation of immigrants, absolutely—the husband was not there. So the woman was raising the children, sometimes with her father or grandfather.

In my life in America, my mother was a strong force, as my father was. They were both forceful people. My mother was a business-woman. Had she not married, she would most likely have been in the department-store business, which does not sound like very much in view of contemporary women's achievements. But consider that in the 1920s, she did not drop out of school at the age of seventeen to get married: She finished high school, left the home to work when girls were not supposed to do that in Brooklyn, married late, continued working, and did not have a child right away. And she never did stop working. In all the years since she married, some fifty years, she has always been a career woman. She likes business, she likes being around people, she likes clothes, selling, even the accounting; she likes going to Europe with my father for the fashion shows. Age, of course, has limited much of this, but she and my father used to go not only to the garment center in New York or Philadelphia, but two or three times a year they attended the fashion shows in Florence, Rome, and Paris.

She always dressed well; she was attractive, pale-complected, and both gracious and sophisticated. She spoke refined English, without a Brooklyn accent. And her handwriting—I can't forget how perfectly clear her handwriting was. I always thought when I was growing up that I had the best-looking mother in the whole town.

My daughters are very aware of being half-Italian and are interested in that, but they do not have a feeling of being a minority, because the Italians, especially in their generation, are no longer such a minority. The sense of minority among all Italians, I believe, will soon disappear.

In one way, I am totally involved in my Italian heritage; in another way, I am not involved at all. Italians are not one thing or the other—we are individualists at the same time that we are a blend of conflicting forces. As a writer, I am always searching for stories, for characters, looking for something that is unusual. Recently, I have returned to my own background, which is unusual. In one way, it is good material, externally. It is also proving to be a discovery of self. In writing about the origins of myself, my parents, the country and the culture that produced my father, I have discovered a greater challenge than I had anticipated, but I believe—and hope—it has a relevance beyond just one person, one family.

Francis Coppola

FRANCIS COPPOLA
Magical Childhood

◇

Now in his mid-forties, Francis Coppola has achieved a reputation as being one of the greatest film directors of our time. His movies *Godfather I* and *II* and *Apocalypse Now* have a tinge of the mythical about them and within a few years of their appearance have become American classics.

A third-generation Italian-American, he is deeply involved in and close to his heritage and was amenable to an interview. He did, however, prefer a written question-and-answer form.

W*here in Italy were your maternal and paternal grandparents born?*

My father's father, Augustino Coppola, was born in Bernalda, in the province of Matera, the region of Basilicata. His wife, my grandmother, Maria Zasa, was born in Tunis, North Africa, of Italian parents. My mother's father, Francesco Pennino, was born in Naples, as was his wife, Anna Giaquinto.

Where were your own parents born?
My father was born in New York City; my mother was born in Brooklyn.

When your grandparents came here, did they settle in an Italian community? If so, where?
It seems to me that my grandparents did settle in Italian neighborhoods: my father's parents settling in Italian Harlem (Lexington Avenue and 110th Street), and my mother's family in Brooklyn.

As a child, did you see much of your grandparents? Did they relate stories about their childhood and life in Italy?
As children we did see quite a lot of our grandparents, especially my father's parents, but as they all spoke Italian fairly exclusively, I don't recall many stories from them. I do remember affection and playing games with them, but not so much in the way of discussion.

Frank Stella and Robert Venturi both said Italian was forbidden to be spoken in their home because their parents wanted to become completely Americanized. What was your family's attitude about speaking Italian?
My parents did not speak Italian to us children, and so we developed no abilities in this respect. Some Italian was used to discuss Christmas presents, secrets, and there were a few expletives when we were in trouble. But other than that, we were not given any of the language.

Do you speak Italian? The Neapolitan dialect?
I do speak a little Italian now, but more from working with Vittorio Storaro and an Italian crew in the Philippines, and a little bit of high school Italian, than any other reason. Again, we have a few dialect words or expressions that come from the stories that my father or Uncle Mike would tell us, but I speak neither Neapolitan nor the Bernaldese dialect.

Many Italians rejoice greatly over the birth of a boy, more so than that of a girl. Did you and your brother, male children, feel in a more privileged position than your sister, Talia?
My parents were very much cosmopolitan Americans, due to my father's work in New York City [composer, conductor, and flutist for Arturo Toscanini]. My mother very much wanted to have a

daughter, and so when a second son was born (myself), she kept my hair very long and I was put in dresses. I was the darling of the family up until the birth of my sister, Talia. She was very cute, and we all made a big fuss over her.

Did your parents try to maintain their Italian heritage in the home as you were growing up? In what ways?
My father was always reading as a boy, and as an adult he would tell us many stories and incidents that related the Italian genius and the tremendous achievements in all the great fields, from mathematics, music and painting, and so on. He always made a very convincing point to us that we should feel a part of a very exalted culture and should in no way feel inferior as Italian-Americans. We ate great southern Italian food, drank wine, were the first in our neighborhood to eat pizza, listen to opera, eat cannoli, and hear about the Greeks and Romans. My father was an expert on Greek mythology, and in fact on mythology in general, being a specialist in the Arthurian legends. These stories, combined with his artistry as a flutist, made him a very magical and formidable figure in our lives.

Your father being a composer and conductor and your grandfather an accompanist of Enrico Caruso, did the cultural ambiance of your home set your family off from other neighborhood Italians?
Yes. Few if any of the people we knew had a professional and artist like my father in their family. Being the first flutist for Toscanini made him a celebrity in our neighborhood.

Who were your friends as a child? Did you stick mostly with the Italian kids?
I spent my time mostly with Jewish kids. In the latter years, as a teenager, I was the only Italian in the crowd. All the others were Jewish (and one of Dutch descent, Larry Poons).

Did you ever feel discrimination for being Italian?
Two instances of discrimination, the only two that I ever observed: one, my father wanted to move and build a house in Manhasset, and I remember his frustration at being disapproved. He said it was because we're Italians, and I became aware that there must be some limitations. Two, when I was fifteen playing with a band, I had a fairy-tale romance that lasted one day. I was walking through the park and talking with a wonderful new friend, who was also beautiful

and who liked me. Abruptly, the next morning she wouldn't talk to me. She tried to tell me that she couldn't spend this time with me, and I never knew why. It was after I met her father, and later a friend told me it was because I was Italian.

What were the happiest memories of your childhood?
My happiest memories were when I attended East School in Long Beach, New York. It was a wonderful school where we told stories and built gigantic structures out of building blocks and where there was a theater that had a machine that could make what looked like lightning.

Did you have an extended family, with aunts, uncles, cousins? Did you see one another often?
Yes, I loved my uncles and aunts and cousins and the times that we spent together. The big dinners and playing with my cousins are very wonderful memories.

Some of the domestic details of Italian life in The Godfather *struck home—i.e., Sonny in the kitchen dipping a piece of Italian bread in his mother's ragú. Was that a scene from your own childhood? What other details of a similar nature from your own experience did you use?*
In truth, it was Jimmy Caan who thought of breaking the piece of bread off and dipping it into the sauce. I had done it many times as a kid and thought it was a great idea.

Do you feel close to Italian-Americans?
Yes, very much. I feel a real sense of shared home with them, and when I meet an Italian-American of a region close to our region or whose style of cooking or behavior are similar to my own family's, I am immediately drawn to them. Martin Scorcese [the film director] is one of the few Italian-Americans who I feel almost as a cousin because of the similar background of family that we share. His parents are very kind. They always took us in and cooked for us, and those nights are very treasured.

You seem to be preserving your Italian heritage by having given your children Italian names like Gian-Carlo and Sofia and Roman. Was that your intention? [Author's note: On the Memorial Day weekend, 1986, Gian-Carlo, who was twenty-three years old, was tragically killed in a motorboating accident in Edgewater, Maryland.]

Well, Coppola is a nice Italian name when pronounced correctly, and Italian first names just seem to go with it. I love the names of our children and think that they are appropriate for their last name.

Are your children particularly aware of their Italian background? Are they happy with it?
Yes, I think our children like the Italian part of their background, but they're much more blasé about it; and I think are pleased to have picked up lots of interesting pointers from my father or my mother. They realize that the Italian strain is a very creative and energetic strain that they have. And the other part of them comes from an Anglo-Saxon, British-Irish direction and so the two are combined in my children, I think, in a subtle way.

What national heritage is Mrs. Coppola?
My wife Eleanor's relatives were in the United States before the Revolution. In fact, they sided with the Crown and made it to Canada and moved across from east to west and emerged in northern California to make fortunes in the agricultural business. Her father went with his family to Mexico and opened a biscuit company right in the midst of the Mexican Civil War and hung on and finally closed the business, and each son took part of the fortune and settled down in California. So my wife's side puts a very interesting bohemian influence in this southern Italian part of the family.

Was there anything in your Italian family experience that led you toward an artistic career?
Everything that impressed me when I was young—my father's stories, my older brother, my early exposure to music and to theater because of my father . . . the individuality and independence that it takes to survive in a place like New York in those times, and other elements of tragedy that happened to poor people in New York during that period all gave me the desire and the ability to make art.

In bringing up your children, have you shown any characteristics of the traditional Italian father: strictness, authoritarianism (coupled with love)?
I hope so. I love our children so much that it's very difficult not to say yes to everything they ask or to make everything easier or better for them. But somehow, because of our Italian and bohemian style of life and belief in keeping our children involved in all aspects of our lives, they have matured and developed grace and a certain Ital-

ian-American style regarding their own lives. Also, though, I think they know if excesses get to a point where they endanger our family or the other kids, which has never happened, that there certainly would be an old-fashioned Italian father drawing the limits and closing everything down.

In your childhood, what part did Catholicism play? I should think the panoply, music, pageants of the Church would have attracted you, as they did Frank Stella.
Catholicism was presented to me in such a frightening, unappealing, dark, anti-aliveness way that I turned from it at a very, very young age. There were times when we had to go to church early on, and we would go, and my brother would flirt with the girls in the church, and it was the worst because there was no real explanation to the proceedings that I could understand. I could only take the figure of Mary to heart. No, I must say that I thought that Catholicism was boring and scary.

What part does it play today?
Now I'd be interested in it more because I understand it a little better, in the same way I'm interested in reading about the Trojan War or reading about Genghis Khan.

Have you ever been moved to do a movie with a Catholic theme?
Yes, I would like to do it. I like the way I think the mysticism could truly be expressed, as it is in Dreyer's films like *Ordet*, or *Day of Wrath*. It would be very interesting to learn more about it now.

How often have you been to Italy? Which is your favorite Italian city?
I would have to say Rome is my favorite Italian city because that's really the only one that I spent any time in. But I loved very much a visit that I had to Lecce, in the south, which is actually where my family originally comes from. I thought it was a beautiful city. I love Milano, and that was the first city I ever visited in Europe. So I am really nothing more than a tourist in Italy; I have no real time in living there. I like Sicily very much, and where we went for *The Godfather*—I thought that was just a beautiful place near Mt. Etna, a wonderful place.

What do you think of Naples? Isn't it one of the great undiscovered cities of the world, with a fantastic concept of grandeur in its buildings and boulevards and the monumental Royal Palace at Caserta?

Naples is such an interesting place, and the architecture and the story of Naples as a kingdom (it was one of the centers of Europe, of course)—but I haven't really spent a lot of time in Naples. Not more than a few days, visiting relatives: a very nice aunt I had who was always wonderful to me, and cousins. I really did appreciate that—meeting these people—and they were all very kind to me. So my experience in Naples is pretty much at their house eating and drinking wine, and I didn't get to see as much of the city as I might have.

Does your lifestyle today reflect any Italian-American influences of your boyhood?
Of course. The things I was taught to dream about—and have since achieved—would impress my father, impress my mother, impress my grandparents and my uncles; the values were made very clear to me. One was that you had to have a big house. Another was that stories about you had to appear in the newspaper. Also, your family had to know a judge.

From the point of view of artistic influences, there was Puccini, Caruso, there was Toscanini, and my father played solo flute for him. That made me immensely proud. I can remember being taken by my father, when I was maybe five years old, by the hand down the dark marble of the NBC building and waiting for the radio concert to begin, walking around the inlaid brass squares in the RCA building's floor. Finally, I was brought into a glass booth below which you could see this great orchestra. And there he was, Toscanini, with white hair, such an imposing figure, and even more interesting to me, there was a knob inside the booth which if you turned it to the left you could hear no sound, and if you turned it to the right you could hear the music.

Bonnie Tiburzi (right) and aerobatics pilot Debbie Gary
alongside an aerobatic Pitts biplane

BONNIE TIBURZI
"In Tuscany, There Was a Tiburzi..."

Bonnie Tiburzi broke barriers when she became the first woman in the United States to pilot a commercial airline. An *originelle* and three generations removed from Europe, she has a whole different set of attitudes about being Italian. The request for this interview led her into a journey of self-discovery. As she talked in her glossy New York City apartment, she managed to feed her baby son, confer with the *au pair* girl, and talk on a white telephone in the shape of an airline.

It's just like being a woman. You have to change the public perception.

P eople usually ask me for an interview because I am an airline pilot. I have never been interviewed as an Italian-American. So when you called me, I was embarrassed at not knowing about the Italian backgrounds of my dad and grandparents. I called Aunt Julie, and she filled me in on all the different things. Of course, my sister had a totally different version of the family history.

Apparently, in Tuscany there was a Tiburzi who was a *bandito*, a Robin Hood, and my sister swears that we are related to him. But my Aunt Julie said, "No, we are not related." He was from Tuscany, and we are from farther south.

Our family is not from north of Rome, as I thought. It is actually from the middle of Italy, from a place called Arcevia, which lies across from Rome. My father's parents were married in America, but they were courting in Italy. My grandfather came over to the States by himself, looked around, and brought my grandmother over. They had all their children here.

My grandfather must have had training as a watchmaker in Italy, though he was not one by profession. He made a watch for the radio team of Amos and Andy, but we're not sure whether it was for Amos or Andy. He apparently got commissions to make watches out of valuable gold pieces and did fine work.

I feel so guilty not knowing more about my grandparents, or even about my father as a young man. But if you think about it, most of the first-generation Italians date back to about a hundred years ago. It really has been a long time since they came in such large numbers. We're diluted now. My husband has a little Scottish blood and a little Irish blood—his mother was Scotch-Irish—and the other half is Italian. I'm fifty percent Swedish and fifty percent Italian, as Mother is all Swedish and Daddy all Italian. Now my son, Tony, who is eight months old, is one-eighth Swedish, one-sixteenth Scottish, one-sixteenth Irish, but his grandfather says he is a hundred percent Italian. Obviously, he has a little Swedish in him—he has blue eyes. [Addressing her son in his playpen]: August Anthony Caputo, nobody is going to believe that is your name. I am very proud of my Italian ancestry, and of my Swedish background, too. But I must say, though, that when people ask me, What nationality are you? I say half Italian, half Swedish, but *all* American. I am really an American living in America.

Italians are a colorful people and they seem to stick together. There is a certain camaraderie among them. I think the Swedes have it, too. Swedes are very family oriented, gentle, and distinguished. You think highly of them. But with the Italians, all of a sudden you think of song and dance. You know the Broadway show *Nine*, a takeoff of the Fellini movie *8½*? It was about Italian men and very colorful. Like my dad—who was an airplane pilot, very cavalier, the Errol-

Flynn-with-a-white-scarf sort of aviator. And he did all sorts of things: He was a race-car driver, he practiced on a rifle range, and he started his own flight school. My mother, on the other hand, was conservative and steadfast. She gave us our stability, whereas Daddy gave us our sense of adventure. Most of the Italians I meet seem to have that zest for life—an open-shirt-and-chain vitality. You walk down the street in Italy and they are all whistling at you and saying, "Hello," and "How are you?" I mean, there's just a certain happiness and excitement about the Italians. You think of Sophia Loren and of Luciano Pavarotti and you say, oh boy, there is a certain glamour, too, and talent. They just seem to be more noticeable.

What I like about them most is the family tie. We always had big Christmases and Easters and holidays because all the family got together. They are family people. My husband was a bachelor until he was thirty-nine years old. [This is Bruce Caputo, the former Republican congressman from Westchester County who in 1978 ran for lieutenant governor of New York with Perry Duryea for governor.] I had big doubts as to what kind of a family man he was going to be. But he is just wonderful. There is nothing more important to him than his family. That is very special about Italians. That part is good.

In Bruce's family, there was an uncle whose wife died giving birth to their third child. My husband's grandmother just took all the children into her house. There wasn't a second thought about it. Until he remarried, they stayed with her. There is such a loyalty. I am trying to think—I do not want to belittle others. My mother would have done the same thing and she is Swedish. She is a real trouper. But there are people who feel that once the kids are away, everyone is on his own and they don't get together. Grandparents go off on cruises, and the grandchildren rarely see them. It seems to me that with the Italians, there is a special tie that never goes away. And once you are brought into the family—you may be Anglo-Saxon or whatever—you are part of the family, *and there is no doubt about it.*

My grandparents didn't speak much English, so Daddy learned Italian. I have to believe they spoke a rather pure Italian because my Aunt Julie used to comment about things like that. Once my sister had a woman working for her who was from Italy. Aunt Julie heard her speaking and said, "Her Italian isn't very good." There were three children in Dad's family—two boys and a girl, Aunt Julie. Dad was born in 1910 and grew up in New Jersey. He barely finished high school and went to work, just as his brother did. The philosophy then was that you went out and you *worked*. It was much more important than a higher education. They weren't planning to be doctors or lawyers—only to make money and keep supporting the family. As a matter of fact, Daddy lived with his mother until he got married, at thirty-one.

Aunt Julie doesn't know when Daddy became interested in planes. First he became a race-car driver and raced both in Italy and in the States. He was also a sharpshooter for the Cliffside Park Shooters in New Jersey and kept all kinds of medals from his sharpshooting days around the house.

"Then one day," Aunt Julie said, "it was a funny thing. He came home and said he was a pilot for TWA."

During World War II, Daddy flew planes for World Transport Command. Instead of going into combat, he did these missions that flew supplies to ports and bases. [Shows a photograph.] This is Daddy when he was a pilot with the Air Transport Command. He had a moustache, dark hair and eyes, and looked like Clark Gable in *Test Pilot* [laughs]. He got into all kinds of exploits.

Perry Duryea once said to me, "I remember your father as a snake man."

He said he remembered Daddy flying into Montauk on Long Island with a whole planeload of eels, which he brought up from South America and left in Montauk to be converted into serum.

"From that time, I always referred to your daddy as the snake man."

My mother was born and raised in Sweden. She came here at twenty to become an artist and got a job as an *au pair* girl. It was during World War II, and at a USO party she met Daddy. After they were married, they lived in Sweden for a few years, and Daddy was a pilot for Scandinavian Airlines. My brother was born in Sweden. My sister was born here just before they left and spent her first three years in Sweden. [Laughs.] Maybe that is where she got her blond hair.

In the 1950s, Daddy left the airlines. Today, pilots, like myself, stay with an airline forever. But years ago, pilots were so much more adventuresome. They were pioneers in so many things. Ernest Gann, a pilot for American Airlines, left and became a successful writer. Charles Lindbergh was a pilot for the airlines, and he left. After Daddy left, he started an import-export business of airplane parts out of South America. He did that for quite a few years, going back and forth to South America. He spoke Spanish, Italian, and could get along in Portuguese. He also had learned Swedish. Imagine, dark hair and dark eyes speaking Swedish. My sister picked up his feeling for languages. She speaks Italian and Swedish and French fluently and can get along in Spanish. I don't have that talent.

I grew up in Ridgefield, Connecticut. Daddy's real friends there were the Italians who were in the grocery business and the construction laborers—they were the people he liked to be with. Today many of these Italian families have big construction companies and grocery businesses. They are substantial, and there is stability and money there. It was not like that then. They were all starting out, and they were hard workers and laborers.

While we were living in Ridgefield, Daddy left the export business and started a flight school in Danbury. Running a flight school was difficult in Connecticut because you had so many months of winter. But that didn't deter him, and in addition, he began a commuter airline between Connecticut and New York, which was a little before its time. But neither was successful, and Daddy had to give up that whole dream of flight school and airline. He ended up moving to Florida and doing consulting work in aviation and he opened a travel agency. Now, of course, the commuter-airline business in and out of Connecticut is booming.

I learned to fly at the age of thirteen in Danbury, when Daddy had the flight school. My older brother also learned to fly then and did solo. He actually logged hours in Danbury. At twenty-one he was flying a stretch as a copilot for Seaboard, a freight airline, in a DC-8. He was the youngest man flying the largest commercial transport of its time. Now, he is a pilot for Flying Tigers, a scheduled freight airline. When we left Connecticut, I was sixteen and knew how to fly in theory and had taken lessons but had not gotten my license yet. In Florida, I continued with flying. But it was a little like the shoemaker's son who had no shoes. I had the urge to continue flying, but all of a sudden we didn't have the airplanes. I learned on my own after that.

In high school, I was advised not to become a pilot because women didn't do that sort of thing. But that was all I wanted to be. I thought of being a dancer, but I'm not that graceful. I thought of being a veterinarian because I love cats and dogs, but the idea of all that schooling frightened me.

What I really wanted to be was an airline pilot like my father. And then they said, "You can't be an airline pilot because there is no future in that for you." I must say that the one thing men had at that time, and women did not, was that men knew that when they became pilots, they would eventually get a job with an airline. I had no assurance of work from anyone, and I thought, What am I doing? Graduating from high school was a frightening time for me because all my friends had an idea of where they were going and what they were doing. I wanted to be something that was not a possibility and didn't know what else I wanted to be.

Still undecided, I went off to Europe as an *au pair* girl. I worked in France for almost a year, went to school at the Sorbonne, and taught English to support myself. My parents paid for the trip over and back, but that was the extent of what they could afford. When I got back to Florida, I worked in a little dress shop—and took flying lessons. I had decided that even if I could only be a flight instructor, which does not pay much—the job security was nil and there were no benefits, or anything—I would do just that. On my father's birthday, I gave him the logbook of my flying lessons as a present—he didn't know I was taking lessons. He, of course, was just thrilled. Shortly after that, I soloed and moved in with my parents because the dress shop paid about twenty-one dollars a week and the flying lessons cost $19 a week. I got my license soon after, and then my commercial and instructor rating. I didn't have an instrument rating—I had just the minimum, and started teaching primary flight lessons. After some bartering, a flight instructor gave me multi-engine time in exchange for baby-sitting. Eventually, I got all my ratings and began applying to the airlines. Just about that time, American Airlines started to hire. Against all odds, I applied, and in March 1973, they hired me. I was the first woman airline pilot for a major airline, first ever. It was an impossible dream come true.

Actually, I have always used being Italian to my advantage. When I was in my early twenties, in the 1970s, some very exciting people were Italian—Pavarotti's name was all over the place, and you heard about Sophia Loren and Claudia Cardinale. And I said proudly, "I'm

Italian," because I think you have to change people's perceptions. Some Americans meet Italians wearing open shirts and lots of gold chains who strut and boast, "Hey, I'm Italiano," and they think, Oh, God, that's Italian? It's just like being a woman. You have to change the public perception. If people want to think of Italians as greasy guys who eat pizza all day, change their minds and portray yourself in a different way and be proud that you're Italian. I got a lot of press saying I was Italian. As a matter of fact, they dropped the Swedish. Use things to your advantage more than to your disadvantage.

Becoming an airline pilot was the same thing. People would say, "You can't become an airline pilot because you're a woman."

"Well, why not?"

"Because nobody is."

Is that an answer? You know, you don't have to be physically strong to be an airline pilot. You just have to be coordinated.

Incidentally, there is a wonderful synopsis by a Professor Finsingmuller from Vienna, who in 1911 wrote the reasons women become better pilots than men. First, because they have scattered attention—which is needed since you have to look at many things at the same time. Secondly, because women can take altitude better than men since their lungs are bigger. It was very funny, but he was serious. So the whole idea is that you have to change people's perception. I even participated in a booklet on the subject of *Why Women Can Become Pilots* that was sent to guidance counselors in high schools and colleges. American Airlines now has 40 pilots that are women. For the longest time, we only had me. In all the airlines, for several years, there were only about 100 women pilots out of 38,000 pilots. In 1986, the number of women pilots increased to 400. People are finally deciding that at the same time, women can have babies, cook, sew, be doctors, lawyers, and airline pilots.

But being wife, mother, and airline pilot—it *is* difficult to be all three. Flying is my profession, but my priorities are my husband and son. I work around them. How does one manage? As I said, I fit my flying schedule around the family, which leaves more time to spend with them. For example, I leave today at 3 P.M., having spent all day at home, and then I'll be home again at 3 A.M. and only miss dinner with my husband tonight. I had breakfast with Tony and

Bruce, and could go have lunch with Bruce. Secondly, I have help —a housekeeper once a week and a live-in girl who takes care of Tony. Each day at 5 A.M., his daddy and I get up, feed him the bottle, and have coffee. It is our two hours to spend together, the three of us.

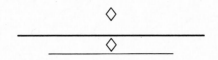

Yogi Berra

YOGI BERRA
"As a Kid, I Just Wanted to Play Ball."

A man who lives and dreams baseball, Yogi Berra chose the Yankee dugout as the place for this interview before a Yankees-Cleveland Indians game in the summer of 1985. As he kept an eye on his players, who were practicing, he spoke about his Italian boyhood on "the Hill" in St. Louis, Missouri.

My father didn't know what baseball was.

He was very strict, but my father was very good. He used to make a time for me to be home. He made *me* make the time— he didn't make it, *I* made the time. If I said I was going to be home at five o'clock, I had better be home at five o'clock. Or like at night, if I said, "I'll be home at eleven o'clock," I'd better be home. If I wasn't, I got it. You see, they wouldn't know where I was. We didn't have a phone. My brothers and me, we were always on time. He let *us* make the time.

For his living, he made bricks in a kiln. He worked for a brickyard. When he first came over, he was a builder, then he went to work for the brickyard.

With my father, we were *afraid* to do something he didn't like. When he said we had a certain chore to do, we had better do it, or else. He didn't use a strap on us. He used his hands. They were like rock.

My parents were born in a town north of Milan called Malvaglia, near the Swiss border. My dad came over to America first, and my mom stayed in Italy until he got established. My two older brothers were born in Italy. I was born in St. Louis. My grandparents remained in Italy, but my mother's sister lived in Detroit. Another sister lived in Italy. She came to Detroit once, then went back to Italy.

We lived on what we called the Hill in St. Louis. They were all Italian on the Hill, so all my friends had to be Italian. We all got along fine. Everybody knew each other and we had good neighbors. You still have a lot of Italians left on the Hill. It hasn't thinned out.

My parents spoke a dialect in the house, a Milanese dialect—at least, that is what my mom and dad called it. I think now, in Italy, it is all one language, Italian, that everyone speaks and the dialects aren't being spoken so much. Before, each town had a different dialect. We had a lot of Italians from all over Italy on the Hill, and I didn't know what they were saying. I couldn't understand them. Some words I knew, but not the way I could understand my mom and dad. We tried to get them to speak American, too. They spoke broken English. But most of the time my brothers and sister spoke Italian to them.

There were four brothers in the family, and my sister came last. We felt all right about her. She was a little spoiled. She married a German and has five children, four girls and a boy.

As a kid, I just wanted to play ball.

My father didn't know what baseball was. He wasn't anxious for me to play ball. My older brothers were all ballplayers, too. He didn't let them go into it, though. He didn't believe in sports. They had to go to work. But they said to him, "Let *him* go (meaning me, the youngest boy). We're all working." And he let me.

All my brothers had the chance to go into baseball. The oldest was the best. He's no longer living. Another brother was very good, too. He also died. But they all had a chance to go and play ball.

I *always* liked to play ball. I didn't need to be inspired by other Italian Americans, like Joe DiMaggio. Anyway, I was a St. Louis fan. Joe, a Yankee, was never my favorite.

Dale, my son, is a professional ballplayer. Another son played professional football for two years, but he had to quit because of a bad knee. He's in his own business now. Timmy, another son, runs my racquetball club. I didn't force any of them to play ball. As for the grandchildren, it's up to them if they play ball or not.

My wife, Carmen, is part English and part American Indian. I didn't choose to marry a non-Italian. It just happened that way, even though I did date Italian-American girls. There has never been any problem in cultures between Carmen and me. My mother liked Carmen, and so did my dad. And I liked *her* parents. We got along real good. My wife had five sisters and they were very close. Usually, girls don't get along, but they were close.

Like my dad, I have been very strict with my kids. We are very close. And they get along with each other. We still get together on the holidays. They consider themselves Italian-Americans. One married a German girl, one an Irish girl, and the third son married an Italian-American.

Carmen cooks everything. I like all Italian food, especially tripe [the walls of an ox's stomach used as food]. My mother cooked a lot of that, along with risotto and ravioli.

My first time in Italy was during World War II, and I went back after the war to Milan to visit the cousins. I saw both my mother and father's relatives. It felt good.

I don't think Italians are lazy. They came over here from the old country and had to work for everything they got.

It doesn't matter to me what color a man's skin is. Just so long as I can talk with him. I like to get comfortable with a guy. It takes a lot for me to get mad, but when I get mad, I get mad. I hate to repeat things all the time. If I tell my players once or twice and I feel they are going to do what I say—fine. If they don't, I get mad—which is a kind of Italian trait, I guess.

Francis Mugavero

BISHOP FRANCIS J. MUGAVERO
Life Among the Irish

The episcopacy of Francis J. Mugavero, bishop of the Catholic diocese of Brooklyn and Queens, New York, has been outstanding for the help and encouragement it has given to the new immigrants who in recent years have poured into these two boroughs from all over the world. Because of his sympathy with the immigrant mentality—which springs from his boyhood as the son of Sicilians—and because of his own prodigious humanity, he helps keep alive the American dream of new Americans.

The happiest moments of my childhood came from being a very close-knit family, living together, working and studying together, eating together.

Why Mario Puzo didn't write me up as part of that book of his *The Sicilians*, I don't know. [Laughs.] My parents came from outside of Palermo, in Sicily. My father was born in Caltavuturo and my mother in Collesano. They are up in the mountains, about twenty-five minutes by automobile from Palermo. I've visited both places, and I'm very glad they came here [laughs].

The first time I went to Caltavuturo—I was a priest in Charities then—was a Sunday afternoon, and the town was having a procession. Summoning up the few words of Sicilian remembered from my childhood, I spoke to people, but they could not understand what I was saying. The dialect is dying out there. The government has decreed that only Italian be taught in the schools and not the dialects. So most Sicilians no longer speak Sicilian. They speak Italian.

Later, I was told by the local priest how to pronounce my name —with an *h*, not a hard *g*. Moo-HAV-er-o, with the accent on the second syllable. He said that way back, about four or five hundred years ago, the name was Spanish because Sicily was dominated by Spain. The Spanish pronunciation is still used in the area. Now in Italian, of course, it is pronounced with a hard *g*. Here, sometimes people say McGovern or Maguire. The Irish identification doesn't bother me at all—I straddle it. When I'm in an Irish parish, you know, it sounds good.

When I arrived in Collesano, my mother's birthplace, about one-thirty in the afternoon, there was no one around. If you go to a place in Italy at one-thirty in the afternoon, everybody is in bed, so forget it. I didn't see anybody.

I am of that small percentage of Italians who never experienced discrimination. First of all, my parents came here as children and they grew up here. My father was a barber, and everybody knew us. I went to parochial school, where the nuns were mostly Irish—there were no Italian nuns then. I didn't see or experience discrimination at school, probably because there were no other Italian children there. It was a German and Irish neighborhood and most of the kids were German or Irish.

On a subconscious level, however, we did feel some discrimination. Living among all those Irish, all those Germans, *you wanted to be like them.* You wanted to be like the class that made it. The Irish and the Germans, they were the third and the fourth generation. They were the people who had made it. In other words, you looked *up.* As I look back, I say to myself, You were crazy to feel like that. But that was the reality of the situation.

Up a few blocks from us, that was *all* Italian. We were not allowed to go on a certain street. My mother and father would say, "You don't go there because they are dirty people."

The street was filthy. And so, you know, you wanted to disengage yourself from that type. You wanted to be like the predominant class.

At home, we spoke mostly Sicilian, though my mother and father could both speak English. My grandmother lived with us—my father's mother. The Italians have the extended family. She didn't speak much English, only the Sicilian dialect. They tell me that when I was about four or five years of age, I could speak perfect Sicilian. When she died, I lost most of it. In fact, on being ordained a priest, I couldn't speak any Italian. And as I was assigned to an Italian parish, it was by listening to my parishioners that I learned to speak the language.

The happiest moments of childhood came from being a very close-knit family, living together, working and studying together. My father worked hard. We were six kids, three boys and three girls. The whole emphasis was: *You study, you study.* All of us received an education. My three sisters and I went to the parish school. My older brothers went to the public school.

As I look back on it, what my parents had was a quiet concern for us—and love. We had a lot of fun in our family; yet there was always a certain amount of discipline. I can remember times, for example, when one of my brother's friends would call—believe it or not, we had a telephone then—and ask, "You wanna go to the movies tonight?"

"Just a moment." My brother would cup the phone and ask, "Hey, Pop, can I go to the movies tonight?"

"You finished your work?"

"Yes."

"Okay."

And it was that kind of thing. They could be strict about certain things. [Laughs.] In fact, I remember one time, soon after I had entered the seminary, my mother said to me—I don't remember whether I had gone to a party or something like that—all she said to me was, "You really want to be a priest?"

"Yes."

"Well then, you'd better cut out this other stuff."

In Italian families, the older brother or sister always commands respect. My father was the oldest on his side, and my mother was the oldest in her family. On Easter, Christmas, everybody came to our house for dinner, *everybody*, my parents being the oldest. Of course, they were helped with the food. And then every Sunday afternoon, my father's friends, mostly couples, and my mother's friends came to the house to visit. In warm weather, they would sit in the backyard, and then they would have something to eat, drink some wine. *And we were there.* We kids were always around, listening, watching. It was very natural.

All these memories are happy ones.

We were poor, in a sense, but we always had enough to eat. We didn't have any luxury—I think my father used to buy a pair of shoes every two years. But *we* had shoes. And there was always money for books—that sort of thing. We were all very good in school and got good marks.

My brother became a bank examiner for the State of New York. My older brother was a linotyper. They all got married, except one sister who died. And *not one of them* married anybody with an Italian name. My brother Joe, the oldest, married a Norwegian girl. My brother Jim, an Irish girl. And my sister Joe married a Kramer, half-Irish and half-German. And the other sister married a Polish guy.

Marrying outside your culture was, I think, part of that *looking up*, that wanting to rise out of your own class into a class that made it. We had a distant cousin who was a schoolteacher and lived in another area. I can remember my mother saying to my brother Joe, who was the oldest, "She is a very nice girl, a *very* nice girl, a very nice girl." She wanted him to marry her.

You know, she might have been a very nice girl but . . . he married a Norwegian woman who *looked* more American. And I think it was that whole business. You marry somebody that is not Italian; this helps your prestige. I think it was there.

My parents were not particularly religious. My father was not in the habit of going to church. You know how Italian men are. As a boy I never expressed much interest in the priesthood, and I first became interested when I met Father Weist. Up until then, it hadn't really entered my mind.

When my father asked me what high school I wanted to go to, I thought about it and said, "Cathedral High School" [a high school for boys who want to become priests].

He said, "Cathedral? What kind of a high school is that?"

When I explained it to him, he said, "Well, let me think about it."

A few days later, he said, "If that's where you really want to go, it's all right. You can go there. But if you ever want to leave, you can come right back and go to a regular school."

Both parents hoped I would change my mind about Cathedral. Their thinking was, What is this becoming a priest and leading a celibate life? Full-blooded, normal Italian boys find a girl, get married, and raise a family.

I don't want to boast, but my mother was a *great* cook. What she did with chicken—it wasn't expensive meat—was miraculous. I remember at almost every meal, we kids would say, "Hey, Mom, this dish is great!"

And we meant it. Kids don't say that to their mother unless they mean it. Every Easter, she made a risotto with chicken and vegetables and herbs that was excellent. And what she did with eggplant! She used it in parmigianas, in sandwiches that she baked with mozzarella and tomato, and with pasta. Ah, her pasta! She made her own—she could make a delicious pasta out of a slab of wood. Her baking was very good, too. But the family never went in much for espresso. Making Italian coffee in a *machinetta alla Napoletana* was unheard of. I myself only learned about espresso about five years ago, during a month in Italy.

My mother had a great love for music, opera particularly. I can remember when she made my sister's clothing. We used to sit in front of the sewing machine as she sewed, and she would tell us stories from the operas as her foot hit the pedal. We would urge her on.

"Hey, Mom, tell us about Aida."

"What happened to Traviata?"

They were the stories she brought with her from Italy as a small girl, and she never forgot them.

Where we lived, the Jews were the merchants, and we gave them a rough time. Our parents said they were not to be trusted, and we believed them. We overturned their ashcans and razzed them constantly. They would come running out of their stores and shake their fingers at us, saying that since we called ourselves Christians, we shouldn't be acting this way. Their faces were full of anger. Their threats scared us, but we went on doing it anyway. You know how kids are.

It wasn't the Jews, though, but the Irish that my parents and other

Italians really disliked. They looked down on the Italians and poked fun at our food and customs. There was real antagonism.

What saved the Italian family, I think, was the love each member had for the others. It was a deep love. Even though they fought —there was a *lot* of fighting, you know—the love was there. It was there even in terms of the extended family. When they had problems, they'd go *within* the family for help. My father was the oldest in his gang, and when a problem arose, they would go to him. He was like a counselor. There was that *concern* for one another.

And there was a sharing. We always learned to share. You know, we had hand-me-downs and that kind of stuff.

Always, always—you realize as you look back—your mother and father cared for each other, no matter what. You could be sure of that. That was a real support for us kids. And they cared for us. We were first, which is maybe not the soundest thing, but you know, we were first.

When I was appointed Bishop of Brooklyn and Queens sixteen years ago, the Italian laity all over the two boroughs—in Bensonhurst, Astoria, and other places—all said, "At last, one of our own, one of our own."

I must say everyone was great. First of all, I was known in the region. Born in Brooklyn, I was the first Italian to be appointed as the diocesan bishop. You see, before this, the first bishop, Bishop Laughlin, was born in Ireland, and he had been a priest in the Archdiocese of New York before he came to Brooklyn. Bishop McDonnell, the next bishop, had also been a priest in the archdiocese. Bishop Malloy was born in New Hampshire, but he studied here. Bishop McIntaggart also came from New York.

For many years, Brooklyn has been known for its Mafia. I remember when I was a kid growing up in this borough, one of them—what was his name, Frankie Yale?—got the Catholic rites before he died and was given a church funeral at St. Rosalia's. Father Cioffi was the pastor then, and he gave a homily saying in effect, What a good man he was, and so on. A lot of people said, "Tsk, tsk, tsk."

Now it happens, even today, that when these men get very sick, they ask for a priest and request the sacraments. They have a *right* to personal salvation. But there is a strictness still about a public figure like that. When this happens in my diocese, priests have to consult *me* whether or not there should be a mass and so forth. A lot of these people think that what they are doing is all right. I really think that they feel this is a way of life. Why get excited about it? Everybody gets excited about it, but *they* don't get excited.

I don't know what it is. Is it in the blood?

I have been asked if as an American bishop with an Italian name, I get preferential treatment when in Rome. [Laughs.] I will say this. When I went over there for the first time as a bishop—I had been ordained in September and went over in November—the head of the Congregation of Bishops was Cardinal Confalonieri, and I went to visit him.

He embraced me and so forth, and then said, "Oh, I am so happy to see you, young man, born in Brooklyn," and then added, "And of Italian parents!"

Pope Paul VI indicated the same kind of sentiment himself during a papal audience. When he turned to me, he spoke to me in Italian and said, "I am happy you are the son of Italians."

To the Italians, it makes a difference.

People say Italians are lazy. There *are* parts of Italy where you are likely to hear, *"Domani, domani."*

You get that here too, sometimes, though I have not experienced it too often. Once in a while, you think to yourself, That guy should get off his seat and start doing something. The capacity is there, the brains are there, the personality is there, but the response is, "Aah, not tonight. Tomorrow . . ."

But you take the Italians up in the north—they are industrious people. And the Sicilians. They are drivers; they are out for position.

Perhaps because I am the son of immigrants, I have always tried to reach out to newcomers, the new immigrants in the diocese. It so happens that Brooklyn is known as the diocese of immigrants. When you have so many, you have got to reach out to them and try to understand their culture. And you have to try to communicate with them *in their own language*. I find that that is essential if they are to be comfortable with you. Lord knows, it is hard, when they first come over, not to know the culture and especially not to know the language.

A perfect example of this difficulty occurred a short time ago in Chinatown, when the Chinese were withdrawing their money in droves from a local bank after a rumor rose that the bank was under investigation. There was a terrible run on the bank, with people pushing and shoving in line trying to withdraw their savings. On television, I saw the police pleading and talking with them, but they were speaking to the Chinese in English. The elderly Chinese, as well as the younger immigrants, *did not understand English*. And there was panic on their faces.

We have to be able to communicate with people like these and that is the reason we have established a migration office in the Brooklyn diocese. Mass is now celebrated in seventeen different languages throughout the borough. In fact, every seminarian who is ordained a priest in our diocese is obliged to speak another language by the time he is ordained. In our intensive language program, the clergy—as well as interested laypersons—can study a foreign language that enables them to communicate with the parents of our schoolchildren. When these newcomers first arrive, we also provide food and clothing, as well as legal assistance and housing and employment guidance.

If we could not communicate with them, we would be of *no* service. I have visited our migration offices and it is interesting to see how a Spanish woman, for example, who doesn't know a word of English comes in and speaks her needs to our staff. At least, *she is understood*.

Fortunately, our ethnic groups have always managed to better themselves, despite the discrimination they have had to face. For example, the Irish immigrants of the 1840s—many of them lived right here in Fort Greene in huts, swamps, and dire poverty— were discriminated against because they were Irish and because they were Catholic. But they rose, and much credit goes to the Church for that in terms of establishing schools and educating the kids. They rose from utter poverty and became teachers, lawyers, businessmen, *and then they forgot*. When new immigrants came in, the Irish discriminated against *them*. It is a hindrance always.

But let's skip to today. Take the Koreans, who make good businessmen. They have been quick to take hold. Over in Flushing and other parts of the city, they have taken over many of the vegetable and food-market businesses. One of our priests is Korean, and he is in the process of establishing a chapel and center for Koreans. They are very religious, by the way, and it is the laity who go out and teach religion and make a lot of converts. How they make such big amounts of money so quickly, I don't know, but they have it. Out in St. Michael's Parish in Flushing, some developers built a row of one-family homes. The Koreans bought them up, and they walked into the closing and paid $175,000 *in cash* for a house. They are lovely people. They are delightful.

The children of our Chinese immigrants are wonderful students. They are outstanding. I know of a Chinese family where the father is still a pagan and the mother is Catholic. They have two boys; one is a freshman in college, the other is a senior in high school. They are both Catholic. Brilliant, brilliant kids, and I've no doubt they will develop their potential to the utmost. They have all the opportunities to do so. And the father owns restaurants. He is such a good man, but his wife would like him to convert. Every time I see them, she will point to him and say, "Bishop Mugavero, pour water over him, pour water over him."

And I say, "Leave him alone. Leave him alone."

I think the greatest contribution Italian-Americans have made to our culture is the example of the caring, close-knit family—of the family that is *concerned* and knows how to make sacrifices for one another. They have also brought to American culture a natural warmth for people, not only for relatives, but for others as well.

As a bishop, I have gotten to know a number of celebrated Italian-Americans in the diocese. Governor Cuomo and Matilda Cuomo, for example. I've known Mario since I was in Charities and he was a lawyer on Court Street here in Brooklyn. I would ask him to serve on a committee, and he was always willing. Matilda, I know quite well. There is a wonderful closeness in the family. They are an ideal couple, and they have raised a good family. To Mario, those kids come first—that is, after Matilda.

Geraldine Ferraro is a member of my diocese. Gerry could provide guidance to other Italian-American ladies who want to combine family and career. All the time she was in Congress, she made sure she was home every Friday night, and the whole weekend was spent with her husband and children. They went to mass on Sunday, and there was the family dinner on Sunday afternoon. She is a very strong person, very strong. I think she has done well in both roles. John, her husband, has helped, but I know Gerry better than I know John.

A wife and mother who takes a job has to give enough time and thought to the kids. This business of the kids coming home from school to an empty house with a key—no, no. At three o'clock there *has* to be somebody there. You *have* to have grandma or an aunt or someone responsible to mind the kids.

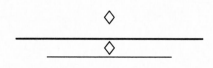

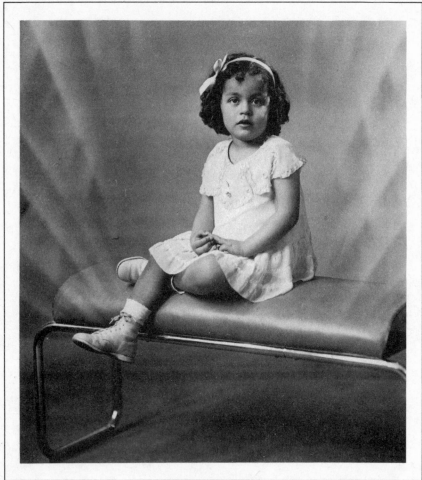

Aileen Riotto Sirey

AILEEN RIOTTO SIREY
A Culture of Matriarchs

Among the new wave of Italian-American professional women, Dr. Sirey is a psychotherapist with particular insight into the Italian personality—of husbands, wives, sons, daughters—and the relationships that exist in the family. She brings to her chosen specialty a knowledge and wisdom rising from a childhood steeped in the traditions of an ancient culture. Dr. Sirey is the founder and president of the National Organization of Italian-American Women (NOIAW).

◇

The strongest bond in the Italian family is the mother-son bond.

In my work as a psychotherapist with Italian-Americans, I've drawn some rather surprising conclusions that are contrary to public perception. Being Italian-American myself, I have a good vantage point from which to observe.

First of all, I have found that the women are feminists *without the label*. They have a relatively conservative view of feminism as a crusade and are reticent of anything that smacks of militancy. However, they are extremely feminist in their views.

The culture is totally matriarchal, in spite of the popular view that it is patriarchal. It is thought that the man has the final word or is the boss. If you were to closely examine the structure of the Italian family, you'll find that it is the quiet little lady doing the cooking who tells the husband what to say, what to do, and how to do it. Italian-American women have a tremendous, innate sense of power. I think the challenge for us is to transfer that power to the world outside: to careers, work, or lifestyles beyond the traditional ones.

Thousands of immigrant mothers were born with fine minds and intellects. These gifts were not wasted. They used them in a very powerful way, a very valuable way—*on their children*, especially the daughters. The children who made good in one way or another were the manifestation of those gifts and ambitions, of the power, ability, and intelligence of their mothers. Daughters were particularly susceptible to Mama's powers. I think Italian-American women make a mistake when they say, "I wanted to be successful in business, so I identified with my father, who was the one who went out to work."

As a psychotherapist, I took part in an in-depth study of ten achieving Italian-American women and found that they identified *with their mothers* because they had the power. There's only one institution of importance in Italian-American life and that is the family. The person who controls that and runs that is the mother. For the most part, the father has gone out to work and concerned himself with earning money. Mothers gave the strong message to daughters—I know mine did. Throughout my life and career, I have felt her influence and drive, more than my father's.

To the sons, the message from Mama was different, but it was loud and clear: "You can't live without me." The strongest bond in the family is the mother-son bond. It is much stronger than the mother-daughter tie, in terms of a connection, particularly in the formative years. Daughters are generally less important in the earlier years. Once they marry and have children, the bond becomes more solidified. They psychologically reunite with their mothers when they establish themselves as heads of households. In the family, the center of attention is the mother-son connection.

My mother was born on the Lower East Side in New York City

and was the oldest of eight children. Her father worked for the Sanitation Department, and as he put it, he "pushed-a the broom." Pushing that broom, he often lamented his lack of literacy and the setbacks he faced. At one point, he moved his family to Albany, and finally settled in Brooklyn.

Although he only got as far as the sixth grade, my father was very bright and spoke without an accent. He loved to read and would engage me, his oldest child, in political argument and talk at the dinner table—to the chagrin of everyone else, who sat silently, listening. He participated emotionally with what was happening in the world. I never felt career limitations or sexism from him. He seemed to want to teach me everything he knew and was very proud of everything I did and supportive of every achievement. He died when I was twenty-five, six months after the birth of his first grandchild, my daughter. I miss his encouragement.

My mother had much more schooling than he did. Her profession was dressmaking, and she was close to getting a teaching license. My grandfather had said, "One daughter is going to be a dressmaker, another is going to be a milliner, and the third is going to be . . ."

I forget what. Everybody was to have a specific trade. My mother worked for some of the better dress houses on Fifth Avenue in New York, including T. J. Simpson, which she used to talk about frequently. It was a store that designed and made custom clothes. At one time, she worked with the designer that did Mrs. Roosevelt's second inaugural gown, and she was very proud of that. The matriarchal influence is strong in my family. My mother wanted to be a teacher—I became a teacher. I identified deeply with her, more than with my father. But as I've indicated, he and I had a good relationship. He made me feel special.

My mother is seventy-nine and still living. Let me tell you—she's dynamite. If I could have her energy when I reach her age! For example, she visits my internist and says, "I'm tired."

"What do you mean?"

"I go to the senior citizens center and now I can only do three dances in a row and I get tired." She tells me she is upset because the doctor laughed. She has no concept of being older. Eight years after my father died, she married again, an Italian, a Calabrese. Perhaps she got married because she can't drive and he can. [Laughs.] A neighbor introduced them; they were both widowed. Now and then, they get into each other's hair, but generally, it is a fine marriage.

For her generation—second generation Italian-American, born in 1906—she possessed a modern way of thinking, an "American" frame of mind. At that time, second-generation children were still steeped in Old World traditions. But my mother is an achiever who was always aware of how things *should* be. She was caught between her parents' generation and her own. Often she found these intergeneration stresses difficult. She told me once, "My mother would send me to the pharmacy for something, but she couldn't give me the word in English for what she wanted. I became embarrassed and I would cry and say, 'Ma, tell me how to say it in English.' I was the buffer between the Old World and the New. It was a tough role to have."

My grandparents, on the other hand, were very happy transplanting the habits of the Old World to the New—that's the way it was, and that's the way it will be. My mother went to school and saw the ways of the *Americani* and—I don't think she would admit this —there lurked in her the suspicion that the ways of the *Americani* were better, more *apropos*. They had something that was special. And we—the Italians—had to become something. *She* had to become something, and *we*, her children, had to become something. She was quite aware of those things.

I grew up in a neighborhood that was relatively mixed, but most of my friends were Italian, including my cousins, who were also my friends. We all lived in the same area. When I got to high school, I became aware that there was a difference between me and the other Italian girls. I went to Lincoln High School, which was predominantly Jewish, and I was upset by the fact that the Italian kids were the ones who were in trouble at school. Not all of them, but they were *not* the achievers. And I think that was the point at which my desire to identify as an Italian-American, all of a sudden, was shaken.

There were two messages I received from the women in the family—my mother and aunts. One was: *Do the best you can in school.* They wanted me to get good marks, and they were very proud of the citations I received and the awards at graduation. The other message was not voiced but was implicit in certain things that were said or commented on, as, for example, when my mother would say, "Cummà Teresa's floors are so clean you can eat off them."

These two messages—*do the best you can in school* and *be a good housekeeper*—were valued by the family. But as I looked at my mother in relation to cleaning floors and cooking and ironing, I sensed that my mother wasn't happy. She gave the impression that she felt these things were important, yet she was upset doing them. It was confusing to me. Talk about the woman's issue: That is it. How do you do both, keep house and use your talents outside the house?

At twenty, I married. My husband and I were both attending Brooklyn College and we lived downstairs in my parents' house. He was Irish, but the name—Sirey—may be French. His mother was born in Ireland, and his father said he was Irish, though his family had been here for many generations. Five years later, my daughter Joanne was born, after I had finished my bachelor's and was teaching. We moved to the suburbs. I was married for twelve years and then divorced.

My family took the divorce terribly. Divorce among Italian-Americans was almost nonexistent then. It was quite a shock to everyone. When my mother first heard of it, she said, "Everything happens for the best." I was upset because nobody talked or asked me about it. Nobody sat down and discussed it. Which is what most people would do, you know. They might have said, "How do you feel? What happened?" Just once my grandmother came up very close to me, looked me in the eye, and said, "Are you all right?"

I said, "I'm fine." And that was that.

It was hard. The years following were particularly hard for my daughter, who was seven at the time of the divorce. I left the suburbs and moved back to the city to a one-bedroom apartment on the Upper West Side near a good school. Joanne got the bedroom, and I got the living room. Of course, I had custody of Joanne. What Italian mother would give up custody of her child? It was hard reestablishing myself and my career and going back to school. I worked first on the administrative staff of Beth Israel Hospital and then for the New York City Health Department as head of a program to train paraprofessionals to do family planning and abortion counseling. I then got my master's and doctorate in psychology and did my internship at Jacobi Hospital in the Bronx. I now spend most of my time in private practice and ten hours a week as executive director of the National Institute of Psychotherapies, a postgraduate institute where psychologists, psychiatrists, and social workers are trained to become practitioners.

It was at Jacobi Hospital that I became interested in Italian-Americans and our problems. During internship, I watched sessions of family therapy with Italian-Americans through a two-way mirror. This took place in the Pelham area of the Bronx, where they live in large numbers. As a rule, they do not have a history of seeking individual treatment and have sought help only in crisis and generally for family therapy. The complaints were usually that husbands and wives didn't get along, children were acting up, and family squabbles were getting out of hand.

Italian-Americans struggle with stereotypes—stereotypes they believe about themselves! The media portrays them as gangsters and illiterates. Youngsters seeing these portrayals on TV and in movies often grow up believing them or they want to disaffiliate themselves from their ethnic roots. The most prevalent feelings expressed are related to not being "smart enough." It's amazing to hear achieving men and women talk about not being "intellectuals" or verbal enough to express themselves adequately. These feelings are often complicated in some measure by being the first generation to finish college or enter a profession.

Another aspect of feeling inadequate seems connected to a lack of true understanding of our cultural background. We *are* different from the WASPs who are held up as the American ideal. Every ethnic group brings its own set of values, traditions, and belief systems from the Old World. They are passed on from one generation to another with "mother's milk," so to speak, and are so much a part of who we are that oftentimes we really don't understand them. The problems and feelings of inadequacy occur when "different" gets translated into "lesser" or "not as good."

In a recent ethnotherapy research project that I worked on with two other colleagues, we were able to document these issues in a scientific way. With three groups of 27 second- and third-generation Italian-Americans tested before and after the sessions, we found that the opportunity to share feelings and experiences resulted in higher self-esteem. It's important to understand our cultural differences . . . and cherish them.

Today, more and more Italians are going into treatment. My clients are now about one-third Italian-Americans. As the population becomes upwardly mobile, we're finding heavy demands from jobs and geographic relocation. This upward mobility seems to be transforming—notice I say transforming rather than destroying—

the ties of the family. In my own case, for example, my aunts lived three blocks away from one another. They were always there for support. Now, Italians are experiencing an absence of that support as they move away from their families.

The extended family is changing. For one thing, the contact is not as intimate and frequent as it used to be. Family members see one another at weddings and funerals, whereas when I was a kid, it was every Sunday. It's different from being at Grandma's house, under the grape arbor in Sheepshead Bay, at the big table, with Uncle Vinnie playing his mandolin. It happened every Sunday. That's not happening right now. But when they *do* get together, it is still there—the joy and power of the family connection.

In modern life, these strong ties are beginning to show themselves in different ways. This may explain my interest in starting the National Organization of Italian-American Women (NOIAW). It is a manifestation of my need for family. I can't have my aunts, uncles, and twenty-five cousins anymore, many of whom have died or moved away or just don't understand my differing needs. Now, these emotional connections are with members of the organization. This is the key to what I really believe: The roles have changed, but the values have not. And because the values have not changed, we find ways in which to construct the same kinds of support and extended family that we had before in our earlier lives.

I had the idea of starting NOIAW after meeting Dr. Anne Marie Valerio, another Italian-American psychologist. We talked about our experiences and the discrimination we had encountered as women generally and as Italian-American women specifically. In my case, I missed connections with other Italian-American women of similar professional achievements with whom I could socialize and share experiences. There *had* to be women looking for the same kinds of connections with people who were not related to them. Who are they, and where are they? We decided on a plan to contact some outstanding Italian-American women to help and guide us in starting the group. Geraldine Ferraro, then a congresswoman, Matilda Cuomo, wife of Governor Cuomo, Roseanne Colletti, newswoman, Bonnie Mandina, law school dean, and Donna DeMatteo, playwright, were present at the first meeting. Everyone was enthusiastic. Mrs. Cuomo thought of the organization's name and came to subsequent meetings to help us organize. Our first office was my kitchen table, then it moved to the maid's room. Now we are located on Fifty-ninth Street in Manhattan and have a secretary.

A goal of NOIAW is to erase the stereotypes of Italian-American women: Mama Ronzoni, Sophia Loren, and Mother Cabrini. Little is known about the *essential* woman. She's not vocal; she's not verbal. I remember meeting with a group of Jewish women and asking them to write five qualities that came to their minds when they thought of the Italian-American woman. They wrote that she was a good housekeeper, good wife, good mother, and so on, but as we spoke, they seemed to be saying they didn't know much about her. She was "invisible," "quiet," "self-contained." No one knew anything about her. Some of that, by the way, may have changed since Geraldine Ferraro's candidacy for vice-president.

Ann Cornelisen, the American writer, wrote a book, *Women of the Shadows*, that dramatizes this invisible-ness. It is very powerful. She describes how women from southern Italy, whose husbands went north to make a living, hold everything together by themselves. They are women *of the shadows*. That image has been our image in America. Where has our voice been? In literature? In music? Now we are beginning to have extraordinary women in the professions: law, medicine, education, and even aviation.

NOIAW's primary goal is to form a network of women who are able to help other members professionally or to help them make career choices. And we strongly believe a woman should have the opportunity to choose whatever life she wants, whether it is a career or home and marriage or all of it! If she's happy being the mother waiting at the doorway, wonderful. But we should *not* deny the woman who wants a career and has the talent for it. Let's not deny her the opportunity to achieve it.

The spirit of the group, by the way, is wonderful. We hired a WASP to help us plan our first national conference in 1985, and she told me she had never met a more supportive group of women—noncombative and noncompetitive. I think that's true. A few months ago I had a new-member meeting of about twenty-five women. I was elated by the excitement they felt about being able to talk to one another and share feelings about what it means to grow up as an Italian-American.

Another goal we've set ourselves is to foster a sense of ethnic pride. In order for a woman to achieve—and I'm an example of this—ethnic pride sometimes falls by the wayside. I think many of us today are attempting to reclaim that pride. One way is to appreciate the values of our background, the culture, the art, the literature, the music. The trouble with many of us whose parents or grandparents were illiterate immigrants is that we have had no connection with the Italy of the arts and literature and music. The only thing my grandfather ever talked about concerning Italy was the size of the fruits.

He used to tell me: "In Italy, they have-a lemons like-a grapefruit."

Everything was always bigger and better there. When I was fifteen or so, I said, "How come you never went back there? What are you doing here, if it was so wonderful there?" [Laughs.]

And that was never answered. He idealized his past.

It is time, I think, to reassure husbands and sons that a woman's career will *not* destroy family ties. These connections—the sense of family—are much too strong. They are durable. In my years of study and practice, no matter what I was doing, I was home every night at six having dinner with my daughter and talking about her day, her homework, and the issues in her life. She, in turn, was very supportive of me. We were, and are, very close.

Recently, I spoke to a group of Italian men and women in New Jersey on the subject of working women. It was a toned-down presentation. You never hear feminist philosophy from me. Afterward, two men, very proper and dignified, came up to me and said, "We have a serious question to ask. If the women go to work, what is going to happen to the children?"

I looked into their eyes and knew, with the intuitive sense of the therapist, that what they were really saying was, "What's going to happen *to me*? Who's going to take care *of me*?" I responded to the question about the children. But in my heart of hearts, I knew they were really concerned with themselves.

Men are fearful for their well-being. I think that is the biggest obstacle to women having choices about their lives. Children are involved, of course. In my case, as a divorced woman, I worked since my daughter was six years of age. From experience, I know it's not the quantity but the quality of the interaction that is significant in raising children. You can have a mother around all day long who is depressed and angry about being at home, and she is of no value to those children. On the other hand, you can have a woman who feels in some way that she is contributing and happy in her work, and she finds she can spend an hour or two with her children and both feel good about it. That's quality; that's the kind of thing we want.

The Italian man is not to blame for the woman's absence of choice. The culture has strong role definitions: what a man is and should do, what a woman is and should do. Traditions like these, which evolve to support the values of a culture, have held us in good stead. Actually, I think men are as much victims of this absence of choice as the women are. They grow up with an idea of what a woman is supposed to be and do and thus limit themselves in their choices of the type of woman they can be with or connect with.

When a male does marry a woman of another culture, he will convince her that he is the patriarch. With an Italian-American woman, he can't do that. She knows better. Similarly, he can accept a non-Italian woman with a broad career interest because she has not been subject to the same thinking about male/female roles that he was brought up with. She's *different*. I think that is a reason for the attraction certain men feel toward the non-Italian.

These seem to be examples of self-hate. If you don't feel good about yourself, you don't feel good about your culture. It is very easy, then, to move into a position where you feel that members of the opposite sex, who are doing what the culture says they must do, are unattractive. In my work with ethnotherapy groups, I've found that Italian men and women tend to desexualize each other when there is self-hate. In their own ethnotherapy groups, the American Jewish Committee found the same kind of self-hate among Jews. But when these group members began to feel better about themselves *as Jews*, they found the opposite sex more attractive.

Italian-Americans in ethnotherapy voiced the problem this way: "I don't feel good about myself as an Italian-American and so I am going to reject my culture, I am going to reject the traditions, and I am going to reject the people of my background, including the opposite sex." At the beginning of the sessions, we found a tremendous amount of conflict and tension between the men and women, but when the two began to hear the issues that each faced, that tension relaxed and they found each other much more attractive.

Let's face it: When you marry an Italian man, *you have to buy the culture*. It's not his doing; he is not responsible for the seeming oppression. When a woman marries within her own culture, she reinforces the cultural ties and yet, in reality, there isn't an Italian woman who doesn't do what the hell she pleases when married to an Italian man. When she marries outside the culture, it is much easier for her to develop herself totally as an individual.

Until we can negotiate a more equal status between Italian men and women, both of us will suffer, but more importantly, the institution we hold so dear, our family ties, will suffer the most. If indeed Italian men and women refuse to understand changing roles and what is going on, both will marry outside the culture and I think our traditions and heritage will be lost. They will marry others because there will be greater freedom from the cultural binds.

Unlike other women, Italian women do not have that same level of anger at the men for having done something to them or oppressed them. They simply do not have that resentment. They have been their own persons for a long time.

Then what are we struggling about? We need to do new things. We need new skills to do these new things. We don't want to change things radically. I think the Italian-American woman values the family and values those traditions and thinks of them as important. But now she needs new skills to negotiate in the corporate world, new skills to achieve in the professions and schools. And there's a further advantage in acquiring these skills, which is explained in the old proverb "When you educate a man, you educate an individual. When you educate a woman, you educate a family."

Alfonse D'Amato (top) with siblings Joanne and Armand

ALFONSE D'AMATO
A Fiercely Prideful Clan

In the hallowed halls of the United States Senate, where decorum and quiet are much valued, Senator Alfonse D'Amato of New York has come to be known as Hurricane D'Amato, or An Ocean of Senate Motion. Called a great senator by Vice-President Bush, he is an activist and practical legislator who *makes* government work for his state and for its citizens. His paternal grandparents came from the province of Avellino in Italy, the same province where John Ciardi's and Rudolph Giuliani's families came from. A Republican, Senator D'Amato is admired by voters of both major parties.

◇

The meals seemed never to stop: first the pranzo, later the pastry and coffee, an hour after that sandwiches, then you started the supper—one meal leading to another, without end.

I t was a fiercely prideful family—the D'Amatos—that my father came from. There were nine brothers and sisters who lived in Newark, New Jersey, and they were deeply traumatized by the experiences of the Depression. To help support the family, my dad dropped out of school a number of times, and when I say school, I am talking about high school. He ultimately finished, and then went to the state college system in New Jersey, entering Trenton State, and eventually transferred to Montclair State College, where he worked his way through with a variety of jobs. He played the piano—he played it much better than I do and was a much finer musician. The Juilliard School of Music offered him a scholarship, but he just simply could not take it because he could not afford to go there. His parents came from the southern part of Italy, the province of Avellino, outside of Naples.

My mother is a Brooklyn girl in the truest sense—born in Brooklyn, with a great Brooklyn spirit. She is feisty and compassionate and has a great love and feeling for family and people. Her father was a real Roman, a *Romano*, and her mother was born in Little Italy in Manhattan. My great-grandparents had come here on their honeymoon and stayed on.

As I was growing up in the late thirties and forties, we lived in Newark, New Jersey, which was at the time a mixed neighborhood and heavily Italian-American. We always lived in a predominantly Italian section. I remember going frequently to Brooklyn to visit Grandpa and Grandma Cioffari in their brownstone on Lafayette Avenue. Every once in a while, I go back and take a look at the house. Of course the area has changed, but somehow the brownstone does not look nearly as imposing as it still does in my mind or as it looked when I was growing up. It was a tradition for all the family to gather in it. I remember the great times we had. Friends would come in also. On Sunday, which was the day for visiting, they all came, and everyone would come *to share*. It would be a total day, a day filled with eating, drinking, women preparing meals, talking, political arguing, storytelling—some of the older people were great storytellers. Of course there were the traditional card games, when the men would break away from the women and play pinochle or poker, while the women would confide in one another about their husbands and their children. The meals seemed never to stop: First the *pranzo*, later the pastry and coffee, an hour after that sandwiches, then you start the supper—one meal leading to another, without end.

Today we do not have the opportunity to spend nearly enough time with our family as we did in those wonderful, warm days of being together and sharing together. We have a society that is so speeded up that we have lost that continuity. Our relatives and friends, brothers and sisters, are often in far different places throughout the country, and it is an exception rather than the rule when we have a drawing together. There are still times at Christmas and Easter and special occasions when we do, and it is a very wonderful feeling. But you do not have the continuity of those experiences, at least in most cases. For families that still manage to meet often, it is a wonderful thing.

Many Italian-Americans, like myself, did not marry Italians, but I think it was only the result of circumstances, especially when you went away to school and met different people. My wife, Penny, is not Italian. I met her at college, though I did date an Italian-American girl in those years. This business of dating was a much different one then. You got married quickly because if you were a year or two out of school and were *not* married, people would look at you strangely. So it was the thing that we did. And that is why you will find many Italian-Americans of my generation who went away to college marrying people who were not of the same background.

Certainly, I have experienced anti-Italian prejudice. When I graduated from law school, I could not get a job on Wall Street because of bias. A lot of it still has to do with what school you went to in the area of law. I went to Syracuse University Law School. Obviously, there are certain law schools—like Harvard and Yale—whose graduates have easy access into the best firms. But I like to think that things are not nearly so bad as they were. Not too many years ago, in a rather short time period actually, if you had graduated from St. John's Law School or Brooklyn Law School or any of the local schools and applied to major Wall Street law firms, notwithstanding that you may have been number one or two in the class, the chances were minimal that you would get a job. You probably would not. Now that is not the case anymore. Stereotypes no longer have a stranglehold. Institutions and their executives are not blinded by them and are not afraid to look at individuals. Thank God for that. If we persisted with biased attitudes, we would be doing ourselves a great disservice.

I remember that as a child, I was on more than one occasion called a guinea or wop—and worse. My reaction was to become very angry. Sometimes I overreacted—I have been known to come back strong. But generally, the effect of these childhood experiences of bias and hate was to get me to try a little harder. That is probably what has driven some of us. We may be overachievers as a result.

Part and parcel of our changing times has been the new role of Italian-American women in our society. A number of years ago, the roles of these women were viewed as being far different than today. It wasn't so many years ago that Italians had a mind-set that no woman could ever run for high political office or, putting politics aside, be an engineer or doctor. Of course, there was always the exception. But I am saying that as a general rule, their role was perceived to be far different. Then, a bright young Italian-American woman—at the most—might be encouraged to go to normal school and become a teacher, as opposed to going on for further study and becoming a scientist or doctor or engineer or other professional. We have seen incredible change for *all* women, and even though Italian women were submerged in attitudes connecting them with home and nonbusiness activity, they also have been part of that great change.

Take my daughters as examples. My younger daughter is an industrial engineer and will be graduating from Lehigh in June 1985. My older daughter is in a small business that deals with computer-oriented software and was in the oil business before that. Twenty years ago, if I had said that my daughter was in engineering school, she would have been part of an infinitesimal minority—maybe one percent of all the women in the nation. This figure has risen dramatically and will continue to do so.

The day of the ethnic candidate has finally come. In my bid for the United States Senate, both in the primary and the general elections, my Italian name was an asset. It would not have been so years ago, and this too has changed for the better. Today you have the emergence of people who have lowered the level of being *anti* or suspicious of those of different cultures and ethnic backgrounds. We are much more understanding and more ready to support people from these cultures than we were years ago. And in addition, there are people of our own ethnic background who are willing to stand up today and be supportive. You have a change of public attitudes —both on the part of the American people as a whole and on the part of ethnic Americans—which encourages the ethnic candidates.

My reputation in politics is more that of a pragmatist, a practical man who acts, than as an ideologue, a man of ideas. There is no doubt that this is the result of my Italian heritage, which has always been concerned with the practical. In politics, why automatically apply some standard or rule to a situation that may sound wonderful and may be fine *in some circumstances*? It may be exciting to talk about it in the halls of the Congress, but as far as relating to the needs of a specific situation, it may not solve anything. Every day, I am confronted with very practical situations that can only be solved with very practical solutions. I do not believe in just making speeches. If you deal with matters in a more realistic way, you are going to achieve some results for people—as opposed to just making big, wonderful speeches. I do not believe in that. A politician should be a leader and should attempt to educate, but I also think that there is a time when he should stop philosophizing and do the business of the people. Why would one want to be in politics if not to help them and do things and work to forge benefits for them? To be a politician and merely have power . . . it is a terrible waste. That would be silly.

Our national strains and individuality should be maintained. I feel very strongly about this. They act as a check on Americans to keep us from becoming all clones, fanatically following the latest fad created by ad agencies that permeate our communications system—television, movies, radio, and so on. It is a terrible thing to have to cut your hair in a certain way, walk in a certain way, wear a certain suit. If someone appears a little different, he is made to feel bad—like an outsider. As a youngster, I used to object to the name Alfonso. It was too foreign-sounding; I wanted to be an American. So I understand this clone mentality. But if we work so hard *not* to be different and we all follow the current mood and dance to the current tempo, that is really a disastrous course. A family's culture and traditions and ways and values act as a very real check on this headlong rush to conformity. They will keep us from becoming a robot society of 225 million clones who all look alike, think alike, and act alike.

Cultural diversity is the great strength of America, and it will save us. We are learning not to be afraid of that diversity. Years ago, the kids in our neighborhood, including myself, were fearful of one another, of the differences and of the strange culture and peculiar habits and language that loomed behind each kid to threaten and scare us. At least today—I will say this for you—that is not quite the case.

Daniela Gioseffi at seventeen

DANIELA GIOSEFFI
Homage to Astarte, Goddess of Earth

Daniela Gioseffi is the only Italian-American woman, with the possible exception of Diane DiPrima, to be widely published as a poet by established presses. Her poems have appeared in anthologies alongside the work of Emily Dickinson and Muriel Rukeyser. Her book of poems *Eggs in the Lake* was praised both here and abroad, as was her novel *The Great American Belly Dance*. For relaxation she plays, composes for, and sings lyrics to the lyre.

A woman of forthright views, she speaks with no holds barred. In a world of resigned acceptance, she raises her voice to protest.

It is all right for President Reagan to have advertised cigarettes, which kill, and been a television spokesman for General Electric, which builds the Mark XII deadly warhead, and to be a PR man for Star Wars, for which General Electric may get a big Pentagon contract, but Geraldine Ferraro, because she is Italian, and a woman, is highly criticized for advertising something relatively benign like Pepsi-Cola.

Women writers who are ethnic Americans, particularly writers with Italian names, have a hard time being validated in a society which is in population overwhelmingly Anglo-Germanic. For example, Frances Winwar, the novelist, was forced to change her name from Frances Vinciguerra, which translates *Win-war*, in order to publish in America. And what American remembers Grazia Deledda, the Italian woman who won the Nobel Prize for Literature in 1926? Not even the feminist movement has reclaimed her! And you won't find her mentioned in American texts on literary art.

Somehow, if you are an Italian woman writer, you are not perceived as a particular ethnicity, or as a writer at all, in this country. No one ever says, "Gee, the discrimination has been hard for you," as they understand it has been for black women writers. There is a subtle discrimination of preference for an Anglo literary tradition here—without question. It involves a tendency to discredit other sensibilities. Helen Barolini, a writer whom I know, explains it all very eloquently in *The Dream Book*, an anthology of neglected Italian-American women writers published by Emile Capouya of Schocken Books, in New York, in 1985. All the scholarship carefully documenting this discrimination against all "ethnic American" writers, with non-British, non-German, non-Irish sensibilities, is there, in her well-written introduction.

My writing is for the general reader. Hopefully, I write universal themes. For example, one of my novels, published by Doubleday in 1977, is a satire on American culture titled *The Great American Belly Dance*. The main character is Dorissa, an Italian feminist who performs all around the country, teaching everyone that the so-called "belly dance" was originally an Etrurian birth dance dedicated to Mother Earth, in imitation of the birth contractions which bring life forth from the womb. Before the Virgin Mary came the Earth Mother goddesses of prehistoric times. Before patriarchal religion of God-the-Father took over, there was an ubiquitous earth-mother deity all around the Mediterranean Sea. Dorissa celebrates the Old Religion of Earth Goddess, whether she be the Roman Ceres, the Greek Demeter, the Egyptian Isis or the Phoenician Astarte, for whom the pagan Easter was named—the celebration of the fertile egg or feminine ovum.

I have a satiric passage in the novel where Mary, in a surreal dream vision, squats down on the earth and gives birth to a female messiah while she is performing belly-dance movements. I'm sure this might seem sacrilegious to some, but for me it is satire on patriarchal religions, which deem the female inferior. You know how we southern Italians are! We don't take the Church too seriously. We see it as operatic pageantry—having lived alongside the various popes, with their ancient corruptions, illegitimate children, massacres of the innocent, *and* what have you for centuries! As a woman, I cannot take Catholicism seriously. Christianity is one thing; Christendom, another. It is far too patriarchal and oppressive of women. There is a theory, which seems psychologically correct to me, that the celibacy of the priesthood, of men *only*, was institutionalized long after the founding of the Church, by either homosexual Medieval monks or mysogynists. It was never deemed necessary in the Scriptures themselves. There is no mention of it in the Bible or the words of Christ.

I've just finished another novel, called *Americans*, which *is* about Italians and partly about the roots of all ethnic prejudice in this country. And it is about my hope that America can overcome all such prejudices—against all groups of people non-Anglo or non-Germanic in their culture. But I wonder, as a woman with an Italian name, whether I will be able to find a publisher for it—even though I had very good reviews, both here and in London, for my other novels. It deals partly with my father's life as an Italian immigrant struggling for sustenance and respectability and the cruel discrimination he had to deal with. It also makes clear that ours is not the only ethnos that suffered or is suffering.

Since it is not about Mafioso sensationalism, which is all Hollywood wants from us Italians, I wonder if America will be interested. We know how terribly the blacks and Jews have suffered, but the pain of Italians, Hispanics, Poles, Asians, and native Americans is just beginning to be understood.

The largest part of our population is *overwhelmingly* English, German, and then Irish, with the far lesser French, fourth, and the Italians, here, *fifth* in numbers.

Out of over 237 million people living in the territory of the United States of America, according to the 1980 census and projections of the *Statistical Abstract* of the United States Department of Commerce and Bureau of Statistics, about 50 million are English and nearly another 50 million are German. Some 40 million are Irish, and the rest of us make up the lesser portion that is left. The French number about 13 million, and the Italians are closer to only 12 million. There are only about eight million Poles and less than a million Chinese, for example.

Other sources claim Italians are about 16 percent of the population, mostly in the Northeast with a small percentage around San Francisco. Besides, I read that 80 percent of Italians born here after 1960 are Italian and *something else*, as my daughter is Italian, Irish-German American. I myself am now married to a Turkish-Polish-American Jew. Perhaps this rapid assimilation explains the discrepancy in the population statistics.

The point is, as Alice Walker, a very fine black American author, has said, we are just beginning to understand "what it means to be an ethnic-American and a woman in a society that validates authenticity in neither."

Some years ago there was an article in *The New York Times* that was entitled, "Bad Image Still Plagues U.S. Italians." Of course, it was referring to the Mafioso stereotype that haunts us, Hollywood-style. But you never hear the people who invoke the term *Mafia* using it for *all* organized crime of any ethnos or talking about that persistent Anglo-American institution the *Ku Klux Klan*, which did plenty of lynching of blacks, Jews, Catholics, Italians—anyone not of the all-American redneck image—right on through this century, *and is still at it*! Are Americans as upset about the Nazi party that persists among them as they managed to be about the idealistic so-called "Communists" during the McCarthy reign? The popular American mind is fairly duped with such imbalances and prejudices.

This kind of mentality persists even among the educated and sensitive. Look at the offensive slurs against Italian-Americans even in a Woody Allen film like *Broadway Danny Rose*, which appeared in 1984 to all kinds of Academy Award plaudits. In it, Italians are portrayed as one-dimensional, Mafiosi vulgarians with loud mouths and no inner feelings. And that is not just my opinion, but the intelligent opinion of a fine movie critic and a poet, a Jewish-American woman, Katha Pollitt, who writes for *The Nation* magazine. She criticized Allen for this shallow portrayal of our ethnos in an otherwise favorable review, and she is the only non-Italian I ever saw make such a correction of this cruel stereotype. An even worse example of this horror perpetrated on our people is *Prizzi's Honor*, directed by John Huston, which appeared in 1985 and rated four stars by the critics. Sure it has good acting and a clever script, but who said anything about how ugly it is toward Italians, particularly Sicilians, and toward Jews and Poles also—because they, too, are the criminals and low-lifes in the film? These films are ignorant and prejudicial slurs on American citizens, and yet they receive accolades, while the Ku Klux Klan persists, relatively unnoticed. I don't know why this wholesale defamation of character is allowed, except that maybe now, since no one dare publicly do this to Jews or blacks, they are using Italians as the smokescreen, the scapegoat for all the evils of the world, diverting attention from the monumental corporate crime of the military industrialists and poison-chemical industries of this country.

Why does this American stereotyping of Italians persist when the great majority of Italian-Americans, like other ethnic groups, are hardworking, ordinary people, not sensational criminals—when Italy has given the world so much culture, where the Renaissance took place to save the world from barbarous medieval bondage, where most of the great paintings of Europe are still housed and many were painted, where music flourished, giving the world the forms and instruments of the symphony? Italians gave birth to Da Vinci, Galileo, Vivaldi, and many great cultural heroes—Paganini, Marconi, Fermi, La Guardia, Garibaldi, and Joe DiMaggio—and still the Mafia image persists to this day.

There is a theory of why it is so. It is the old tactic of divide and conquer. Keep ethnic groups—the "Rainbow Coalition" of American minorities—set against one another, while the wealth remains in the hands of the same few who have always controlled it. The bulk of the wealth is still held by the same few, and it is distributed very much as it was in 1913, when my father first came from Italy. He came as part of the hordes mainly imported by profiteering steamship companies as cheap labor—to break up the labor movement, which was begun by immigrants who had arrived earlier.

It is so ridiculous for Jews or blacks or Italians or Hispanics to be set against each other when the bulk of American industry is militarized and the war-weapons industry is controlled by the executives of General Electric, Westinghouse, Rand, Bechtel, Lockheed, Honeywell, Grumman, Hughes, or what have you—all the big Pentagon contractors who are likely to blow us "ethnics" all to kingdom come with greed and the profit motive. In my estimation, *that's* the truly scary organized crime of our time. Corporations like Union Carbide poisoning people, with *no* accountability for their crimes. The most a corporation gets is a fine in dollars, which it can usually afford, but some little "ethnic" in a ghetto who steals a piece of bread is clapped in jail—and Hollywood throws up a Mafia sensational smokescreen to blame all crime on Italians and we sit and take it. Should we? How many Hollywood films are exposing the Ku Klux Klan?

It is all right for President Reagan to have advertised cigarettes, which kill, and been a television spokesman for General Electric, which builds the Mark XII deadly warhead, and to be a PR man for Star Wars, for which General Electric will get a big Pentagon contract, but Geraldine Ferraro, *because she is Italian*, and a woman, is highly criticized for advertising something relatively benign like Pepsi-Cola. It's a funny world, growing up Italian! I mean, Pepsi-Cola doesn't build the Mark XII warhead the way G.E. does, while it hypes with a slogan:

"We bring good things to life,"

and the Mark XII warhead is the most deadly evil weapon in history—*sizzles billions in an instant*. Still, Ronald Reagan has gotten away, very well, with being the G.E. spokesman through the years—but look at the criticism of Geraldine Ferraro, in comparison!

That's why it is difficult growing up Italian in America! It is difficult for any ethnos that doesn't fit the all-American Hollywood image. The American popular vocabulary is full of ethnic slurs— ugly pejoratives that we carry in the backs of our minds.

My father came from Apulia, on the Adriatic coast, across from Greece—a little village called Candela, because it looked like candlelight on a hill at night, a one-goat mountain village. His father, Galileo, was an artisan of the town, and his father before him, the mayor. In those days, a town craftsman was well respected. He handcrafted all sorts of leather goods and gold-leafed them in Florentine style. Unfortunately, when he arrived here in 1910, my grandfather found America had no use for craftsmanship. The Industrial Revolution had created the assembly-line shoe or purse. He was devastated to end up a shoe repairman, a mere cobbler, in a large city like Schenectady, and later in Newark, rather than a respected artisan of a small village community. He was soon frustrated and broken by America and put all his hopes for the American dream into his sons, my father being the oldest and, therefore, most burdened and responsible to *la famiglia*.

The name Gioseffi, by the way, was misspelled by an immigration officer, like so many names of immigrants from southern Europe, and the name became Josepha. There's no *j* in Italian. Later, my father researched the original spelling in his homeland. His Christian name, Donato, was changed to Daniel and so I am called Daniela, actually an Anglo-Saxon version of a Hebrew name. His real name was Donato Gioseffi.

His mother probably came from Naples; her mother definitely was Neapolitan. But we are not sure whether it was Naples proper or a village outside the city. She was such a humble, gentle soul, Grandma Lucia from Naples. My paternal grandfather was a blond, blue-eyed Italian and there are many such. After all, the Swiss Alps are not so far away, you know—you can walk over the Alps. My father was blue-eyed, with very pale skin, like me. Some aunts and uncles are blue-eyed and some are brown-eyed. Grandma Lucia, on the other hand, was olive-skinned and had black irises, very dark brown eyes. Half the children came out olive-skinned, and the other half blond and blue-eyed.

Family legend has it that we are Greek Albanian Italians and that we are descended from the Etruscans, the truly indigenous people of Italy, the pre-Roman Italians. With our new ways of cracking language codes, I believe it has been discovered that one-third of contemporary Albania is ancient Etruscan. Many of the Roman edifices and amphitheaters we know were built over Etruscan ruins. The Etruscans were closer to the Greeks in civilization. They had a marvelous civilization. D. H. Lawrence admired them, traveled a great deal in Etruscan Italy, and wrote *Etruscan Places*. Many feminists are interested in the Etruscans because their women were equal to their men and the civilization was of matrilinear descent.

When my grandfather Galileo, who had arrived in America first, went to meet his family at Ellis Island, he was heartbroken to find that my father, Donato, was hospitalized with scarlet fever and diphtheria and that his daughter, Raffaela, had died aboard the ship of scarlet fever or diphtheria and had been buried in the ocean. He couldn't even read the English-language message an official stuck into his hand as he waited, pacing back and forth, wondering what had become of the family he had traveled miles from Schenectady to greet:

"Your five-year-old daughter, Raffaela, died and was buried at sea," it said, in effect, "and your wife, Lucia, and son, Donato, are quarantined in the hospital. Come back in thirty days to see if you can meet them for entry."

Can you imagine my grandfather's sorrow—how devastated he was! Remember, many of the immigrants who arrived here diseased were healthy when they boarded the overcrowded steamships, but because of the close quarters and bad conditions aboard ship, they often contracted illness by the time they arrived at Ellis Island. Some died at sea. Very simply, the steamship companies were profiteering. They would go to the Old Country and advertise that the streets of America were paved with gold: "Buy your passage from us, and have all your dreams come true!"

What they were actually doing was overbooking, even in crowded steerage, and making big profits. They imported people like tangled worms and gave them slop to eat. They gave them filthy conditions to travel in. They had to stay in overcrowded, disease-ridden cabins below deck, with a stench and very little water to wash themselves and very little fresh water to drink. Water was rationed. On the deck, they sat in the rain and wind. God bless America, land of liberty! They were imported like cargo by big industrialists for cheap labor to break the unions here. That is why we were brought over from southern Italy—not to give us freedom in the land of the free and the home of the brave. Sure, we were starving there, too, but at least under blue sky. At least we were not treated like worms, like cargo, like slaves. We were brought over in better conditions than the black slaves, but many were indentured servants when they came. Somebody would make an illegal contract with them: "If you work for a penny a day, we will let you have a job over there." And there were a lot of immigrants using one another after they arrived. The ones who had learned to speak English used the ones who hadn't to make a profit from them.

Let us be realistic about this home of the brave and the land of the free, this land of "Bring me your poor, your tired, your huddled masses!" Though there is a grain of truth in that—hopefully, some-day this will *really* be the land of the free, free of ethnic prejudice and stereotyping, and maybe there is something here more hopeful than in Russia—the truth of the matter is that we were herded here to break the unions because the immigrants who were already here had wised up and started to unionize.

And there were lots of battles going on. People were still being shot down in the streets. The Vanderbilts or Morgans or Carnegies or whoever were fighting each other for control of the railroads or whatever and hiring guns to shoot labor leaders and one another, too. A lot of murder and violence was going on. As late as the 1920s in America, you still had Jews and Italians and blacks and Catholics being lynched by white Anglo-Saxon Protestant Fundamentalists in the South. One of the few words that made its way back across the sea into the vocabulary of Italy's Italians was the word *lynch*. They heard about how Italians and others in America were suddenly "lynched" for no reason, accused of nonexisting crimes.

Do you think Sacco and Vanzetti really deserved the death penalty? And did the Rosenbergs? Or were they scapegoats for the moneyed and powerful evil in the land?

My father was a miniature Horatio Alger. When he came here, he was lame—he had fallen in Italy and injured his leg—and couldn't speak English at all, but he graduated Phi Beta Kappa and Sigma Psi from Union College in Schenectady. He won honors in science at Columbia, too. This little, lame Italian immigrant came from such poverty that sometimes he didn't have food to eat. At Christmas, the biggest present he ever got as a child was an orange, and on some Christmases there wasn't even an orange. He had a large number of brothers and sisters.

It's not well known that many immigrant Italians were starving in America. There was no Social Security, there were no pensions then, there was no unemployment insurance. They rarely applied to social services in any case, because there was a code of honor that you did not accept charity from anyone except your sons. This is part of the pride of the Italian male. Perhaps it's a noble characteristic. My grandfather would sooner starve than ask the government for money. So he was often starving. In Italy, you simply had a lot of children, and your wealth was your children. It was a way of life. They helped you work the land or run your business or whatever you did. Discouraged with life in America, because he was so discriminated against and had no friends or *paisani* or money, my grandfather became very ill. Then everything fell on my father, the eldest son.

You will not find many American sons supporting their parents and brothers and sisters anymore. You don't find that kind of familial closeness. Two attributes of Italian-American families are that the divorce rate is low and very few Italians put their old people in nursing homes. Even today, according to statistics, we still take care of our old in our own homes. In this, we are even more adamant than Jewish families, according to an article in *The New York Times*.

As a boy, my father took care of the *entire* family. How did he do it? Every morning he walked six miles in wind, snow, and sleet, and six miles every evening, delivering newspapers, and he was lame in one leg. He earned a penny apiece for each paper delivered. And he brought the pennies home to put bread on the table for his brothers and sisters. He also brought home baseballs to sew from the factory. The family sat around the kitchen table sewing baseball covers on the baseballs. Baseball was becoming a huge fanatical thing in America, as it has become a multibillion-dollar sports industry. In a three-room cold-water flat, they sat every night by the cold stove, seven brothers and sisters, mother and father, sewing baseball covers at the table.

They sat in the kitchen, talking to one another, being together. My grandmother would tell them Italian fairy tales while they sewed the covers on the baseballs for a few cents apiece, or sorted and sewed other items, doing whatever they could to earn money so that the family, *la famiglia*, could survive. And they stuck together and made it.

And yet my father was so anxious to be an American. This anxiety to become Americanized on the part of many Italians is responsible, I think, for the continuing prejudice *because they have not fought to get rid of the prejudice.* How many of us kept a hold of our language? My father learned American history from A to Z, and who were the people he quoted to me as I grew up: Shakespeare and Lincoln! Not Dante, but the great English Bard, and the best President America ever produced if he'd lived long enough. He learned to speak perfect American/English in a resonant voice. His diction was impeccable. There was no Italian accent. And while he was delivering newspapers supporting the seven children in Schenectady and his mother and father and bringing home food for the table, he worked his way through Union College, working in the library, working at night, never sleeping, almost, sleeping less than Thomas Edison. Not only did he put himself through college and feed *la famiglia* while he did it, he also earned Phi Beta Kappa and Sigma Psi. And it still brings tears to my eyes to say it.

He became a chemical engineer. Along with Dumont, he helped invent television in a garage. He invented Sylvania soft light, and softened the incandescent harshness of Edison's bare bulb to eliminate the eye strain of factory workers. An inventor with a nearly photographic mind, once at college he helped a whole classful of fellow students pass an exam. The professor was a bore. The women sat knitting and reading magazines in class while the men slept. One day, the professor announced, "We're having an exam tomorrow on the entire history of education."

My father went home and, sitting by the coal stove with the kids throwing things and making a racket in the kitchen (there was no other place to study), he memorized all the salient facts in the entire eight-hundred-page textbook. Next day, his friends sat near him to get the answers, and they all passed the course on my father's brain. And that stupid professor deserved it.

By the way, what did my father get for the patents on his inventions? One dollar. The corporations used him. He died without a pension. Imagine how difficult it was for him, a handicapped person, to get that Phi Beta Kappa key and to speak English as perfectly as others. And yet, he died without a pension, after all that hard work.

My mother never managed to become educated and was kept "barefoot and pregnant." But she also worked in the factory, like most Italian women. They were allowed to work in the factory, but not to have *careers*. They only thought of work as a way of putting bread on the table for the family, supplementing the income. They never thought of it as self-fulfillment.

I am the first college-educated female of my whole family. When I was going around this country trying to be a poet and giving poetry readings, I met a Professor Falbo at the University of Buffalo. He said, "Do you realize you are a pioneer?" He made me aware. I never looked at myself in this way, until well after the age of thirty, when I became aware that I was the first woman in the family to go beyond grammar school. I was the first Italian-American woman besides Diane DiPrima to make any sort of name in the history of American poetry.

On the positive side of the Italian ethnos is our love and respect for music, art, food. They are also part of the warmth of the Russian peasant and other Eastern or Southern European peasants. You give all the food you have when a guest walks in the house, and this is how you show your wealth—by putting your food out on the table, and you give of it very generously. The kitchen is a place of cleanliness, where good things are created for the family. It is the center of the home. Even when the Italians got a little bit better off and everyone was working and bringing in a paycheck from the factory and all the kids were grown up, they would still meet for feasts in the kitchen.

My relatives spent much more time in the kitchen than in the living room. Unfortunately, Italian living rooms were often covered with plastic. They are such a strange thing to us. The southern Italians really didn't have a parlor in Italy, and they don't know what to do with it, so they display it like a museum. The house where my father grew up in Italy was one room with loft beds arranged around it and a brazier in the middle for chilly evenings. My grandparents lived in a tenement here, and when their children were all married, they kept the parlor to entertain guests. My grandmother was always scrubbing the floors, and everything was spotless in her house. On special occasions the family would gather there, and my grandfather would have his guitar leaning against the wall and he would sing and play, and the family would join in the old songs. As he played, my grandfather would have some of his homemade wine, which he kept in a bottle in the icebox, with the ice chunk melting in a pan. And still my grandparents would have starved in their old age if my father hadn't helped them, because they had no Social Security or pensions. They would have refused welfare. They wouldn't think of asking anyone but their *son* for charity.

Perhaps the Italian who has contributed the most to American political society was an early immigrant, a writer, and a close friend of Thomas Jefferson. His name was Filippo Mazzei. Translated into English, his work was read by Jefferson and had a big influence on his thinking. Mazzei's statement *"Tutti gli uomini sono di natura ugualmente liberi ed indipendenti,"* which translates, *"All men are by nature equally free and independent,"* is the foundation of democracy and was echoed by Jefferson in the Declaration of Independence. I think it is important for us to remember Filippo Mazzei, who influenced Jefferson, and know that many of our democratic ideals were part of his writings.

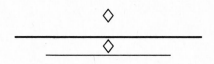

John Ciardi with Concetta, his mother

JOHN CIARDI
The Difference Was Love

Some months before he died on Easter Sunday, 1986, John Ciardi was interviewed in his home in Metuchen, New Jersey, where he spoke with wit and feeling of his Italian upbringing. Poet, essayist, and professor (Harvard, Rutgers), he was internationally acclaimed for his translation of Dante's *Inferno* (1954). The author of some forty books of poetry and criticism, including many volumes of children's verse, John Ciardi served as poetry editor of the *Saturday Review* for sixteen years. He aptly fills the description of American man of letters.

◇

My mother—she was a medievalist and securely born in the Middle Ages—let her hair grow down to the backs of her knees.

I'm in between, in a way. When I'm in Italy, I get along for a while and suddenly someone will say, "You're not really Italian. You're a goddamned army sergeant." [Laughs.]

As I tell them: *"Sono un italiano diracinato."* I'm an uprooted Italian. I was born in the North End of Boston, but we moved out when I was a baby. I spent some time in Italy and loved it there. But I recognized something . . . I recognized the emotions. It's a little like the times I would return home after being away for a while, when I found myself astonished by my mother's dialect. I have written a couple of poems on this subject—it's quite moving, in a way. She spoke with a very broken Avellinese dialect; she had no education. And I could recognize what she was saying and I was remembering. I couldn't say it myself by then. I had twisted my Italian, or rather straightened it out, and hers remained twisted. *Yes, that's the way she used to say it. That's the way I used to say it.*

It made me think of James Baldwin, who once spent some time writing in Switzerland, where they had never seen a black man. He sat and listened to Bessie Smith recordings to get Mama's cadence, to get the idiom, the beat, because he had been to Harvard and had lost his first tongue, so to speak. And suddenly he heard it again in these songs. He sat there for a long time and wore out the record.

I recognized that feeling because before my mother died, when I returned to speak to her, it was something of that experience. I had been away and when I heard her speak again, I could remember . . . and so when I am in Italy, I tend to recognize the emotions, but I am as much amused by them as taken. I'm in another world.

At home, I spoke Italian in order to speak to my mother. You see, my uncle who lived with us used to take the newspaper *Il Messaggero*. (My father was killed in an automobile accident when I was a baby, so I know nothing about him, or practically nothing.) I was always interested in reading and found that as soon as I learned to read English, I could read *Il Messaggero* because Italian is so phonetic. And I straightened out a lot of things.

My mother couldn't read. If I read something to her out of the paper, she had trouble recognizing it. I was terribly divided in this way because I loved my mother very dearly. She would give me advice, for example, on how to behave out of the house, and it was loving advice, and I accepted it as such. But it was just dead wrong. She didn't know what she was telling me. So I learned to lie. I learned to be deceitful from the start and do what I had to do in order to get along. The neighborhood was primarily mixed Irish and Italian, and had I done what my mother said, I would have had a broken nose and black eye every day of my life. So for survival, I did what I had to do outside the house and lied to her about what I had done because if not, we'd all be in trouble.

That started a division in my mind. The house was one thing, and the world outside something else. And there was another division. We had a lot of cousins and relatives back in the North End in Boston—it was a clan—and from time to time, I would go back to visit. But it was like going abroad—things were different. Or they would come to Medford and find *us* different.

We had left the North End after my father died in July of 1919; I was just past my third birthday. He had made a down payment on a house in Medford, which was then a rather rural town on the Mystic River. I grew up on the banks of that river and watched the whole town grow up around me. Fields where I used to play turned into blocks of tenement row houses, mostly three stories. There were lots of three-story, three-family tenement houses then.

When my cousins came up to visit, they would take a trip out to "the country"—six miles! It *was* country at that time. One of our neighbors kept a cow, another neighbor had bees, we kept chickens. My mother, aunt, and I ran what seemed to be an enormous vegetable garden. We had two lots, and one lot, on which there is now a house, was a huge garden. One of my jobs was to collect horse droppings along the street [laughs], pile them and spade up the soil. I worked at the garden, tended the chickens, and that sort of thing.

These were divine mysteries when my city cousins came out from Boston. I remember my cousin Vinnie—Vinnie Arcomante. (I don't know what on earth has happened to him; we lost track of that family.) He walked along the street one day and saw a dandelion growing through a crack in the pavement.

"Look, *cicorias*!" he said. [Laughs.]

In Medford, at least, the streets were paved, not with gold, but edible stuff. He had seen them in boxes in front of grocery stores in the North End. These things, by the way, grow wild. They are edible but not when they flower, because then they get bitter. They are not really *cicoria*—they're dandelions, but they're called *cicoria*. Chicory is something else. *Cicorias* have a blue flower, and I used to pick the shoots along the river and toss them into salads. My mother, aunt, and I spent enormous time out in the garden picking new dandelions. They made delicious minestra.

My older sister Ella had gone to nuns' school in Boston—I was too young for that—where the nuns warped her with a sense of guilt from which she is still not completely recovered. I don't know what it is. Those old nuns must have believed that children were the devils' brood or they were twisted themselves or they were convinced that they had to scare the hell out of us for the good of our souls. I was afraid of them. My sisters had a bad time with them, but I escaped and was brought up by Yankee schoolmarms in Medford.

As they grew up, my sisters had something else to put up with. This is a special case; it has nothing to do with being Italian. When my father died, my mother, who was a sort of hysterical woman, heroically so, decided that I was his reincarnation *and I became my father*. I was the man of the family; they were just girls. I was the only son of the Italian family, and that meant that I got what I wanted *at their expense*. No one questioned this. I was an insufferable brat, but I had been trained to be. Three times my mother had borne a child, and alas, it was always a girl. And finally, the sacramental son arrived, and she could give the man the son he had a right to, to bear his name, to be his immortality.

It was a very twisted, but ancient, formula. And the girls accepted it, and I accepted it. My mother insisted upon it. Of course, the impression it made on my sisters was questionable, but that was the order of things. You did not have to like it. That was what ruled.

Two of my sisters married (the third one died). One sister had two sons. You know, a generation makes a lot of difference. The older boy was a very good scholar. He went from first grade through the Massachusetts Institute of Technology without getting any grade less than an A. He is a very successful chemical engineer and is now running a plant in Alberta, Canada.

Had my father lived, I probably would have been a different person. I would not have been cast in this special role as the man of the family, the wet-pants man of the family. In the old tradition, my mother—she was a medievalist and securely born in the Middle Ages—let her hair grow down to the backs of her knees. She had to work enormously hard—remember, she was a widow with four children in a land whose language she hardly spoke—and just messing around with that hair all the time took an hour every day. The girls kept insisting that she bob it, which was somehow sinful in those days, but it became less so. She waited until my sixteenth birthday and asked my permission to cut it. [Laughs.] Of course, I gave it to her.

We had street gangs in Medford between the Irish and the Italians, but they were not really gangs as we know them today. We had fist fights, but there were never knives or clubs or anything brutal. Now and then, mischief went over the line and they decided to do something that could be criminal—to break into some place. And I always pulled out, even though they called me chicken, because I could not bear the thought of doing that to my mother if I got caught. The thought that my mother or my sisters would have to come down to get me out of jail was just too much.

It seems to me that if you are a child growing up on Mulberry Street in New York's Little Italy, there is a dissociation, there is a certain anonymity on the street, and you fade into that anonymity. Once you are out of Little Italy, it's another world. In Medford, all the kids were known. We went to the same schools, and although the Irish and the Italians fought, there was the Catholic Church in common, though very early I had little to do with it. We played on the same teams, did things together. And then there came as a sort of natural consequence, an inevitable consequence, a huge number of Italian-Irish marriages. My sister Cora married Tom Fennessey and hers was the fertile branch of the family. When we have a reunion, it is more Irish than Italian.

As a child, I was loaded with guilt for various things. I was commissioned to pray for my father in Purgatory, and my mother insisted on that. She was really a Greek colonist set down in another place, and Catholicism had put a new vocabulary on her basic paganism. But the words of it were very important to her. She would insist on this.

When she moved to Medford, she suffered two enormous shocks. First, she met a priest who could not speak Italian. Priests in Medford were Irish. She was convinced that she had met a fraud. How can the man speak to God? So she had nothing to do with St. Joseph's, which was Irish Trinity. She used to go into Boston to do the shopping, and there she would stop at the Italian Catholic church to say a prayer at the altar where she had been married. But she would not go near an Irish priest. She distrusted them. And this was permission for my uncertainty about them, though she insisted that I go to Sunday School, mass, and that sort of thing. I did, but always with a reservation because I never met an Irish priest I liked. They seemed to be suspicious of Italian boys.

The other shock was that she heard some laborers outside the window once early on and, with my sister's help in translation, made out that they were digging a ditch for a gas line and talking about how falling-down drunk they were going to get that night. For her this was ultimate truth of bestiality. A man might start to play cards with his friends, the winner getting a glass of wine, and he might get a little rowdy or loud, as boys will be boys, and he might say something a lady had to pretend she had not heard. But to plan, in sober sweat, during the day to go out and make yourself into a drunken animal—that was ultimate bestiality. She was a quick generalizer; she always was a quick generalizer.

Fraudulent priests and bestial laborers—she would have nothing to do with the Irish.

She was instantly suspicious of Tom Fennessey, the man my sister Cora married, when he came around. She even turned out to be right. He said he was a guard at Deer Island Prison. He was a young punk from South Boston who was running hooch from a bootlegger. I don't know where she got the money, but she put detectives on his trail and got the proof and in some scene out of demented opera, she confronted my sister Cora and my future brother-in-law with it. And he broke down and admitted everything and swore to Cora that he would quit and get a job. And he did! He was a good man and worked hard. Cora was sure that her love could straighten out this man—those are *her* terms. He was a handsome boy—*and it did*. As a matter of fact, he worked like hell at terrible jobs during the Depression, but stuck to them.

In my childhood, it was always *two* worlds. I have always felt that when you have a second language, you have three things: the first language, the second language, and the difference between them. That occupied some of my attention; I was fascinated by that. And the other was that there was home and there was the world and the difference between them. That occupied my attention from the start because I realized that out of my necessary deceit, I had to use a double standard: one thing out-of-doors and another thing indoors.

It did not always work that way, that peaceably. Sometimes, in this generation gap, Italian boys especially, realizing that their parents were dead wrong, became nastily indignant. That led to shouting matches in which the kids and the father, sometimes the mother, said terrible things to one another. Two or three of the boys I grew up with ran away and were never heard of again.

The difference is *love*. If you had enough love, you could forgive this obvious difference. I knew my mother was wrong and ignorant, *but not by her lights*. Had she told me what she was telling me back in her native Manocalzati on the mountain, it would have made sense. She had not been able to make the shift. I had to allow for it. Knowing my mother's limitations, I had to make up my own mind about things. There was nobody to tell me what to do. I did what I wanted to do or what seemed to be necessary. But I loved her very deeply and I always knew what sacrifices she was making. And again, had there been a father, that would have changed the equation. This was all the parent there was. I spent a lot of time as a boy and early adolescent looking around for any large male who would let me attach myself. I needed a father, see. There wasn't any.

There was an uncle, Alessio, who lived with us. He had married my mother's sister. He was good to me in ways I did not recognize at the time. An uncle by marriage is a sort of unacknowledged kin. I remember, for example, on my twelfth birthday, he brought me a single-shot .22 rifle and a little puppy in a basket. [Laughs.] But he was gone most of the time. He was a barber, and he would be up in the morning and gone. I was also fond of my Uncle Pat— Pasquale—who lived in another town. Later, he retired to Hollywood, Florida, and died recently. I used to stop there every year to see him.

My mother was a sort of matriarch of the clan, either because of her character or because she had a house within an elevated and street-car ride where you could come on Sundays. Relatives used to come from Boston and visit and bring their problems. Not that she was a court of law, but she had a certain authority within the clan.

I shunned Italian girls. It was a natural reaction, in a way. All of the relatives, my godfather and mother and all the cousins—there was a tribe of cousins—were determined they were going to find me a nice Italian girl. And the natural reaction is, "The hell with you. I'll find my own."

It was a declaration of independence. Don't tell me what you're going to find for me. I'll find my own. I didn't marry until the age of thirty. I had to go into the army, and there was nobody around that I wanted to marry. I turned out to be an aerial gunner, and it wasn't a good idea to leave any widows around. But on leaving the service, I met Judith in Kansas City and we got married. Mother fell in love with her instantly. Judith is from Missouri. When Missouri was opened, one line of her family, which is Pennsylvania Dutch, came down and settled there. The other side, southern Baptists, also moved into Missouri territory and cleared the land. Her father was a Missouri farmer.

My being Italian had little or nothing to do with my becoming a poet. Some people assume that Italians have a patent on feelings. What about German artists and German poetry? The English have not produced a great visual art, but they are marvelous poets. The French? the Greeks? Every nation has its poets and artists.

In my poetry I have not drawn much on my childhood. It would be a kind of arrest to write exclusively about one's childhood. And I have never been inclined to be a confessional poet. Such writers as Kerouac (should we call them writers, typewriters, typists?) who wrote about everything being absolutely wonderful because it happened to sacred me—that is a tone I just dislike. There is a certain validity in writing about childhood, but there are other subjects in life. A writer doesn't usually choose what he will write about—he writes what comes; at least that is what a poet does. A novelist may block out an area he wants to explore, and that can be exciting, perhaps. I have never tried it.

It's generally thought that poets like Dylan Thomas, Robert Lowell, Frank O'Hara, Delmore Schwartz (who were more or less of my generation) led unstable, disordered lives. I have not lived that kind of existence. From the start, I knew that I had to be on my own and was concerned, in a sense, with supporting my mother and helping her as soon as possible. This gave me a kind of purpose. And there is no question that a loving Italian family situation is a steadying influence. I had things I wanted to do. I am a word freak. Language has always excited me, the way music does a musician or a composer. Because I always had to be self-dependent, I felt I could face whatever it had to be.

Poverty was a mess; I remember the lousy jobs I had to suffer through for a dollar or two. The army put death into the question, but you find you can face that. By the time I had survived the Catholic Church, poverty, and war, I felt reasonably self-reliant. I did not marry until the age of thirty, which gave me some time to think about things. It has been a happy marriage. I chose with blessed fortune. How much all of this is a result of being Italian and how much is personal, I don't know. I have always been a family man.

Italian families tend to be close-knit. But German families tend to be close-knit, as do French families, English families, and so on. This is a human thing rather than an ethnic one.

Now, these are personal equations. To refer back for a moment to Dylan Thomas. He was a very orderly man inside the poetry, entirely dissolute outside it. My guess, as nearly as I can make it—and it's from the poems—is that Dylan grew up as an immortal boy. He was happy roaming the countryside and larking and doing things, and then one day, somewhere in his early twenties and maybe before that, he made the astonishing and soul-blasting discovery that he was going to die. I don't know what tipped him so—it seems fairly common news—but it so distressed him that he spent the next twenty years of his life drinking himself to death. A self-destructive existence toward death in an alcoholic haze in order to get rid of this thought that he was going to die. It's very deeply in his poems from the time he was Prince of the Apple Towns, to roaming Wales, to the time he drank himself to death in New York, chugalugging a whole bottle of Scotch. I think he was moved by a strange and unusual terror of death. He had no control over this terror.

Now, what can I tell you? If one has put up with the army and the shooting war, these invented terrors don't have a hold on you that the real terrors do.

As a kid, I occasionally ran into people who had anti-Italian feelings. And my reaction was basically: "There's something wrong with him." At one time I had a job with a local gent. It was a night job during my postgraduate year in high school—I stayed in high school an extra year because there was no money to go to college. Well, I hadn't seen this gent for a while, and on coming back from Michigan, I had a broken-down model-A car. Passing him on the street one day, I stopped and gave him a ride. And he gave me a lot of stuff like, "You goddamned Italians coming over here and getting all the cars, while native Americans like myself don't have one."

What could I say? There's something wrong with this guy. This was a seventy-dollar car that I was tootling around town in.

Now and then, that kind of bias came up. I published a poem in the *Atlantic Monthly* once about Italy and Mussolini. It was a bit of satire on Italian *orgoglio* and all those chin-thrusting plaster images of Mussolini—and about an Italian background. Robert Lowell, the poet, wrote me a note saying it was the best Italian-American poem he had ever seen. And I thought, "Does that son of a bitch think he is more American than I am?" [Laughs.]

Where did he think I was brought up? Because my name is Ciardi, he decided to hyphenate the poem. Had it been a Yankee name, he would have thought, "Ah, a scholar who knows about Italy."

Sure, he made assumptions, but I can't grant for a minute that Lowell is any more American than I am. I was brought up here and had Yankee schoolteachers. I have lived in this country and have been abroad now and then. I was in the American army and out of it, thank God. And I'm an American man of letters. There's no hyphenation in that.

Growing up in small Italian communities or Little Italies, so to speak, some people have felt a strong antipathy toward anyone who breaks out of that community. I myself have never really lived amidst Italians and have been to the communities only as a privileged visitor. I got to know the North End by visiting my cousins and relatives there, but I always lived *outside*. And by the time I had grown up, there were so many Irish-Italian marriages that ethnic wholeness and that disapproval of breaking out of it just weren't there. At least, not in my experience. Had my father lived and had I been brought up in the North End instead of moving out, that would have made a difference. It was always a case of visiting the Italian community, never being a part of it.

I avoid Italian food in restaurants. My mother did it better. But I can get tired of Italian food even in Italy. Perhaps I'm just thinking in terms of my mother's cooking. She was an excellent cook. She had learned all the recipes natively. And when she got to this country, she found there was meat to put in them. On the whole, I don't think of Italian cookery as the ultimate end. My favorite food is Chinese.

There are things I like, though—peasant dishes, for example. Judith makes a johnny-cake and we boil up some fat, meat, and cook mustard greens in the pot liquid—and we have the American equivalent to pizza and minestra. It's the same in the South here as in southern Italy.

Every ethnic group has made a contribution to our society. I feel that instantly, always. By contribution, I am not speaking of skills such as masonry work or tailoring that result in beautiful buildings and clothes, but something of an *ethnic* nature. I have an experience that illustrates this. I have done a lot of traveling along the lecture trail and once found myself in Texas doing a series of Texas colleges. They were normal and dull until I got to the University of Texas at El Paso. There I had the sense of a European university. There were things going, there was a cultural life, and suddenly there was a marvelously different, fluid cutural association by virtue of the fact that practically everybody there spoke *both* English and Spanish. Here the Spanish (or ethnic) culture and the gringo culture (that of the *norteamericano*) came together—one contributing to the other—and wherever you get that kind of meeting, things flower.

Now I was blessed from the start by being put in that "meeting" because there was one culture at home and another culture in the world outside. And I was aware of this difference, *interested* in the difference. It was a learning experience.

This separation is good. It sensitizes you to things outside, you see. When my friends did certain things my family did not do, I recognized that difference and noted it. One of the reasons there are so many good Jewish writers is that the sense of alienation makes them more perceptive. And as a boy, I certainly felt some alienation from my friends. They did things differently, and I took note of that. So that you might say I saw them more carefully than they saw themselves.

We are an anthology of ethnic groups in this country. The three things we have in common are TV, Kentucky Fried Chicken, and McDonald's. And maybe an abused sense of the Constitution.

For some reason—I don't know why, because nobody else in the family turned that way—I fell deeply into books and lived a lot of my life in books. This, curiously, produced an enthusiastic, if tacit, consent from my mother. My father had had some education in Italy, far more than she had had. They both came over as children. He worked first as a laborer, from what little I could piece out, then he was briefly a tailor. Meanwhile, he went to night school and studied and became an agent for Metropolitan Life Insurance back before World War I. This was simply "running a debit," so to speak, and he went around with a big black book I noticed from other insurance men who came later. They collected nickels and dimes for burial insurance. At least, he had learned English well enough to work for

Metropolitan and to file reports, read insurance policies, and that sort of thing.

And he read books. My mother was very proud of the fact that he was president of Figli d'Italia, a fraternal group. He and his brother Ciccio, who died at almost the same time he did, used to take turns being president and vice-president.

He read books. From the little I could piece out, he was a sort of syndicalist in the Sacco and Vanzetti tradition. But he read whole books, and this impressed my mother. The memory of him sitting at the kitchen table to read a book was awesome to her—she had never read a book in her life. And not only was I made over in his image as the man of the family—and I was supposed to be exactly like him, a duplication of him—but when I turned out to be a reader, this reinforced her idea that I was in my father's image. She remembered *him* reading. It made her feel good to watch *me* read books.

And I was generally pretty good in school. I got a double promotion and I was in a special class, that sort of thing. Books were as important as what was going on around me. At first, I had no discretion at all about them—I read Frank Merriwell, Dick Merriwell, the Rover boys, Horatio Alger, *Gulliver's Travels*, Hargraves's *Golden Treasury*. Whatever came along: Stealthy Steve, the Seven-eyed Sleuth, and the Quest of the Big Blue Diamonds—I remember being impressed by that for a time.

In Italy, Ciardi is a foreign name. All names ending in *ard* and a vowel are German. It's a rendering of Hardt. The name started as Gerhardt and it became Gherardi, Cerardi, Ciardi. I would say about thirty-five to forty percent of Italian surnames, especially in northern Italy, are Germanic in origin. You give me the German name and I'll give you the Italian equivalent: Reinhardt, Renati; Theobald, Tebaldi; Doenitz, Donizetti.

In the fifth century, King Albuin, the head of the Longbeards, known to the Italians as Lungobardi, came down from Bavaria with two tribes of Saxons and subjugated a tribe the Romans called Capidae, and conquered all of northern Italy. They started the kingdom of the Lungobardi, Lombardia. For about three or four centuries these were German-speaking provinces and in the Alto Adige, still today, there are a lot of German-speaking Italians.

Bit by bit, the conquered land conquered the conquerors, and they ended up with Italian voiceboxes. Unless you've been to school, a person with an Italian voicebox has trouble with German names. Mussolini spoke German, but in the south, very few Italians do. If your name is Gerhardt and you're a southerner, you can't pronounce it. When I was at the American Academy in Rome, a man named Plotner was also there. Instantly, without the batting of an eye, the servants had him named Plotonieri. They simply could not say Plotner. The Italian voicebox insists on putting in some vowels. Even in Dante's case, a couple of generations earlier, the family name was not Alighieri but Aldighieri, and how far north do you have to go before that becomes Aldiger?

I was curious how the name Ciardi, with its Germanic origin, got to Manocalzati, which is the mountain behind Vesuvius in southern Italy, where my parents were born. When I visited, I discovered that there were the remains of an old Lombard tower in the area. At about the ninth century, some Lombard lordingly had been given a fief in the south and my paternal ancestors must have come down as his straw bosses and henchmen. After the tower fell apart and he was gone, they blended into the population. There's still the stub of that tower standing there, with goats grazing on the land around it.

There's no tracing my mother's name, because the name is DeBenedictis. That is Latin and was given by priests and nuns to foundlings left at the church door. The same applies to names like DeAngelis, Della Chiesa, Diodonato, Della Dona, Didio. There are many such, either in the Latin form or the Italian form. It means that sometime in the Middle Ages, an unmarried mother left her bundle at the church door and went off crying into the night.

I have been asked how I was first drawn to the idea of translating Dante's *Divine Comedy*. I took a course at Tufts in medieval literature. We spent a lot of time on Dante, and I could not figure out Dante's old Italian, his fourteenth-century Italian, but with a very bad translation I could get some of it. We used the Temple Classics, which was a prose literal translation—Italian with the English text—and neither one made sense, nor did the professor. He didn't know what he was talking about. I audited a second course on Dante in another school, and the same thing. There was something fascinating about this enormous poem that the professors couldn't tell me about. I got to the University of Michigan graduate school, took another course in it, and concluded that professor was a dope. He was not getting to it. Either I was stupid, or he was wrong and did not know what he was doing.

I began to collect the various translations and look at them and they were abysmally bad, one after the other, and I thought if this is the best that can be done, I've got an open field. If I can't do better than this, I will quit. I began it. I also realized that it had never really been done by a poet—except by Rossetti, who was too delicate, and Longfellow, who was too genteel. Dante is not genteel. When he dips a sinner in excrement, it ain't "excrement." There is a difference between the genteel and—what should we call it?—the aristocrat. The aristocrat calls a spade a goddamned spade and not an agricultural implement. Longfellow's error was obvious: He was trying to make Dante conformable to the modes of the Cambridge living room, and it's a terrible mistake to assume that your sensibilities are genteeler than Dante's, your language finer, and your moral distinctions nicer. It made it a rather prissy translation.

Now and then Dante gets raunchy, and those are the test lines. For example, in the canto of the drafters where Malacoda, the sergeant in charge of the fiends, lines up some fiends to escort Dante to the next passage, Dante at one point says, *"Ed egli aver al cul fatto trompetta,"* meaning he had made a trumpet of his ass. [Laughs.]

It's just as straight as that. But look through the translations, and compare that line with, "And he did trumpet from his nether parts," or, "And he replied with signal base and low."

It misses the whole context of it. Now, on different levels—that's a dramatic example, I suppose—on different levels the translators prettified, got away from the facts of the poem, got away from the tone of the poem. And I decided that it could be done better.

Avellino, where my parents were born, is the capital city of the province of Avellino, known to the Romans as Abellenum. The Greeks called it Irpinia. It was a Greek colony for a time. Then native tribesmen and surviving Roman slaves made this population mix that created Pompeii. There's no mystery about who the Pompeians were. Look at my cousins, and you're looking at the people of Pompeii. We spent a couple of days in Avellino. It's a nice place to visit, but I wouldn't want to live there. Every night at about five o'clock the natives do what they called *la passeggiata.* You walk up one side of the main street and down the other, the boys look at the girls, and people say, "Buona sera."

My daughter Myra was in her teens and pushing the miniskirt to its limits. When she walked down the street with her cheeks out, they (the cheeks) stopped *la passeggiata*. Everybody followed us. And when we went to Monte Vergine, the shrine to St. Mark on top of a nearby mountain, they wouldn't let her into the church because of the miniskirt. She was insulted. At the Vatican, she had not been allowed in and we had to get a raincoat somewhere. It was transparent, but somehow that covered a lot.

My mother had spoken frequently about Manocalzati, a mountain in the vicinity where she was born. Her stories played in my mind, and I wrote a poem about it. The mayor of Manocalzati heard about this—there are a couple of scholars of American literature there—and he got all excited, had the poem set up on a plaque of Carrara marble in bronze letters, and it's in the *municipio*. We were planning a grand tour of Europe at the time, and we were invited to the unveiling of this plaque in the *municipio*. We went and put up in the Jolly Hotel in Avellino. I wanted to go to Manocalzati right off, but the mayor would not let me get into the town. I was to have my first view of it at the ceremonial.

And what a ceremonial they made! My kids were standing by, nudging one another and saying, "Can you believe that? Can you believe that?" We pulled into town and our way was blocked by the 7th Fleet Band. The consul-general, Homer Morrison, was in from Naples and had brought the band with him. Everybody in the province who had a uniform was lined up, wearing a sash: judges, officials, *pompieri, carabinieri, bersaglieri, guardia stradale, guardia forestiere*. And the people were lined up.

We were stopped by a procession, got out of the car, and the mayor pointed across a ravine to the house where my mother was born. While we were being photographed, a fireworks cannon down in the ravine fired twenty-one times. Suddenly, my cousins, whom I had never met before, descended with great hugging and crying, and everywhere there was a sense of operatic rejoicing. And my kids kept saying, "Can you believe that?" We marched up the street in the parade. Judith was given about four dozen American beauty roses. She looked like Jackie Kennedy walking up the street alongside me. People were throwing flowers from balconies. They renamed the street we were on from whatever it had been to Viale degli Stati Uniti. We walked up to the Monumento ai Caduti, and I was given a wreath to put on a grave.

When we got to the *municipio*, we saw a sheet thumbtacked to one of the walls. Judith was given a cord; she pulled it and the sheet, thumbtacks, and a little plaster came off the wall. And here was this gorgeous plaque. I had sent them some money to help pay for it, but not until they were going to do it, anyhow. There it was, very handsome—a translation of the poem. Next came a great deal of oratory about having survived *la furia tedesca*, and that sort of thing. When the ceremonies were over, the town and the nuns served a repast—beer and fruit drinks and little pizzas and cookies.

It was about to break up—the 7th Fleet had drunk up all the beer—when RAI, Italian television, showed up. They were late. But it didn't bother anybody. They formed up again; we marched *down* the mountain. People picked up the flowers, went up to their balconies, threw them down again. That night, we watched the procession on RAI. Where else, except in Italy, would that happen? You re-form the parade and run it backward for the tardy television cameras.

They made me an honorary citizen of Manocalzati. I have a huge illuminated scroll upstairs in my study—for having brought the name of Manocalzati to "international literature."

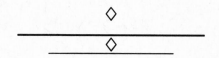

Helen Boehm with her first employer, Nathan Gillis

HELEN BOEHM
Ariel's Call

◊

The unusual accomplishment of Helen Boehm, an Italian-American woman who knows kings and queens, popes and heads of state, springs from a strong desire *not* to become the average Italian housewife. Her drive was to free herself from what she called bondage and make use of her enormous entrepreneurial talents.

Like the bird-in-flight sculptures she has made famous, Helen herself seems in constant flight. During a brief respite before taking off for Europe, she was interviewed lying on her stomach as a masseuse gave her a massage in her hotel apartment in New York City.

Freedom was important to my future happiness.

T he more prominent the individuals, the easier it is to talk with them. It is so much more comfortable to talk with Prince Charles, as I have done, than with a person who has made it but still has a beef, or a black part of his life, on which he is hung up. People who are "up there" are used to dealing with all kinds in society. Prince Charles speaks not only with royalty, he speaks with the sick and the crippled in hospitals and the poor in slums. He has to go up and down on all the social levels. And having studied this and applied it to my own circumstances, I feel comfortable meeting all kinds of people. I am at ease with children, with secretaries, with mothers, and yet I can talk with the sultan of Brunei and feel relaxed.

What helps is the ability to like the person you are addressing. I think that is a particularly Italian trait—Italians like people. And they have a disposition to talk. When we were kids and would gather round the dinner table every night, my father *expected* us to talk. It was important for us all to express ourselves, whether we were complaining or chatting about happy things or talking about a person or event. We were all very vocal, and I think talking like that around the table gives you confidence. It prepares you for the outside world.

When you meet new people and overcome the initial shyness and awkwardness, it is like a candy store. You don't know what candy to choose. I love everybody and want to talk with everybody. People are my energizer. If you give me an audience of two thousand, I give my heart all the way. But if you give me a lot of empty chairs, I cannot give my story fully.

My father was from Florence and my mother from Palermo— north meets south. In our culture, it is a big plus for a southern woman to marry a northerner. They married in Italy when they were young and then came to Ellis Island with two small children by the hand. Talk about courageousness! Would I go to China or Russia with two small kids to start a new world for myself without being able to speak the language? How did my parents know it was going to work out here? It was only rumor they heard that there was gold on the pavement.

The two children were my older brother and sister. I was born here. We were seven children in all, and my mother always referred to us as *"i miei gioielli,"* my jewels. The only jewel she ever had was the gold wedding band on her finger. Real jewels were not what she wanted. The most important thing to her was to be a good mother and give her husband and children love and support.

My baptismal name was Elena Francesca Stefania Franzolin. There was no "i" at the end of the family name because if there had been, my father would have left it there. His family originally came from Corsica. Look at this picture of my mother and father [points to a photograph in her book *With a Little Luck*, published in 1985 by Rawson Associates, New York]. I love it. In these old photos, the man usually sits and the woman stands. She was five feet, two inches, and he was six feet four. She always wore her hair in a big bun like that, and my father once told her, "If you cut your hair, I'll cut your head off." That is the way it was in those days—women *had* to have long hair.

They settled in Brooklyn. My father, who was good with his hands, was a cabinetmaker and he finished and refinished furniture. His first job was at Namm's in Brooklyn Heights, where he worked for more than ten years. But his life was cut short by a fire in the plant, when he had to jump off a fourteen-story building. He was badly hurt, and we watched as my strong papa of six feet four lay in bed and deteriorated before our eyes. He died when I was thirteen years old.

To help support the family, my older brother and sister, who were teenagers, went to work. My mother was skilled with the needle and took in sewing. She did embroidery and men's suits. When we came home from school, it wasn't skating or playing for us. We all had chores to do. My job was to shop for the evening meal from a list of things my mother had written: bread, veal cutlets, fresh tomatoes, and so on. Setting the table was another chore. We were all trained in helping in the domestic part of life—housecleaning, preparing food, cooking, sewing. In the Italian fashion, we were also preparing for our future by learning skills necessary to be good wives and mothers, thereby assuring domestic tranquillity in our marriages.

Until the age of fourteen, I went to parochial grammar school and then entered New Utrecht High School. I liked the nuns, but don't know whether I would like them today. Nuns in the traditional sense, they wore the habit and you respected them. Yet they could be motherly and helpful. All this current talk against these older nuns —it is not all true. We rarely questioned them—even when they said something we thought was funny—because that showed disrespect. You just might go home and tell your mother and father, but that was about the extent of it.

Your mother would say, "Your teacher is right."

And your father would say, "Your teacher is right."

What they were saying was, Respect your teacher. Today, it is another story.

There is a lot of permissiveness in the Church today, and some of my older Catholic friends resent the fact that when they were small, they were restricted in what they could or, more usual, could *not* do. To them, I say, "So accept it and move on. What can you do about it? Why worry about something that took place a long time ago? Be accepting." As a girl growing up, I resented my brothers being so strict with me. Hatred and rebellion surged within me, but I held back and told myself, Helen, tomorrow you will be on your own. You know that that day will come in your life, and the sun will shine.

Memories of my Catholic schooling are good and positive. The discipline was appropriate to the time. But I would not accept that kind of discipline today, because it is different now. I enjoy the more relaxed atmosphere in the Church. Take my monsignor. I have dinner with him often and go to parties with him. Tonight, at the Boys Town Dinner at the Waldorf—where I will be one of the ones honored—two other monsignors, also friends, are coming to New York for the occasion. The Church has changed. Priests socialize with parishioners and are less formal. The mingling of the clergy in the social life of the people has helped a great deal. The clergy and the people are getting to know one another much better—all to the good.

When we were growing up, we lived in a mixed neighborhood. In our minds, the people around us were classed into two groups: *gli americani* and the Jews. It was a funny thing: Among the Jews and Italian kids, you never stopped to think who was what. You just had friends. Today, people are more conscious of it. Then, you were friends with all.

Because she was a widow, my mother was always worried about her children's future. After graduating from high school, I remember going to an oculist for a checkup—accompanied, as usual, by my mother. When she heard that his receptionist was leaving to be married, she pounced on the occasion and told the oculist what a terrific person I was, smart and responsible and hardworking. He hired me on the spot. His office was on Bedford and DeKalb avenues, which was a lovely area at the time. Today, you can't get near there without four guns in your pocketbook.

If there was anything wrong with growing up Italian for me, it was leading a sheltered life, with *no* freedom of movement. On every appointment, every trip outside the house, my mother or sister had to come with me. Usually, my mother was my chaperone, I was my sister's chaperone, and she was chaperone to another sister. My brothers were very strict and acted like bodyguards. Life was miserable. After I met my husband, my mother went out on *all* our dates. It was like living in a novitiate.

In our community in those days, *if you were Italian, you married an Italian*, knowing that he would be very strict (like my brothers) and would not let his wife go from here to there without being accompanied. I could not bear to have my life continue under such strictures. Freedom was important to my future happiness.

And then I met my husband, Edward Boehm. He promised, and gave me, the longed-for release. It was a beautiful thing to be promised your freedom and the chance to find out *who I was* and *what I was really all about*. He said he was going to give me a beautiful life.

"You will know what freedom means because I know how confined you have been," he said, sensing that there was a lot in this Italian girl to be developed, to unfurl, like a flower.

He was true to his word, and he nurtured my potential and, in return, I helped to bring out his creative genius.

In those days, it was a big thing to have an *americano* in the family. Ed's family had been here for four generations. They were from Germany originally. He and my mother got along beautifully. She was with me when I met him while we were visiting my brother in army camp in upstate New York. Ed loved my mother, and she loved him, because *he* was attentive to her and because he was an orphan whom *she* could mother. When Ed and I met, he was a farmer. He had never gone to college or studied art, although he liked to sculpt animals out of clay. On leaving the orphanage at the age of sixteen, he worked on a farm and at night took courses in animal husbandry. By the time he was twenty-one, he had his own animal farm, and before he went into the army, he had acquired a large Guernsey breeding farm. While he was in the service, the farm was destroyed by fire.

After we married, he stayed close to his beloved animals by becoming a veterinarian's assistant, and in the evenings, he continued to do the clay animal sculptures. We were young and ambitious and felt there *had* to be a way whereby he could devote himself to his art and I could help as his business partner. We kept our dream alive, and the day came when Herbert Hazeltine, the sculptor, took Ed on as student and protégé. Ed began spending hours in the libraries ferreting out information, wherever he could find it, on the art of porcelain making in ancient civilizations. There was no porcelain making in America. After much study, he unlocked the secret of making hard-paste porcelain.

From then, we found our way. He began creating beautiful porcelain sculptures of animals, birds, and flowers, and I sold them—the shy artist and the aggressive salesperson. We challenged the English, German, and Asian ceramicists who had dominated the field exclusively for thousands of years. Today, Boehm porcelains are in 150 museums throughout the world, including the Metropolitan Museum of Art in New York. Three life-size mute swans, all porcelain sculptures, are on exhibit in the White House in Washington, D.C., the Vatican Museum in Rome, and the Great Hall in Peking, China. Our sculpture is in the private boudoir of the Queen of England.

In the Western world, fine porcelain has been the medium of kings and queens since they first admired Chinese specimens of this art hundreds of years ago. They set their chemists and alchemists to work to attempt to duplicate the Chinese formula, and by the fourteenth century they had established their own factories and studios. Later, royalty established the Meissen factory in Germany and the Sèvres factory in France. And here am I—an Italian woman from Brooklyn—in a field that was monopolized by monarchs.

Through his art, my husband helped me find myself, my own potentialities. I became a successful entrepreneur by bringing his beautiful porcelain sculptures to the attention of the entire world. Breaking into the porcelain world was my big challenge. Ed and I had to take on Europe and Asia to bring our porcelain into the position it holds today. Thirty-four years ago, America was the last on the list of fine porcelain makers, and today, because of Boehm porcelain, we are the best in the world. We went into unknown territory, into a field never explored by an American. What I am producing today—even after my husband's death—is a porcelain art based on his genius, and it will live forever because art lives forever. His sculptures document the natural beauties of nature with a somewhat sophisticated approach. Yet I have worked it out to a level where an average person, a child even, can collect Boehm porcelain and appreciate it. Anyone can understand it. Thus, we were able to bring our art to everyone, not just the affluent and heads of state—though, goodness knows, we need the affluent.

In all my years as an entrepreneur, I never felt that there was a door closed to me because I was Italian or that I was being discriminated against for that reason. First, I project myself as a human being. After succeeding in that, then I talk about Italians and how great they are. But first you make it as a *person*.

Feminism has never been an element in my life. Very simply, I did my thing and did it in the best way possible. Certainly, I am *all* for women advancing and being paid equally for their talents. But joining women's organizations and supporting them require time which is not available. Doing your own thing, and doing it successfully, can be helpful to other women by providing a role model.

In my married life, all I knew was the Italian way. A wife does everything she can to make her husband a success. She *overloves*, *overfeeds*, and *overhelps* her man. But I was more fortunate than most wives because my husband helped me to realize my own abilities as an entrepreneur and businesswoman. Such mutual help does not usually exist in Italian families. Now, it is true that not all women need to fulfill themselves outside the home. If the family means everything to them, then they have succeeded. But if the mind starts to wander and a woman thinks, "Ah, if only I could design dresses," "If only I could have a gift shop," "If only I could write," then you are in trouble. If she wants to be more than a housewife, then what is going to happen to that marriage? How is her husband going to accept it?

Usually, we think of big names, like Frank Stella or Gay Talese, as Italians who have made it. To my way of thinking, there are thousands of Italians throughout the country who also have made it. Unknown private citizens, they form a bulk of American life, a solid segment that is dependable and loyal to American ideals. They educate their kids, go into the army, get better and better jobs, and enjoy the kind of life their immigrant parents worked for them to have. They form a broad base and give support.

Of all the celebrated people I have met, the ones I was most comfortable with were two—President Sadat of Egypt and his wife, Jehan. He was a man of very humble beginnings—that may have been the reason for the attraction—yet he was a noble man, one of courage and compassion. His going to Israel for the sake of peace, sitting down on the floor and crossing his legs with the Israelis, impressed me deeply. Jehan Sadat, whom I love and admire, has a doctorate in Egyptian and Arabic literature.

Once I asked her, "Jehan, when you got your doctorate, did your husband call you Doctor?"

"Never," she said.

It was almost like she was an Italian wife.

Coming, as I do, from a similar background, I am often asked my opinion about Geraldine Ferraro. Frankly, my reaction to her wanting to be vice-president was negative. It was too soon for her to make a bid for the White House. She should have stayed at the level of congresswoman and slowly built a reputation for accomplishment and achievement. As a congresswoman, she did well for her community, but suddenly she was going national and international, areas in which she had small experience. The vice-presidency is not a training position. It is not for trainees. If you asked me what woman would make a good candidate for vice-president, I would say Jeane Kirkpatrick or Elizabeth Dole. These are women of proper experience. Geraldine took a big step forward for women, particularly Italian-American women, but it was too high a step. Would you feel secure if she answered that red phone in an international emergency?

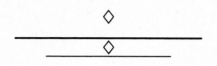

Ken Auletta (right), at fourteen

KEN AULETTA
Between Two Families: Jews and Italians

Ken Auletta's growing up was an unusual amalgam of two rich cultures—the Polish-Judaic and the Italian-Catholic—which were dissimilar and yet, oddly enough, alike. Mr. Auletta is the author of several books on the financial world, including *The Streets were Paved with Gold* and *Greed and Glory on Wall Street: The Fall of the House of Lehman.* He is a contributor to *The New Yorker* magazine, weekly columnist for the *Daily News,* and political commentator for CBS-TV.

◇

Although I identified as an Italian, I also identified as a Jew.

My mom is Jewish, but I was brought up as a Catholic. My dad is Catholic. They were married in a civil ceremony. I was really free to do as I wished. As a kid I went to Our Lady of Solace Church, which was half a block from our home, and knew the priests and the sisters. My dad would go to church, but my mom would not. We were not devoutly religious at all. Today I am not a Catholic.

I was born in Coney Island, Brooklyn, on April 23, 1942, in a predominantly Italian section—on West Seventeenth Street between Mermaid and Neptune Avenues. Basically, that was in the Italian enclave of Coney Island, which comprised four blocks from Seventeenth Street down to Stillwell Avenue and over from Surf to Neptune Avenues. On our street you started to get a few Jewish families, and on Nineteenth Street, there were some Irish families. In the 1920s and 1930s the area was heavily Jewish. Now it is black and Hispanic. And yet the Italian enclave remains. That four-block area is still almost intact.

My dad's parents were born overseas; he was born here. His father was from Salerno, and his mother was also from that part of Italy. His family actually came from a town called Auletta, which I visited. There are no Aulettas in Auletta, which makes me think that his name was taken from the town name.

Although my dad speaks Italian, I learned very little of it. I have no facility for languages and blame it more on that than on my dad. Remember, he was born here—he was an American and spoke English with no accent. His father was a barber who died when I was about four years old. We saw a lot of Nonna, his mother, who did not live far from us. In her house she surrounded herself with statues—she was very religious. We would have Sunday dinner there, or she would come to our house. She and my mother's parents were very friendly—Mrs. Auletta and the Tannenbaums. My mom's two sisters also married Italian men, by the way. So I rarely witnessed any tension between the Italians and the Jews, the "they-killed-Christ" sort of thing. The only way I came across that was with my friends—the tough guys I hung out with when I was younger. Many of them were anti-Semitic. They basically thought of Jewish kids as fags. They did not mean anything sexual, only that the Jewish kids were weak. They were not tough guys like them. The Jews were sissies. There was some of that, and I would speak up against it. But I was of a torn mind. I was around eleven years old and so I identified with tough guys and did not want to identify with someone who was perceived as weak. And yet I went to their defense. It is interesting. In general, though, I found harmony between Jews and Italians—on the kids' level and on the parents'. They are really a very similar people. The enmity was between the Italians and the Irish. It was much stronger between them than the Jews. I think it had a lot to do with the Church.

The Tannenbaums, my maternal grandparents, were immigrants. My grandfather was from Poland and his wife from Germany. When I grew up, we lived with them. They had a little candy store, which was very popular in the area. Although I identified as an Italian, I also identified as a Jew. I always knew that if they were going to come for my grandmother, or any one of the Jews, they were going to come for me. I had a rich experience living with them and also feeling Italian. We lived with my mom's family for about thirteen years in a house with a stoop.

Then we moved, thinking it was a great opportunity, into public housing on West Twenty-ninth Street and Surf Avenue by the water. My sister's room and my parents' overlooked the ocean, and my brother's and my room was in the back. Oh, it was wonderful— the music of the waves and the roar—we were thrilled. This shows how differently public housing was perceived then. It was really lower middle-income public housing. We were lower middle class and relatively poor. My mom and dad worked, and still do. It tells you how much things have changed. I remember there were five buildings and only one black family that I knew of—a black school-teacher, who lived on our floor. There was a lot of nervousness on the part of the neighbors—you know, *the-blacks-are-moving-in* sort of thing. Of course, today, almost the entire project is black. It mirrors our changing perception of public housing and also the racial and ethnic composition of neighborhoods.

Being a real opportunist, I used to take off both the Christian and the Jewish holidays. I felt more Italian than Jewish, but I always felt Jewish. Not just for the holidays. I *identified* with them. Sometimes I sensed in some of the Italians a feeling of looking down on the Jews. They would remark, "They're weak," "They are not strong," "They don't fight." I do not want to overstate this because, in general, it was a fairly harmonious period in terms of ethnic relationships. But it was less so among the teenage kids.

Among the boys, it had much more to do with turf and things like that. What was manly to the Italians was physical prowess— strong hands, fights, athletics. The Jewish kids who went to school with us tended to concentrate more on books, which we did not value, than on athletics, which we did. My brother, Richard, who was the first member of the Auletta family to go to college, was very bookish. He graduated from high school at fifteen, two years earlier than most boys. And I remember I was *embarrassed* by my brother. Many of my friends had older brothers who were tough guys. If they got into trouble, the brother would come in. This was a gang culture and you wanted to be part of it when you were eleven or twelve years old. My brother was in school, he was reading books, he was always studying. And I was embarrassed by that. When he went to Brooklyn College, these kids would ask him, "What are you going to college for?" which again tells you how much things have changed.

I was athletic—not at all bookish—and a little bit of a wise guy, not cruel, but nevertheless a wise guy. My peer group pressures were more important to me than family pressures. We are talking about when I was from eleven to fifteen years old. My grades were not good. Once in a while I would do well, but I was *not* a student. High school for me was a place where I could play football and baseball and hang out at the sweet shop. In my junior year, I got into trouble. I stole a book of passes from the dean's office and was suspended from school. My parents were absolutely appalled. My mother was the understanding one; my father was the shouter. Every once in a while, when he got mad, he brought out the shaving strap, and two or three times in my life he used it on me. Even as a teenager I feared my father. He was about five feet seven and I was taller than him in my teens, but I feared him because of that strap and because he was my father. I was brought up within a certain structure.

In any case, they went to see the principal, Abraham Lash. He is about seventy-eight years old now, a wonderful man, who saved my life. He said to my parents, "If he agrees to work in my office for three hours a week rather than go out to the sweet shop, I will lift the suspension and he can stay in school."

"No way," I said.

Lash, who was a brilliant psychologist and understood what was of interest to me, said, "Ken, if you are suspended, you can't play football or baseball with the school."

That had not dawned on me. He had me trapped. You don't think of consequences at that age. So I worked in his office, wound up graduating and got into college not because of my grades—it was a 64 average—but because I had a good sports record and the coach at the University of Oswego in Oswego, New York, helped get me into a program called Industrial Arts. At the time I thought that was art; little did I know it was woodworking. In college, I became more interested in studying.

Friday night was always man's night out, and my dad would go to Garguilo's, a wonderful Italian restaurant where I still go, or to a little pizza place around the corner called Tatonne's, where he would eat octopus. He would always have fish on Friday night with the men, and sometimes my brother and I would go along, but we had to be invited. My brother and I did not like fish much, so we would have a pizza at Tatonne's and my father would go back into the kitchen, where all the men were, to eat octopus. We thought it was disgusting and would tell him, "Don't come back to the table near us while we're eating pizza."

We always had Sunday afternoon dinner with all the family. I still have vivid memories of having dinner at three o'clock with the aunts and uncles and cousins, very much in the Italian tradition. There were relatives I did not even know. And after dinner the men would fall asleep.

Actually, my mother—who was Jewish—did the cooking. She was a much better cook than my dad. I have still not had a better plate of lasagna than my mother's. I think she learned it from Nonna. But Dad had to take over when she made meatballs. To her, they were just chopped meat. With his hands, he would work the meat for several minutes, then soak the bread, bring out the water, sprinkle the parmesan cheese on heavily, sprinkle the parsley, garlic, salt, pepper, and so on. The time I am describing was in the early 1940s. Life was all very natural and undisturbed. One never felt that there was a war going on.

I always love the fact that as a kid, I hugged my dad, and still do. When my parents came to visit me at college, we would embrace and everyone would look at us. My father and I would kiss each other on the cheek, and the students—there were not many Italians at Oswego—would look at me and say, *"Weird.* Kissing your father on the cheek? Kissing your mother, we understand, but not your father."

It is a nice tradition we have, using your body—your hands, your arms, your mouth—in greeting. It is a warm tradition. Raising your arms to greet someone—it is a gesture of warmth. More than other people, Italians speak without words. My father does not have to say anything to me. I know what he is thinking about just by looking at his face. For a book on Wall Street, I am studying the faces of the men who work there and they give me nothing. They are hard. Their expressions are calculated *not* to give you anything. The chief executive sits in a meeting, the investment banker sits in a meeting, and what they are trying to do is *not* communicate. They are trying to hold off the decision. They are trying to ponder, they are trying to negotiate and, therefore, bluff the other side. Everything is designed *not* to communicate.

The large number of Italian names you suddenly see everywhere stuns me. The Wall Street area seems to teem with young Italian-Americans. And they do not look like the stereotype, the dago stereotype of twenty years ago—you know, black hair slicked back, narrow tie, and pointy shoes. People are not looking anymore for Frank Nitti, the great Italian-American stereotype who was the gangster in the Elliot Ness/Robert Stack television series *The Untouchables* years ago. He wore custom clothes, black silk suits, and pomaded hair, and lifted his waist with his forearms, rubbing his nose. When people protest stereotyping on television, they often refer to Frank Nitti.

These young people are assimilated not only in how they dress, but in their actions and attitudes, which has negatives in my judgment because they forget their roots and who they are and become like all the others. I suspect that if these kids on Wall Street knew who they are, they would not rush headlong into this transactional world, where loyalties are less important than the transaction. Loyalty, I feel, is part of Italo-American culture, and there seems to be a break-up of that. In any case, they are assimilated in the more positive sense of power. They are VPs and in many cases are running major enterprises—Lee Iacocca, for example. And they are active in other areas—look at the credits on movies and television shows.

It is really important for me to know where my family came from, and to understand that and to understand their rich traditions and have a sense of roots. One of the attractive qualities of Mario Cuomo, and one of the reasons he is such an attractive public official, is that he really knows *who he is*. He is in a business where people tend not to know who they are, because they are defined by the last election or the current quotas or by the mail they get. Here is a guy who remembers his father's store, remembers working behind the counter, remembers how to speak Italian, and speaks to his mother in Italian. His children have roots—they were brought up in Queens, in the home their grandfather built. He knows the neighbors—his next door neighbor is a cop. He has a sense of the past that he always carries with him. A lot of people I have met over the years do not have that and are really rootless, which can be damaging. They have no mind-set as to what they will *not* do, what they should *not* do. They do not have memory, or enough memory. I think memory is very important to the continuation of society.

Do you join the mainstream, or do you keep your group identity? The subject of group loyalty *vs.* society loyalty is an area that is fraught with tension. Personally, I do not think there is enough memory on the part of ethnic groups in this country. On the other hand, it is also important not to get caught up in ethnic life and organizations and to remember that you are part of a larger society. You are always an American as well as an Italian or a Pole or a Hispanic, and somehow you have to balance that. Bilingualism, for example, can go too far, and while it is important to welcome the immigrant, there have to be certain standards whereby people are expected to learn English. If you do not have that, you are not going to have the degree of assimilation that is really important, and you might well have a continued polarization of society or lack of integration, which is damaging. The new immigrants that are flooding our shores give our country an energy that is profoundly important. But even though immigration is good, you have to strike a balance, that is to say, you cannot have completely open borders. There is always a tension concerning open borders and standards, and between ethnicity and the good of the larger society. If you have completely open borders, you would not be protecting people *who are already here*. You would be menacing them. And that would create great consternation.

Despite Senator Moynihan and Milton Glaser's book *Beyond the Melting Pot*, which claims assimilation has not worked, from my observation it has. Try and tell me people have not assimilated down on Wall Street. Jews and Italians were outcasts on Wall Street twenty years ago. Today, there are Jewish partners and there are Italian partners. If that is not assimilation, I don't know what is. There *is* both assimilation and integration in America. Of course, in some cases there is not. You will find neighborhoods that are not assimilated—Moynihan and Glaser are right about that. But there are many other neighborhoods that are.

One of the good things about the ethnic-consciousness movement that started about fifteen years ago is that Italians are happier with their heritage than they were then. Some of these groups were spoiled by the efforts of Joe Columbo, a known Mafioso, who gave them a bad name, but before that, in the 1960s, I remember going to meetings of these organizations and attending their consciousness-raising sessions. Stephen Aiello, Frank Arricale, and a whole lot of good people were involved. There was a feeling that Italian-Americans needed more of an identification, that they had to raise their consciousness, not only among themselves but among society in general. There is less talk of that today, partly because that effort was soured by the Columbo experience, but also because there *has* been progress.

When you start having role models like Mario Cuomo, Lee Iacocca, and Gay Talese, by their presence on the scene they are sending a signal to Italian-American youngsters that there *are* opportunities in lots of different areas. You do not have to think of yourself as a sanitationman or priest or schoolteacher. You can be head of Chrysler, you can be governor of New York, or a great writer. Implicit in their presence is a teaching experience.

Having gone to Italy many times and comparing that country to other places and considering my life experience, in general I find Italians more open, warmer, less uptight, and less defensive than others. In Italy, even without speaking the language, I feel much more comfortable than I do in France because I can get by with hand gestures and touching people. Italians touch one another, the French do not, and a lot of other ethnic groups do not.

What openness and warmth I have comes in part from the cultural experience of being Italian. Feeling close to people helps me as a reporter—it helps to make others feel relaxed and comfortable so they can talk to you. Whatever ability that is, I learned through osmosis. There was no one teaching me and saying, "This is the way you ought to behave." It really comes from the way we lived.

Many people have attacked Mario Puzo's novel *The Godfather* for stereotyping the Italians. Before that book came out, Puzo wrote a wonderful novel called *The Fortunate Pilgrim*. It is about an Italian-American mother and the focus is on her, the woman, not the man, which is unusual. As you read it, you might think it is a Jewish woman—Jews often make that point about the matriarch, the domineering person. It is a fine, sensitive book, so when Puzo is accused of stereotyping Italians, it is obvious that the accuser has not read the other book. Years before women's lib had taken over, he was showing the importance of a woman, a strong woman, among Italians, even though she was a housewife. It was the woman who imbued that family with its values and strength.

The Godfather is a great read. We should not forget that. I remember reading it on vacation in St. Thomas. I *gulped* it down, reading it so fast and enjoying it so much. There were scenes about the Italian-American experience that were *real*, with a true sense of the family and loyalty.   .

Speaking of loyalty once again, I want to stress that it is a strong trait of our culture. Perhaps because they feel in part that the world is against them—even in church, because the priests are often Irish —Italian Americans have developed an intense loyalty toward family and friends. *Together, we have to be together, we have to unite to fight this world.* Whatever sense of loyalty I have comes from that experience. I treasure loyalty. I prize it.

The Godfather is also noteworthy for portraying the unattractive part of the Italian-American experience that I lived with growing up. And that is the celebration of the Mafia, of the mobsters, *by the Italians.* Coney Island was, and still is, a place where parts of the mob are very powerful, and I remember that they would hang out at an Italian coffee shop on Mermaid Avenue, about two blocks from our house. My father would tell me, "Walk on the other side of the street. Don't go near them." But in fact, a lot of the Italian families worshiped and treated these people with respect. They were killers, and they would shake down storekeepers. They were terrible people. And I remember how some members of our community celebrated Joey Gallo and how there was talk of making a play out of him and heroes of the mob. They were bums. They are bums. There is always that strain in the Italian-American experience that is standing together and not knocking even the bad people. You see some of that in the Puzo book.

Michael Andretti

MICHAEL ANDRETTI
Ferrari Is My Favorite

◇

Son of Mario Andretti, one of our most celebrated race-car drivers, twenty-three-year-old Michael Andretti has himself achieved distinction as a car racer by qualifying in his first effort for the Indy 500. At Indianapolis, not only did he qualify, he posted the fastest speed ever recorded by a rookie. During this interview, Michael was joined by his grandmother, Rina Andretti, who added a few reminiscences of her own.

The interview took place in the office of Mario Andretti's split-level home in Nazareth, Pennsylvania, where the author caught a glimpse of the trophy room on the lower level. It was filled with what seemed like hundreds of trophies under glass, a bar the length of one wall, and glistening blue mirrors—a racing fan's heaven.

Among the foreign cars, Ferrari is my favorite, mostly because to have a Ferrari is saying something.

Being a race-car driver, I have to say that what impresses me most about Italy are the cars and the way the people are into racing so much. I think that's really neat. I'm in a profession that over there is considered very big. I mean, as big as football is here, racing is over there. It's a unique experience for me to be treated as a hero by the Italians. They know more about my racing than Americans do.

Why Italians are so wrapped up in racing is hard to say. Maybe a lot of it would have to do with Ferrari, Enzo Ferrari, the man who started Ferrari sports cars and race cars. I know one thing—an Italian grows up idolizing race drivers and dreams of being one the way an American kid dreams of becoming a baseball player. If Italians don't become race drivers, they sit behind their wheels and turn into speed demons. The fascination with speed seems to be inborn. With me, racing is in the blood. I saw my dad do it, and that was one of the incentives. Money isn't what lured me to the track. I might be racing even if there was no money in it. If you love anything enough, you'll always do it anyway.

My father was born in Montona, in Trieste. He and his family emigrated here in 1955, ten years after the end of World War II. I've been to see his hometown and I think it is unique. It's very small and has walls built all the way around, dating way back. Very old, really unique. My dad definitely has the Italian in him. He is a very proud person, and I think he is proud of his background. On the other hand, he is happy to be an American—he was naturalized in 1959.

In a lot of ways, you could tell that as a father, he was from a European background. He was a bit more of a disciplinarian than other dads, for example. But not a lot. He has always been behind me in anything I have chosen to do. As long as he knew I was giving it my best effort, he was happy. He has quite a few Italian-American friends. They enjoy being with him, and he enjoys being with them. I think Italians are very tight and seem to attract other Italians. Mostly, his friends are not in auto racing, they are local businessmen. As I was growing up, my own friends were not usually Italian but whatever they happened to be.

As a child, I was in a unique situation because my father was not around much. Racing keeps you away from home a lot. But when it came to the time we did spend together, it was more a question of quality than quantity. In some ways we ended up being very close because he wasn't here all the time. When he was around, we valued our time together a little more.

We had a place—we still do—in the Pocono Mountains that was like our own resort. We had a lot of good times up there. Whenever there was a free weekend, we were in the Poconos. We had minibikes and motorcycles and snowmobiles around. I guess my dad supervised us. I have a lot of good memories when the whole family was there—and friends as well.

I'm probably the most Italian-oriented in the family. Maybe it's because I'm the oldest—besides me, there are Jeffrey and Barbie. Actually, I'm half Dutch. My mother is Dutch-American. Her parents were born here; the Dutch ancestry goes back. But there hasn't been much of a Dutch influence. Although I feel it in some ways, I feel closer to the other heritage. I don't know why. Probably because of the name. That has a lot to do with it. Also, my father's parents live just down the street, and they speak Italian. My father always speaks to them in their own language. I grew up with that.

Jeffrey's in between, I think. I don't really know, not having ever noticed whether's he's more one thing or the other. As for Barbie, she considers herself just plain American, maybe because she's the youngest. My fiancée, Sandra Spinozzi, is from an Italian family. In fact, she's more Italian than I am, even though both her parents were born here. She is third generation, I am second. I knew Sandy for a long time because her parents are friends of ours. It's funny how it worked out. We finally got together about six years ago. She lives here in Nazareth, about a mile away. I'm building a house, which we plan to live in after we're married.

I like my grandmother's food a lot—particularly her gnocchi. With meat sauce—I love that. My mother cooks Italian, and she's pretty good at it. But she cooks a little of everything. Sandra is a very good cook. She learned pretty much from my grandmother and cooks the same things she does. She wants her to teach her more.

All the schools I went to while growing up are right across the street here. I went to the public elementary school and the junior high school. For four years I attended Catholic school. My grandparents had a big influence in my being sent to Catholic school. I think, looking back, it was good. I don't regret it now. After I got confirmed and everything, they transferred me back to public school. I graduated from Nazareth High School. After that, I went to a local junior college for two years. That was about when I was getting into racing and had to go into it full-time. I attended two racing schools in the United States, the Bertil Roos School and the Skip Barber School. In Belgium, I attended the André Pilette school.

Besides my father, I don't have any special sports heroes. I'm not a follower of baseball, I'm more into football and like hockey a lot.

Among the Italian-American entertainers, I enjoy Dean Martin. To me, he is a funny man. I like him a lot. I don't feel close to any of the singers. Most of them were before my time.

I don't have any painful memories of growing up Italian. Not really. We are subject to jokes and things like that, but I think a lot of it is done in fun. You know, there are racial jokes, and they're said about anybody. It doesn't matter who you are. If you're Polish, you hear the same thing. I did grow up hearing a lot of that, but I don't think it was done maliciously. It was all in fun, you know, and I can put up with it. I never took it to heart. Maybe if I was full Italian, I would have. But growing up in America and being half-Italian, I wasn't affected by it quite as much as others, perhaps.

The word *ethnic* doesn't upset me, either. I'm an American. It probably would have bothered my father because he did come from another country. But not me personally. I never considered myself one.

Up to a point, I think the Mafia is a joke. But then all of a sudden—if you really think about it—it is a little scary at times.

Montona in Trieste, where my father was born, near the border of Yugoslavia, was part of Italy at the time. But that whole area was taken over by the government of Yugoslavia after World War II and came under Communist control. My grandfather owned a lot of property, which was taken over by the Communists. The family was left penniless. They were put in a relief camp in Lucca and lived there for I don't know how many years. My father was just a young boy. When they were given a chance to emigrate after seven and a half years . . . my grandmother is visiting us today. She talks about this a lot. Let me ask her to come in.

[He leaves and comes back with his grandmother, Rina Andretti, a diminutive woman with dark brown hair, fashionably dressed. She has a bright-eyed, youthful look. After introductions, at Michael's urging, she begins to speak softly in English with a precise accent about life in Montona before World War II and afterward—and about the food delicacies of her native land, which she still cooks for the family. Her remarks are in italics.]

Before the war, we had a lot of land. I have no idea how many acres; we brought the map with us. My husband administered the property. He was left an orphan when he was four years old. His father and mother both died of pneumonia, his father in 1912 and his mother in 1914. Then he lived with two uncles. One of them was a priest. So his uncle priest raised him. (There was another uncle priest in our family called Andretti.) The one who raised my husband was from his mother's side. These two uncles owned all this property, and when my husband grew up, he managed the land and supervised all the families who worked on it, twenty-one families in all. They provided the families with seeds and fertilizer and equipment, and there they were working.

After the war, the Communists of Yugoslavia came over to where we were living in Istria, to Montona. For three and a half years we were living under Communist regime. We had to stay there during those years, but after that time, they gave us the option to leave. We decided to go because things were so bad. And we left—not only us, but thousands of people throughout the territory left. We lost all our property—everything.

My husband tried very hard to get work. He went all over looking—to Rome, where he had a cousin—to see if he could find a job. But it was impossible; he couldn't have a job there. He had other cousins in other places, and even they couldn't help. Of course, it was very hard at that time. It was after the war, in 1948.

From 1948 to 1955, we lived in a relief camp in Lucca in Toscana. The government gave each person a little money every week. Living was pretty bad there. After a while, my husband and the other men were given work planting trees. For a dollar a day, the equivalent, I mean, they were working for eight to ten hours a day. They had no choice but to go and plant these trees. Remember, we were in a relief camp.

Then we decided to get out. I had an uncle in America, my father's brother, and he was living here for fifty years, since 1908. He sent me a letter and he said that you have to choose: either you come over with your family, or your brother comes with his family. He gave the option to my brother first. But my sister-in-law was teaching school, and she had her parents there, and she didn't want to leave. And we came to America, to Pennsylvania—my husband, Mario, Aldo, his twin brother, myself, and my daughter, Anna Maria.

It took five years before I learned English—I mean, to understand it. I started to work in a blouse factory three years after we came, in 1958, and I started to understand a little bit. I wanted to go and work and be with American people and learn the language. I'm always trying to learn more, and I ask if I don't know something. When I hear something new, I ask, "What mean that?" And I try to remember.

I went back to Italy four times because my parents were there, my mom.

Until she died, I went back. My husband is retired, he's seventy-six. I'm seventy-two. I'm retired for six or seven years. We live down the street from Mario. We had a lot of influence on our children. When the boys were fourteen and began to show a little independence, their father said to them, "While you live under my roof, I'm your father and I'm the boss. Then, when you marry you will be on your own."

I fight with my son Mario and Dee Ann, his wife, to send my grandsons, Michael and Jeffrey, to Catholic school, and for a while they were going to Catholic school. We are Catholic. We have two priests in the family. When we left Italy, the cousin priest said, "You hold up your religion." He knew in this country there are so many religions and Italy is ninety-nine percent Catholic, so he said, "You hold up your religion." I go to church every morning when I can, almost every morning. I don't want to miss the church.

In the beginning, my husband and I were not happy that Mario and Aldo choose to race cars. They were twin brothers, and they were both race-car drivers. Aldo was in two big accidents, and then he had to quit.

When my dad and uncle first started racing, my grandparents didn't know they were racing. They kept it a secret. When my father came here at the age of fifteen, he was already into racing very heavy. He was following it in Italy and raced a little bit there, but he didn't have any money. And he was still young. They used to go to a lot of races. In fact, his real hero was Alberto Ascari, who was at the time the Italian Formula I driver. Formula I driving is the top level of racing on an international scale and it brings the world title. In 1978, my father became a world champion in Formula I. Alberto Ascari was his inspiration.

Aldo is living in Indianapolis. He runs a family business, a warehouse business. I have a daughter in Florida; she studied art. She's a very good artist. You can see the picture at the top of the stairs. It's very nice.

We still celebrate Christmas and Easter in the Italian way. At Christmas we have the presepio, the manger. And tortellini. That comes from Ravenna. I make the famous frittole. They are like little fruit cakes. You put yeast in them and they puff up, then you fry them, turning over once. They come from Montona. We make them only the night before Christmas. We fry and eat them while we are waiting to go to midnight mass. We have the frittole then. At Easter, we have the pinze. It is an Easter bread, round, but sweet. We cut the dough in the shape of a rose, and when we put it in the oven, it puffs up in the shape of a rose. This originated in Montona also, but it is popular in Trieste because people from Montona went to live in Trieste and they started to make it there. Everybody liked it and they made it. Frittole and pinze are both found in Trieste.

When we were in the relief camp in Lucca, all the people there came from Istria, where these sweet breads were made. There were twelve hundred people living in one building, one family in a room, two families in a room—it had been a college dormitory before. But we didn't have any ovens in the house, so all these people talked to the bakers of Lucca and told them they would like to have pinze for Easter and they gave them the recipe. The bakers made them and then they were selling the cakes to everyone. All the people were loving them and buying them. At Easter you saw all these displays of pinze in the windows. They were really good—made with butter and eggs.

I am glad Michael is marrying a girl from an Italian family. She is a wonderful girl, she is. And a very good cook. She learned cooking pretty much from me and cooks the same things I do. She wants to learn more. Her mother and father are both good Italian cooks. My son Mario doesn't like to cook. And my husband doesn't like to, not even to fry an egg. He knows how, but he won't bother.

I tried so much to teach Italian to Michael, and then to Barbie, his sister. When she was small, she did speak a couple of words. If she asked me for something, I would say, "I can't give it to you unless you ask me in Italian." And then she learned pretty good. But when she started to go to school, she didn't want to do that anymore. You see, with me and with their father, they could have spoken it. But Michael understands a couple of words. And DeeAnn, his mother, understands a lot. She can't speak it, but she can understand it.

Yes, and my mother enjoys Italy. She loves visiting, but she wouldn't be able to live there. I've been over about six times—mostly in the northern part, from Rome up. My dad doesn't go so much anymore. When he was driving Formula I, he went over at least once a year. Now he hasn't been there for a few years. In the next year or so, I think we'll be heading back. The whole family, probably. We'll see. I hope to be in Formula I soon, and I'm sure we'll be able to do some family outings over there in Italy.

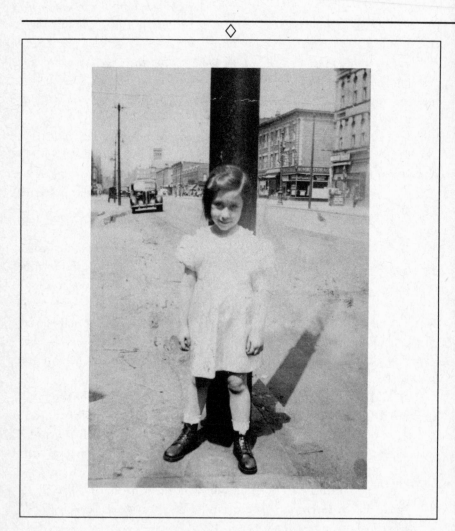

Loretta Di Franco, age five

LORETTA DI FRANCO
"Fa-la-na-na Bambin"

Despite exotic looks and a Metropolitan Opera career as soloist singing such roles as Mimi in *La Bohème* and Lauretta in *Gianni Schicchi*, Loretta Di Franco maintains a relatively simple lifestyle that is close to that of her upbringing and free of the excesses of success. Wife, mother, and churchgoer, she is the classic Italian-American of the second generation transplanted in glorious costume and panoply to the stage boards of the Metropolitan Opera House.

Music was our family background, our entertainment, and a continuous presence in our lives.

As a soloist at the Metropolitan Opera, I sing in many languages, including German, Russian, French, as well as Italian. Learning languages is part of Met training. Right now, I'm singing Marianne in *Der Rosenkavalier*. I have studied German and sing in many German operas and auditioned in Germany. I have sung in Swedish—and in Russian, in the role of Xenia in *Boris Godunov*.

Actually, it is very nice singing in Russian once you get past the Russian *l*, which is sung back in the throat. I used to study with the late, great Russian bass Sidor Belarsky. He was an immigrant to America and taught voice at the university in Salt Lake City. Years ago he heard me sing on the radio and took me on as a student. Famous for his interpretation of Jewish music, he also taught me Yiddish and Hebrew songs and coached me in music interpretation and diction. I have sung Yiddish and Hebrew songs on WEVD radio and at Jewish community gatherings.

Needless to say, I most enjoy singing in Italian. But I wasn't "born" into the language. My father, who came here from Palermo, Sicily, at the age of seven was so determined to be an American that he rarely spoke Italian at home. My mother was born in New York. I did hear a little Sicilian now and then, but not enough for it to stick. I'm sorry I didn't learn Italian—it would have been such an advantage in opera. Later, I studied it and now speak it fluently.

Italian-American singers at the Met are growing in number. There is Joanne Grillo, a mezzo soprano who has sung *Carmen*. She's from Brooklyn, like me. There is Claudia Catania, a mezzo soprano from Philadelphia, and Catherine Malfitano. Charles Anthony is an Italian-American tenor who sings character roles and has been at the Met for many years. And there is Anthony LaCiura, a young tenor with a remarkable flair for comedy.

More and more, Italian-Americans are developing into classical singers of quality. I was amazed at the skills shown at an audition of these singers that I was asked to judge recently. One young woman, a lyric spinto, had a truly fabulous voice. A lyric spinto has a full-bodied lyric sound. It is not overly dramatic but has more weight than a light lyric and could do some of the heavier roles, like *Butterfly* and *Tosca*. This performer sang from Catalani's *La Wally*.

Music was our family background, our entertainment, and a continuous presence in our lives. My mother's family, who came here from Messina in Sicily, was musical. Her father was a violinist and played at the Sherry Netherland in New York. My Aunt Concetta was a pianist and was preparing to give her first concert at Carnegie Hall when she died at nineteen of tuberculosis. Another aunt was a coloratura soprano. As a child, I remember talking with this aunt about music for hours and hours. At home, my mother played music, Neapolitan songs and Italian opera, on the Victrola all the time. I began imitating the singers I heard on records, both male and female, including Caruso and Galli-Curci. Whatever I heard, I would sing. I am still quite good at tenor arias, like "E lucevan le stelle," Cavaradossi's aria from *Tosca*. I sang and poked fun at the singing at the same time, and one day a friend of the family heard me and said, "You know, you sound good. Why don't you take lessons?" That started me on the way, but I never thought then of making a career of it.

Actually, my first lessons were in pop music. I was studying to appear on a TV program called *The Star Time TV Kids* with a bunch of teen-age hopefuls. I was fourteen at the time and had to travel all the way from Brooklyn to Jamaica, Long Island, for lessons. My father always came with me because he refused to have me travel all alone on the subway for that long a distance. He and I quickly got tired of the long commute and I never had a chance to appear on the show.

Soon after, I began studying arias with a lady teacher in Greenwich Village who was recommended by a neighbor. I can't recall her name. What I do remember is that she kept a bottle of wine on top of the piano and took swigs from it during lessons. My father soon decided that this bohemian atmosphere wasn't conducive to learning or to a proper upbringing.

At sixteen, I began studying with Maude Webber, a wonderful teacher, who lived at the Buckingham Hotel on West Fifty-seventh Street in Manhattan. An opera singer herself, she was very dramatic in her manner and the way she dressed. I remember she always wore huge wide-brimmed hats festooned with plumes that she kept on her head during lessons. But she was a wonderful teacher, and I learned from her.

During these years, music meant a great deal to me, but it was still a hobby. I was in high school and taking secretarial courses to make a living, which served me in good stead when my father died. To help support the family, I left school and worked as a legal secretary on Court Street in Brooklyn. But I kept up with my singing lessons and, whenever I could, sneaked away during lunch hours to Manhattan for auditions. When the telephone operator went out to lunch, I sneaked away, and Madeleine Ansalone, a co-worker, would cover for me. The auditions were usually for Broadway shows, but I never appeared in one. At these auditions, I simply walked onstage, was looked at, and told, "Thank you. Don't call us. We'll call you." Often I didn't even get a chance to sing. I wasn't the type they were looking for. Girls with dark hair and eyes have a better chance in opera than on the Broadway stage.

By a fluke I got into the Met at the age of eighteen. I had been at work with Maude Webber for two years and wanted to become a member of the American Guild of Musical Artists, which is the union for singers. In answer to my application for membership, the guild sent me, by mistake, a notice of auditions for chorus at the Met. Maude Webber saw it and suggested I go anyway and try to audition just for the experience. I had never auditioned for opera before. Maude had allowed me to join a group of her students who met once a week to learn chorale opera numbers, providing me with a small knowledge of ensemble singing. At the Met audition, when I was asked whether I knew any chorale numbers from opera, I said yes. I sang, and they were apparently impressed—mostly, perhaps, because I knew these numbers at such a young age. They hired me, and I joined the chorus.

At the Met, there was an unwritten law that once you get into the chorus, you stay there and are never given a chance to sing as a soloist. I wasn't aware of this—ignorance is bliss, as they say. Each year, I would try to audition for the Metropolitan Opera National Council auditions. They are held every year for promising young singers. One year, I made the preliminaries but did not go on to the next level of auditions. Another time, I went from the preliminaries to the next level. By the fifth attempt, I managed to get into the finals. They asked me to learn some new arias since I always sang my favorite aria for the auditions, which is "Caro Nome," and they simply wanted to hear me sing something else. I did Norina's aria from *Don Pasquale*, and at the semifinals, I sang "Una Voce Poco Fa" from *The Barber of Seville*. In the finals, though, I did sing "Caro Nome" because it was my favorite and I *wanted* to sing it.

I won first prize. In retrospect, I probably had an edge over the other entrants because I had the experience of singing on the Metropolitan Opera stage and felt more at ease. Besides receiving a contract to perform as a solo artist, I was awarded a two-thousand-dollar scholarship. But what was most exciting for me was that I made history at the Met by becoming the first chorister to be "promoted" to solo performing artist.

In my first appearance as soloist, I was scared stiff. I couldn't say what was going through my mind because I was so concentrated on the conductor that I had to remember that there was a huge, if silent, audience in the black pit out there. From the stage, you look out into what seems like a black hole, you know, and you don't see too many people, perhaps just a few faces in the front row. Mostly it is darkness, with a scattering of lights. You are totally involved in what you are doing and you don't really see anything beyond the stage. You are entirely concentrated on the conductor, the scenery, the costumes, and the characters you are singing with. I sang Chloe in *Pique Dame* (The Queen of Spades) by Tchaikovsky. The opera was sung in English at the time, I think. Since then, it has been done in Russian. Dressed as a shepherd, I sang a pretty little duet in French, while the opera ballet corps performed a lovely pastoral.

I grew up at the Met. It has been my home all these years. After winning the National Council Auditions, I took acting lessons at the Met's Catherine Long School, where young singers were taught how to perform and act in opera. We also studied fencing and languages. Today, the Met has the Young Artists Program, in which young singers can train more extensively and in greater depth with coaches and voice teachers. To be eligible for this program, young singers are screened by the Met through a series of auditions. It is wonderful learning experience for anyone preparing for solo performing careers.

When the Metropolitan Opera took its singers to Paris in 1966—it was my first trip abroad—I sang Barberina in *Le Nozze di Figaro*. When the tour ended, I asked my mother to fly over and meet me in Rome. She had never been on a plane before, but she flew by herself. It was her first time in Europe—she had always stayed home in Brooklyn. While there, we decided that it was a good time to visit my father's family in Palermo. Dozens of cousins—I counted about thirty-eight of them—met us at the airport. It was an exciting week, and they didn't want us to leave. One thing I remember was riding on a *carozza* to a little market where we ate raw fish. I think they called it *polpi*.

In 1972, my husband and I spent the summer in Venice. We had a *pied à terre* right on the Grand Canal. While there, I studied with an Italian coach, learning to sing Italian opera and Neapolitan songs. The coach's studio was in a palazzo and it was wonderful singing in the grand salon, looking over the canal and the gondolas passing by.

At each session, I sang "Aprile" by Tosti and also learned a wonderful Venetian lullaby in the local dialect called "Nina Nana Bambin." I loved that lullaby so much that I sang it constantly: "Fa-la-na-na bambin" [she sings it]. It was so beautiful. Nine months after I came home, in April, my daughter Lavinia was born. I think it was because I kept on singing this song "Aprile" and then the lullaby—Italians believe in this sort of magical thing. I was going to name the baby La Veneziana, or if she had been a boy, Marco, after San Marco. But I decided on Lavinia, my mother's name. [Laughs.]

By the way, for most of her life, my mother thought that her name was Loretta. I was named after her. For some reason, when she was fifty-five years old, she had to have a copy of her birth certificate and discovered that her baptismal name was actually Lavinia. She called her older sister, who dug into her mental archives and remembered that when her younger sister started school, someone—for reasons unknown—changed her name to Loretta and she became known by that name. Her middle name is Feryll. That's certainly not Italian. Apparently, her mother was fascinated by some English novel about a family called Feryll that she was reading when she was pregnant.

Lavinia, my daughter, who is twelve, has been on the opera stage since the age of three. She is in the children's chorus at the Met now. She debuted with the New Jersey State Opera in Newark in *Madame Butterfly*. At five, she appeared in *Butterfly* at the Met playing the role of Trouble, Cio-Cio-San's illegitimate child. She had to have special permission for this because children have to be at least seven to perform at the Met. She didn't sing, of course. She was a super, which means she did acting, without lines.

Since then, she has performed in several operas in the children's chorus at the Met and the New York City Opera. She is also in the Preparatory Division at the Manhattan School of Music. She is very much involved in music. And I am determined that she learn Italian. I started teaching her, but to little avail. She needs to be taught by someone else, in a more structured way.

I have good friends at the Met and see them socially. But my life is centered around my daughter and husband. I am also quite involved with church and parish work here in my area. Our church, the Church of the Blessed Sacrament on West Seventy-first Street and Broadway here in New York, has an active parish with lots of programs, activities, and special functions. I am a eucharistic minister and a lector and assist during the mass. I have been the chairperson of the entertainment committee and a former vice-president of the parish council. On Saturdays, I teach liturgical songs to students as part of religious education.

My husband is also Italian, born in Brooklyn. He speaks Neapolitan, a talent which suddenly emerged and flourished for a few days while we were in Italy. One day, he was a linguist, conversing in his Italian dialect with Renata Scotto, whom we visited in her villa outside Milan. At home, he and I share a lot of the cooking. Like some Italian men, he loves to cook. If I have two performances in a day, like Saturday, I am really exhausted by the time I get home and he usually takes over.

I have always had an independent spirit. And I am very sympathetic to a number of women's liberation causes. Rehearsing, studying, performing, traveling, and touring take me away from home a lot. Even though I come from a culture that frowns upon such a lifestyle, my family accepts it and is supportive of my career. My husband accepted my career interests when we married, and he has encouraged me. He did not dare not to. Nowadays, the idea of a woman staying home as a full-time keeper of the house, as my mother did, is no longer *de rigueur*, even with Italian-American men.

Growing up in a large Italian family is an experience I wish my daughter shared. She has not had much opportunity to enjoy the pleasures of large family gatherings, especially during the holidays. These were particularly happy times, spent eating and playing with cousins. Our family used to get together every Sunday for a veritable banquet of homemade goodies. After a marathon dinner, we'd gather around the piano and sing or we'd just sit around and exchange jokes and stories. But she has Italian qualities—she's warm, loyal, and affectionate. She loves music and opera. And in just one generation I am going to reverse things. Just as my father was determined to be an American and raise me as one, I am just as anxious to have my daughter grow up with a deep sense of her Italian heritage.

Robert Venturi, age ten

ROBERT VENTURI
Upbringing Among Quakers

◇

The writings and buildings of Robert Venturi are credited with having initiated the shift of architecture away from modernism onto more humane ground that reflects our eclectic, pluralist culture. An Italian-American who was born in Philadelphia and works from there, Venturi is perhaps America's most admired living architect.

Among his firm's recent commissions is a co-designer role in the $400 million state mosque in Baghdad, which, if built (depending on the Iran-Iraq War), will be among the largest works of architecture in history, and the extension of London's National Gallery, considered Britain's most prestigious new building project.

I have not easily connected with ongoing and established ideals.

In a way, I am an architect who doesn't fit into any major category. Not belonging applies to my life as well. I've been called an outsider. As someone looking in, I tend to see things from a different perspective. I like the expression *nerd*, and I loved the movie *Revenge of the Nerds*. A nerd is someone who is awkward on the outside whose good points are not visible because they are on the inside. I feel like a nerd. Although I am not a WASP but an Italian-American, I don't fit easily into that mold either, having not been brought up Catholic and being married to a non-Italian. Yet I feel strongly connected with Italy and Italian tradition.

As an architect, I must love Italy. Few will argue that Italy has not been the fountainhead for architecture in most of Western history. My book, *Cmplexity and Contradiction in Architecture*, led some people to believe I was against the austerity of modern architecture. My background may explain that. Even as a child, I was interested in architecture, and Italian architecture always attracted me. As an architect, I have been consistently connected with, and very much inspired by, Italian architecture and its urban qualities. How much that is the result of background and of feeling at home in Italy, I don't know.

I have a more general interest in Italy, too. I think I have made over thirty trips there and we go there as a family once or twice a year. Italian art has greatly influenced me, and Italian opera is my favorite music (after Beethoven). There isn't time to go to performances, so I listen to opera in my car. I love Italian cooking. Last night, Denise was out of town and Jimmie was out for dinner, so I made myself a pasta with only good olive oil on it; that dish was, for me, elementally delicious.

My father was born in Abruzzi, in a town called Atessa. Abruzzi is a province that lies east of Rome on the Adriatic Sea, where the Apennine Mountains are at their highest. Many Philadelphians are Abruzzesi—at least, that is what I have been told by our Italian consul.

My mother was born in Washington, D.C. Her family came from Puglia, which is in the heel of the peninsula. Through the centuries, Puglia was invaded by Normans and Germans; that may be how I inherited blue eyes and a light complexion. As a child of immigrants, my mother also did not fit the mold. In high school, she was much influenced by a teacher, Florence Carroll, who died soon after I was born. Miss Carroll took a great interest in my mother and became her American role model. When my mother had to leave school because her family did not have the money to buy her a winter coat, her teacher continued to befriend her. As a young woman, my mother became interested in literature and socialism and liberal causes. She loved the Fabians and Bernard Shaw and the Webbs. Norman Thomas, the socialist, was her choice for President the five times that he ran for that office. Although her parents were poor immigrants when they came here, they were of a slightly higher level of education than many of their peers and probably encouraged her in intellectual pursuits.

Though her lifestyle and cultural interests were "WASPy" my mother was in a way a "Jewish" mother. She was the dominant parent. When I look back now, I realize my father was influential on me too, but not in the direct ways she was. Now I find myself thinking more of him than of her. I wish this had happened before he died.

My mother and father were born Catholics but did not practice. When I was about five years old, they decided they needed a religious affiliation for my sake. Being a pacifist, my mother was attracted to the Quakers because of their stand against war, and so she became a member of the Society of Friends. My father went along with her, and the three of us went to meeting on Sunday morning. I was sent to a Friends School in Philadelphia.

I never went to a public school; pledging allegiance to the flag—"coercive patriotism" my mother called it—was anathema to her. So she wouldn't send me to a school where that kind of ritual was performed in the morning: This was an expression of her pacifism. Also, she and my father wanted me to get a very good education. I went to the Lansdowne Friends School until I was ten years old; then they felt that the Episcopal Academy was more appropriate for an older child—it was more structured—and I was sent there.

My maternal grandmother, whom I loved very much, was the only grandparent I knew. She was the one ethnic I had any contact with. She spoke with an accent and was the typical *nonna*—stout and jolly. She didn't live with us, but gave me some connection with what I could call the normal second-generation experience.

My father arrived in America at the age of nine, but when I knew him, he had lost any immigrant characteristics. Like most sons of immigrants, he had to work very hard when he was young. He was sixteen when his father died, and as the oldest of four children, he assumed the role of father to his younger siblings, and he quit school in order to run his father's fruit-and-produce store. Over the years, he made it into a successful wholesale enterprise, although the world of commerce was not to his liking. He was not a born businessman, but he was a person with an enormous sense of responsibility and commitment to his family.

The melting-pot ideal of his time meant a great deal to him. He was very much of his generation in that respect; without disowning his roots, he still felt that one did everything one could to become typically American. His lifestyle showed this: Most of his friends were not Italian or other ethnics. He "assimilated." The appellation *ethnic* would probably have made him uneasy. My wife says my Italian-Quaker parents were not involved in upward mobility but in vertical take-off.

Although both my parents knew Italian, they did not speak it at home. We never lived in an Italian neighborhood. By the time I came along, my father—who married late and was reasonably well off by then—chose to live in a middle-class neighborhood that was not ethnic. The only Italian I know is what I learned in college, with the help of my mother's tutoring on the side, and from a few years of postgraduate study in Italy. My Italian is very limited, but my wife speaks a fair amount of it.

In my childhood, I knew my cousins well and have kept up with them. They are middle-class people, most of whom went to college and some of whom have been extremely successful in business and academically. We were closest to my mother's sister, and our two families got together for holidays. Each family had one son. We shared a vacation house in the summer.

As a kid growing up, I loved Italian food. But I didn't get much of it. My father's inclination was to shun what we would now call ethnic cooking, and my mother was into nutrition, which was unusual in those days. She thought pasta had no nutritional value, and so I grew up in a household where the emphasis was on natural foods, a diet more typical of today than of the thirties. My mother was a vegetarian for part of her life, and at these periods, we ate lots of fruits and vegetables. I was always starved for pasta (spaghetti we called it), and I loved eating it at my three aunts' houses, where I could indulge myself.

Both my parents were very much interested in architecture and undoubtedly encouraged my absorption in it—my mother was also interested in fashion and furniture and had very good taste. But their influence was not overt. They never said, "You should be an architect." My father loved to point out his favorite buildings—he once impulsively stopped the taxi as we were passing Penn Station in New York, when I was around ten years old, to show me the grand interior there based on the Baths of Caracalla. I will never forget that first impression of that awesome space, and I now treasure the memory of it. My father's father was a builder in Italy, but when he came here, he went into the fruit-and-produce business. I know my father would have become an architect if he had had the chance. I have just learned from the architectural historian George Thomas that Phineas Paiste designed my father's store; a later renovation of it was designed around 1922 by Edmund Brumbaugh, both well-known architects of their day who were friends of my father. From a very early age, I knew I wanted to be an architect—I still remember noting my favorite buildings on the bus route to grade school.

My only connection with the immigrant outlook was through my maternal grandmother, and as I didn't see her much, I never fell under its influence and felt no conflict between American and ethnic values. If anything, my mother's attitudes created a conflict in me that was somewhat the reverse. She was more liberal than most of the Americans I knew—as a pacifist and Friend and devotee of liberal causes. But that wasn't a big problem for me. I was never affected, of course, by what you could call Catholic conservatism.

My own son goes to a Jewish Sunday school. My wife is Jewish. She feels very strongly that if you are half Jewish, you ought to really know about Judaism so you can deal with anti-Semitism. Then, when you grow up, you can decide which way you want to go. I go along with that. I like the Jewish religion and admire it. I feel comfortable about the situation. On the other hand, I want him to know about his Italian heritage. He goes to Italy frequently. He was there last Christmas and in the spring and summer. He is fourteen years old. So far, he is not interested in architecture—he calls it architorture. But I think he is absorbing things Italian. I have no particular desire to have him learn Italian—he should do what he wants to do in that respect.

We keep up with my mother's family in Puglia. They live in Foggia. On our trips there, everyone shows us great hospitality. My mother's cousin is an elderly bishop and a fabulous person. From what I have seen, the members of our family who remained in the old country have done at least as well, economically and in terms of education, as those who migrated. This may be more typical than we realize. If my recent ancestors had the gumption to get up and go, leave one country for another, then initiative is possibly a family trait. The ones who stayed showed their initiative in other ways.

Italian-Americans have been important to America, but until recently, they have not been as influential as they might have been. What the reasons are, I don't know; although I am not a historian or sociologist, I have some ideas on this. From my observation, clichés like *Italians are idle* are thoroughly false. In the recent past in this country, many Italians had to work at hard labor. Some who could not achieve immediate satisfactions in their work lost ambition. Another problem may have been that the Catholic Church in this country did not acknowledge higher education as a priority for enriching experience and for getting ahead. Also, most Italians came from rural and small-town environments. This hardly prepared them for the nineteenth-century American city.

I have never noted any particular prejudice because I am an Italian-American. There have been other problems that sprang from, for example, not having the right connections, but that is different. No, I have never felt discrimination, and I am rather touchy. It may be partly because I have been well educated and because I don't look like people's stereotype of an Italian. This is not to say that prejudice does not exist or that I am unsympathetic to people who have felt it. There is a parallel with feminism. My wife, who is a feminist, is saddened when she hears successful women say, "As a woman, I have never felt discrimination and have had no unusual trouble achieving success in a man's world. I don't know why women are involved in the feminist movement. *I've* never had any problem." This kind of thinking is, at the least, insensitive.

However, I do not want to be labeled and pigeonholed as an Italian-American. I am an architect, not an Italian-American architect. This does not mean that I lack emotional feeling for people like me, people who come from where I come. Here is another analogy with the feminists. Women who have an emotional feeling of sisterhood with other women may not wish to give their achievement a gender. If they happen to be writers or architects, they want to be considered as such, not as women writers or women architects.

And yet I feel good when I hear of Italians in America who are doing well and achieving respect in their fields. I find I like it that one of Yale's presidents, A. Bartlett Giamatti, is of Italian descent —this is a purely emotional reaction. And I love Italian women. I know more of them in Italy than here. It is bad to generalize, but I love Jewish women and Italian women.

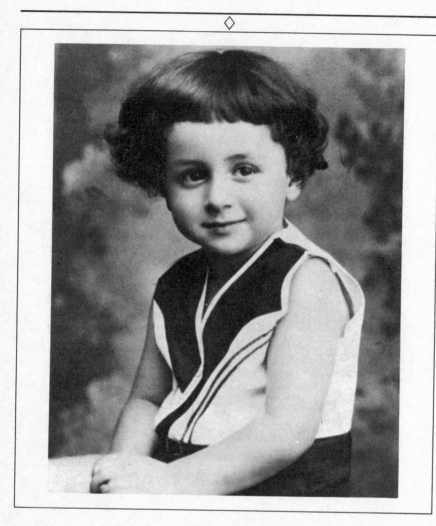

Arthur Caliandro

ARTHUR CALIANDRO
A Methodist Boyhood

◇

In October 1984, Dr. Arthur Caliandro succeeded Dr. Norman Vincent Peale as minister of the Marble Collegiate Church in New York City. An Italian-American, he is now the head of one of the oldest Protestant churches in America. Dr. Caliandro, who is himself the son of an Italian Protestant minister, is a unique blend of an Italo/Yankee upbringing in Portland, Maine.

◇

Her parents had learned she was dating an Italian and forbade her ever to talk to me again.

It is natural to assume that all Italians are Catholics, but that is not so. I am an Italian-American Methodist minister. My father, who was born a Catholic in southern Italy, became a Methodist minister. His three brothers turned Protestant, and a son—myself —became a minister.

When my father was studying in Rome as a college student, he had a dramatic conversion experience. Usually, in Italy, conversions to Catholicism are the norm, but this was the reverse—a conversion from Catholicism to Protestantism. As a Catholic child growing up in the small town of Ciegli, near Bari, he had a couple of unfortunate spiritual experiences with the local priest. He would tell me about this town as being quite medieval in attitude and culture, and when I went there, I found that to be true. Nothing seemed to have changed in centuries. Being a sensitive boy, he was greatly disturbed by the priest's attitude and manner.

One of the things that happend concerned the Bible itself. His older brother, who had gone to America, sent a copy of the Bible to my father, who was twelve years old at the time. He was very proud and happy to have it because he realized the importance of the Bible in Catholic scripture, and he decided to show it to the priest. The latter responded by insisting that the boy burn it. That was the medieval touch. It bothered my father greatly, but being a dutiful child, he obeyed and burned the Bible, keeping the cover, however, because he felt something was wrong with what he had done. And that was the beginning of the change. There were other things that had gone wrong, but that is what started his spiritual pilgrimage.

Years later, when he was studying in Rome and searching for something spiritual, he and a friend took a walk one Sunday evening. They happened to go by a Methodist church that was, and still is, located near the railroad station. The windows were open and people were singing—Methodists are great for singing hymns. [Laughs.] They wandered in, out of curiosity, and when they were inside, were received very, very warmly. It was this warmth, this friendliness, and the openness of the people that really captured their hearts.

They were Italian Methodists. Rome is a cosmopolitan city, of course, and there are two or three Methodist churches there now. But at that time, this was *the* Methodist church for Italian Methodists, and how they ever survived, I do not know. My father and his friend were converted. Later, they both felt a call to the ministry. They came together to the United States and attended Drew Theological Seminary in New Jersey on scholarship. That was 1924, when my father was twenty-three years old. It took them four years to get through a three-year program because during the first year, learning

English took up most of their time. Although they came to the States intending to return to Italy, they both stayed.

Each time a Greek person or someone of Greek heritage hears my name, he will most likely say, "That's Greek." The name comes from two Greek combination forms, *kalos* meaning good, or beautiful, and *andro* meaning male, and can be translated as *good man*. My father was born in the vicinity of Bari on the Adriatic. Over the centuries the Greeks and Italians did a lot of warring in that part of the Mediterranean, and obviously some Greeks settled there. The name became Italianized, but there are still in that part of Italy settlements where Greek is spoken and there is much Greek influence.

In my father's family, there were four boys, and each came to the United States at different times. In those days, the firstborn would come over and he would send for the next son, paying his fare and seeing to his welfare, and this son the next son, and so on. Eventually, all four brothers came and they all turned Protestant.

My mother's family is Catholic—she is the only Protestant. She came from a small village in Sicily, and her religious background was not very strong. There was no religion really, except culturally. Her family settled in Greenwich Village and she worked as a seamstress for twelve to fifteen hours a day in the garment district. What happened was that her friends, who lived in the same house she did, were Protestant and they were in the habit of going to the Judson Memorial Church in the Village. She started to go to the church with them—this was around 1916. My father was doing his seminary field work in that church. They met and married.

My father's first church after graduation from the seminary was in Portland, Maine. It was a tiny mission church for the very few Protestant Italians in Portland. At that time the Methodists had what they called the Board of Home Missions and they worked with Italians. There were Italian Methodists in Boston and some in Hartford and various cities in the Northeast. Each of these cities had an Italian Methodist church. New York City, of course, had several. And my father was assigned—in the Methodist system, you are *assigned* a location—to that church in Portland in 1928 and he stayed there until 1950. I was born and raised in Portland.

My father always craved association and friendship with his Roman Catholic colleagues, but he never achieved it. This was one of the things that hurt him throughout his life. He never had any bad feeling about the Catholic Church: He had simply had an experience that brought him to another setting, spiritually. The best opportunity he had for this kind of friendship was during World War II, when he was a chaplain in the service. The army was the most ecumenical of all societies, and the Roman Catholics, the Jews, and the Protestants got along well together.

He would have been pleased to know—and I believe he probably did know—that at his funeral the monsignor from the local Catholic parish was present. That kind of thing is what he wanted all his life. He himself never had a sense of division, and he was always hurt when a priest would judge him for crossing over.

From the very beginning, my father leaned toward being more American than Italian. So much of what we were about was pure American. As the Italian-American is coming more and more into a place of leadership and prominence, I am aware of how much was missed by not being raised in an Italian culture, and I regret it very much. Not learning the language, for one thing. My mother and father spoke it together generally, but we children did not even attempt to listen. We wanted to be American kids. Each time I am in Italy, after a few days I can pick up the gist of what is going on, but that is the extent of it.

Living in an Italian community which was ninety-eight percent Catholic, we as Protestants were isolated. My association with the Italian kids was only in school and not in the home, because they were Catholic and we were Protestant and the two groups did not socialize. There was no extended family for us. As a minister, my father was assigned to that community, and there were no Caliandros around us. His brothers were all in New York. If we had lived near a grandmother or grandfather, aunts or uncles, we would have had more of the Italian culture. It was not passed on to us.

In the seven- or eight-square block area of Portland where we lived, there were also Jewish people, Armenians, and Greeks. These ethnic groups lived side by side, like a small melting pot. I did not realize the richness of it at the time.

The only educated Italians I knew were a lawyer and a druggist. All the others were laboring people. My image of the Italian was not a good one. The juvenile delinquents of these growing-up years were the Italian kids. Living right next door to the police station, I was aware of all the kids getting into trouble and being picked up and put into jail. Ninety percent of them were Italian.

This embarrassed me. As a result, I did not socialize much with the Italian kids. This affected my own self-image when I went away to college. The high school was pretty ethnic and we were all the same, although the Italians seemed to be at the low end of the socioeconomic and educational scale. At Ohio Wesleyan in Ohio, where I went to college, there were very few Italians, just about four or five. And I don't even remember them. My older brother and I went there at the same time and we were very much a minority. I changed my name from Arturo, my birth name, to Arthur. It was uncomfortable saying Arturo Caliandro in an Anglo-Saxon setting.

The first awareness I had of any prejudice happened in my freshman year at Ohio Wesleyan, when I was dating a girl from western Pennsylvania. We might have had eight or ten dates. I liked her and she liked me. After Christmas vacation, she refused to see me or talk to me. This upset me because I did not know why. Later that year I found out. Her parents had learned she was dating an Italian and forbade her ever to talk to me again. That hurt, and it fed some of the feelings that I had—that there was something wrong with being Italian.

The entire thing was cleared up almost overnight the summer after my graduation from college, when I spent a month in Italy with the Peale family, Dr. and Mrs. Norman Vincent Peale and one of their children, with whom I had gone to college. It was after being in Italy for two or three days that I said to myself, "*This* is my heritage?"

I was filled with excitement as I saw evidences of the culture, the richness, the charm, the beauty that is Italy. Almost overnight, I said, Wait a minute. You don't have to feel shame. And pride became part of my emotions. Later I became aware that before the mass migrations of the late 1800s and onward, the Italian people in America were the artists, the creators, the musicians, and they were regarded as very special people. It was the migration of the poor and the needy and the uneducated that affected all this. I struggled with feelings like these.

As a very young boy, I would stare at a map in one of the rooms of my father's church. The church comprised two large rooms on the ground floor of a wood frame house, and we lived upstairs. The map was hung on a wall, and on the bottom of the map, were the words "America, the Melting Pot." That concept seared itself on my consciousness. I know there is a lot of debate now on whether or not the melting pot has succeeded in America. In my mind there is more truth to it than not. Unfortunately, it has not worked for the blacks. Color keeps up walls for too many people. But I think it has worked for every other group, including the Hispanics, who are light-skinned enough to have had an easier time of it than the blacks.

The mix of peoples has made this country rich—so many cultural influences, so many ideas. One of America's beauties for me is that so many different people, a miniglobe, can live together side by side. We do extremely well with the various national groups, even the ones whose native countries are warring with one another. We live peaceably here. Down in Chinatown and Little Italy, there has been very little conflict between the Chinese and the Italians. I have asked some of them, "How do you get along so well?" The best answer so far is that there is the same emphasis on family in both cultures that creates a bond. And so they get along. People are becoming even more tolerant and understanding and eager to see things work. Despite television and radio, which have had a big influence, I hope that everybody does not become the same or speak the same. A certain standard accent of television and radio announcers exists that influences people's speech patterns. What is vital is to keep the unique features and speech patterns of our backgrounds.

As the father of one of my college friends, Dr. Norman Vincent Peale came to know me well in college and later on in the seminary. We always related well, and I became a close part of the family. He was like a father to me. When I was thirty-three years old, he asked me to join the Marble Collegiate Church.

This is the oldest church in America with an unbroken ministry. The congregation is the continuation of the original church in New York, which was founded in 1628 by the Dutch East India Company. Unbroken ministry means that there has been worship every Sunday since then and there has been a ministry continuously, whereas other churches, which are older, have had a break in the continuation. It is the Reform Church of America, the church of the original Dutch settlers. Peter Minuet was the first elder.

I am the forty-sixth minister in a long line going back to 1628—and the first *Italian* minister. I may be the last, I don't know [laughs]. It is a little bit like being the first Italian president of Yale University. And recently I read about the new dean of the Yale Law School. His name is one of those wonderful Italian names [Guido Calabresi]. It touched and excited me.

Dr. Peale stuck his neck out when he planned the succession. After I had been here two years, he put his hand on my shoulder and said, "I want you to succeed me." My being Italian seemed to make no difference to him. He is not that kind of person. And it took six years for the succession plan to be made official. Once it was, then I was freer, he was freer, and he gradually began to pull back and do less and less. When he finally left in early 1985, relinquishing the pulpit, I was familiar with everybody and everybody was familiar with me. The relationship had already been tested. So it has not been a difficult transition. I have been here now for eighteen years.

Some years ago an elder of the church, and a very significant alumnus of Yale who graduated top of his class from the Yale Law School, came to me one day and said, "You know, Arthur, you're a good person, in spite of being Italian." He was serious and sincere, and I did not take it offensively, knowing it was the Yale, the Ivy League, the Anglo-Saxon, presence that was speaking. It was obvious that he liked me, and this was the best way he knew of to express his feeling. I haven't seen him since they have an Italian dean at his alma mater. I'd like to talk with him about *that*. [Laughs.]

In terms of my relationship with the church, I don't worry about being Italian anymore, though at the beginning I wondered, because it was so different from my background and so Anglo-Saxon. It has become a church where there is an enormous mix of peoples, even though there are very few Italians. The national groups, the religious backgrounds of the people, are so varied that I feel very normal and natural. And it surprises and pleases me that my not being a WASP does not make any difference to some of the old families of New York who are members. Not any that I am aware of, because they continue to come and the relationship we have is warm and open. And this is a melting pot, all right? There is something that is fusing and connecting—perhaps it is because of New York. I do not know.

My two sons, ages twenty-three and twenty-one, have been to Italy. They sought out their grandfather's birthplace even though they barely remember him, because he died when they were very young. They have not had the same kinds of experiences or sense of isolation that my generation had in growing up Italian. They have never met any prejudice or had a feeling that something was wrong.

On meeting an Italian, I find myself saying, "Hey, paisano!" That is a good feeling. The thing that is missing is that we did not grow up with the Italian culture. I don't know all the dishes, for example.

In an Italian restaurant, friends will say, "Arthur, you should know what to order." But I do not, any more than anyone else, because the Italian foods of my childhood were the few dishes that happened to be my mother's favorites. With an extended family, we would have had many more and have learned a wider range of dishes. I'm happy, though, about knowing pizza before anybody ever heard of pizza, because pizza didn't really happen here until about 1950, after World War II.

I feel an affinity—I do—with other Italians and admiration for people like Mario Cuomo based on the sense he has of himself and for the very natural and easy relationship he has to his heritage. He doesn't flaunt it but holds it naturally, which is pleasing and acceptable to all people. And admiration for Geraldine Ferraro, particularly for her ability to be very honest, personally, and to put things on the table. She is a woman of spunk and courage and she handled herself beautifully when running for vice-president.

Part of my embarrassment at being Italian led me to avoid dating Italian-American girls. Although we lived in the city, every girl I dated was from the high school, which was in the suburbs, the nicer area. The idea of marrying a woman of your culture was conveyed to me by my parents, but they were not referring so much to the Italian culture as to a basic value system that springs from similar socio-economic backgrounds. In other words, they were encouraging marriage to someone with the same values we had. And my father suggested that we date Protestant girls because, he said, "You will have fewer problems." Now in our day, that would be different because it is easier to intermarry. Catholics and Protestants cross over more easily and naturally. In my era, the Catholic kid was not allowed to step into a Protestant church, and there were generally some real differences between the two churches. And I myself thought that stepping into a Catholic church was a sin. When my father encouraged us not to fall in love with a Catholic girl, he was not being anti-Catholic.

My wife's name was Brown. She is from Louisiana and is of German, English, and Irish ancestry. The family goes back a long time in the South—they emigrated in the early-to-middle 1800s. I keep saying to her, "Gloria, if your name were still Brown, you would be just like Jones or Johnson or Smith and couldn't be distinguished too easily. But with a name like Caliandro—once they know that Gloria Brown is Gloria Caliandro—no matter where you are, they're going to find you." My sense is that my wife has never felt anything but a natural acceptance and pleasure in her married name.

She is a fantastic Italian cook. It took her a while to *want* to learn but she did finally learn from my mother. For years, my mother said to me, "I will not teach your wife to cook until she asks me." Very stubborn.

After six or seven years of marriage, my wife said to her, "Nana, will you please teach me?" Now she makes the same sauce I had as a child, the same pizza. And the sauce is everything.

Today, as an Italian-American, I feel whole and enjoy people, love people and am at ease with them. There is in me a passionate appreciation of great painting and great music, and a special kinship with them because so much art and music came from Italy. Despite being isolated from the culture as a child, I have traveled and grown older and wiser and realize that these precious things—music and art—are a heritage from that culture. I am connected.

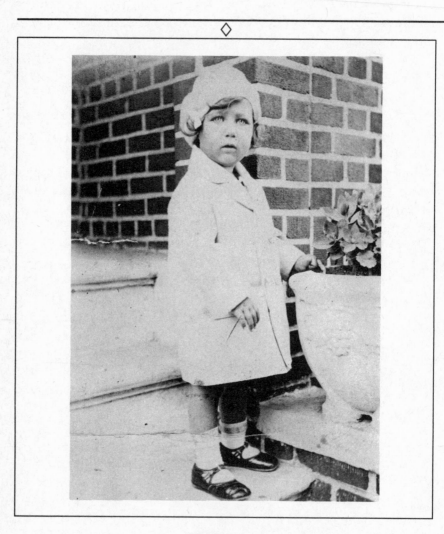

Julie Bovasso

JULIE BOVASSO
Protecting the Inner Core

In the inner circle of the avant-garde and off-Broadway theater, Julie Bovasso, playwright and actress, is a name to con-
tend with. The first to introduce the Theater of the Absurd
into America, she is a highly principled woman who has
been known to walk away from a role or directorial assign-
ment rather than do something damaging to her professional
integrity.

Among her movie roles are Mrs. Manero, John Travolta's
mother, in *Saturday Night Fever* and the nurse in *The Verdict*
with Paul Newman. On television she played Rose, the first
Italian-American heroine of television soap opera, in *From
These Roots*.

◇

*The best of all possible worlds is to get beyond being Italian, or
being black or being Chinese, and arrive at the point where we
are simply people . . .*

Bovasso is an Albanian name. I suspect that somewhere along
the line, there might have been an *s* on the end of it. My father's
family were Albanians who emigrated to Italy some four hundred
years ago. In Italy, they continued to speak Albanian in the home,
and even today they speak Albanian as well as Italian. They came to

the United States in the 1880s, earlier than my mother's people. My father was born on the Lower East Side in New York City.

My mother was born in Rome. Most of the Italians who came here were from southern Italy, and my mother's mother, who spoke the Roman dialect, could not communicate with them because they spoke different dialects. Before she came here, her husband made several trips to New York alone, leaving her and their newborn baby in Rome. He sized up the territory and worked on the railroads. At the turn of the century, he brought his family over and settled on the Lower East Side in Manhattan. They did not *just come*.

After working in a paper factory for many years, he developed a tumor in his lung, which I suspect was a result of the work. His salary was six dollars a week, or something ridiculous like that. There is no question about it—they were poor. My mother was four years old when she arrived. My father's family was better off and more settled—my grandfather had a job with the city and was well salaried. They had a better standard of living.

Soon after my parents were married, they moved from the Lower East Side out to Brooklyn, to a better environment for their children. It was like moving to the suburbs, to Westchester—Brooklyn had trees and good schools. I was born in Bensonhurst. At that time Jews, Italians, and a smattering of Irish lived in Bensonhurst and the atmosphere was healthy. My friends were mixed, mostly Jews and Italians. Sonia Gold was my best friend. For the longest time she was curious about the Roman Catholic Church service and and she would come to church with me until her mother found out. [Laughs.] We are still good friends. Anita Steckel, the artist, is from the same area in Bensonhurst. I may occasionally see one of my Jewish girl friends, but I don't see any of the Italian girl friends now. They got married and followed in their mothers' footsteps, whereas the Jewish girls became professional women—like Sonia, who is a rare-book dealer, and Anita, who is an artist and painter.

As a child, I rarely heard Italian spoken. My mother and father never spoke it except when they wanted to keep a secret. He spoke both Albanian and Italian, and when he wanted to keep a secret from my mother, he spoke to his own family in Albanian. [Laughs.] I grew up with foreign languages being used when secrets were told. A mysterious thing. My maternal grandparents who spoke Italian lived on Staten Island and we saw them rarely. No one took the trouble to teach us the language, and I was not interested enough to ask.

People take me for a northern Italian because of my blue eyes and blond hair. You know the cliché—all Italians have dark hair and eyes. In my business, the movies, the cliché still holds. I did not get an acting job as an Italian until after changing my hair color. Someone said, "Dye your hair black, for God's sake, and you'll get a job."

In our family, there were just two children, my older brother and myself. He was the prince. He was *maschio*, the male, who would carry on the family name. I was *la feminuccia*, little female, to be loved, coddled—and set aside. I was not aware of any resentment on my part, but it manifested itself in my behavior. I became detached, and what probably happened was that I refused to accept my role as this little female. I really did not like being adored in that way, and resented it. Deep down, I felt they are doing this to me for some silly reason and there is more to me than that. I was aware at a very young age that there was more to me than they were letting on, even *knew* about. At the age of six, I remember thinking, They don't know anything about me, all these people. They keep giving *him* the bigger piece of cake. That's ridiculous. I became independent. And they loved it. They let me be. More fortunate than my brother, I was free of the myth of passive femininity, but my brother was still a *maschio*, and he had to live with that. I think this kind of thinking exists in Jewish and other families as well. This myth is not exclusively Italian-American. Women like me are fortunate—we have not allowed ourselves to fall under the spell of the myth which, spelled out, says, "Girls are put on this earth to look pretty, marry, and raise children." If the myth sets off some spark of resentment, it can lead a girl to rebel and find her own way.

At public school in Bensonhurst, our classes were grouped by ability: Class number one had bright students, number two had slow learners, and number three was the intermediary class. I was always in class number one, and that was ninety-eight percent Jewish. Class number two—the dummies—had all Italians. [Laughs.] Being assigned to class number one with all the Jewish kids and not to class number two with the Italians kids was weird. I adjusted to it by thinking, Yes, I'm Italian, but I'm better than they are because I'm smarter. Until one day my mother got hold of me—because I had grown a little too arrogant—and said, "They are *not* in that slow class because they are stupid. They are there because they have families with lots and lots of children, and their mothers and fathers can't help them with their homework. The Jewish people had only one or two children, so they can help with homework. You just remember that." And *that* was that.

Once she also explained poverty to me. Why was it, I asked, that the poor kids were always dirty, or seemed to be. In my kind of logic, washing clothes did not require money. Her answer was, "When you're poor, you get very sad and you don't feel like doing certain things, like washing."

At public school, my teachers *pushed* me, they really pushed. I would not be in the theater if it had not been for Mr. Steinfeld and and Mrs. Schaef. From the age of eight, I appeared in school plays and won poetry contests because I used the most "expression." They called it expression in those days. I recited poetry with a passion. The teachers recognized something that was kind of special. They began to lean on my mother to give me lessons in this, lessons in that. Which I would not have had if she had not *allowed* herself to be open to their influence. She was enlightened in her way. A bright lady, my mother was a bright lady.

For example, she was the first one in our family to send her children to public school. Most of my cousins went to Catholic school. She would not have any of that. Public school was where all the Jewish people sent their children, and they were all smart, and that is what *she* did. [Laughs.] She was right, because I received a better education. My parents were Catholic but not practicing ones. And they were believers in a way that most people who are raised Roman Catholic are—out of suspicion and the fear of God. They were not churchgoers. We were made to go to church until the age of fourteen or so, and after that they felt we could decide for ourselves. Which I did. But I suspect that the reason she sent us to public school was that she did not have to pay. That had a lot to do with it. Not so much idealism—but she didn't say that [laughs].

Books about nutrition fascinated her, even though nutrition wasn't the big thing it is today. She was a fanatic about food. During the week, she served American food that was nutritionally balanced, and on the weekend we had meatballs and spaghetti. I think it was just to remind us that we were Italian. The meals were balanced by color: a yellow, a green, a red, and so on. Actually, her food interests provided us with a good foundation, even though she did not know *that* much about nutrition. We *always* had orange juice and milk. She was aware of all that.

As I began to show interest in things theatrical, my family accepted this and even encouraged it. When I showed a musical bent, my father himself said, "We'll have to buy her a piano." This must have set them back a lot, and the lessons especially. They gave me every opportunity to develop. But there was something else. My aunts and uncles on my mother's side were all creative people, even in Italy. One aunt wanted to be a writer, an uncle was a marvelous dancer and wanted to go on the stage. When I was ten, my aunt brought me Charles and Mary Lamb's *Tales from Shakespeare*. Not to be outdone by her relatives, my mother bought me *The Complete Works of Charles Dickens*.

My Aunt Connie, the writer, was one of my favorites, but her political views put me off. My father was conservative and his attitudes influenced me, while her liberalism was frightening. As I grew older, I appreciated her more. The person I adored was my Aunt Maureen, who was English and married to my Uncle Paul. He was a printer by trade, but it was the Depression and he was out of work. Every time his name came up, someone was sure to say that he was out of work. Aunt Maureen was a dancer, an ex-Ziegfeld girl, beautiful and wonderful. Her influence strengthened my leaning toward the theater. She is still living in Greenwich Village and looks like an eighty-five-year-old Ziegfeld girl, batting her eyelids as much as ever. [Laughs.] She is a real trip, very healthy and alive.

All my relatives loved to talk politics. We were deep in the Depression when they had political battles. My father was a teamster and ultraconservative, and there was constant clash between him and the others. My brother and I found this stimulating and sat still as these wild arguments would go *on and on* in our house. We sat in a suspended state, absorbing it all. I recall the word *communist* thrown about and me sitting there, wondering, What is a communist?

I was the only Italian girl in our neighborhood to break away from her family. There was terrible conflict. But I was helped by my brother, who broke ground before me. He went to the High School of Music and Art in Manhattan and became a painter. They were about to send me to a commercial high school for secretarial courses, but somehow I managed to get into the High School of Music and Art instead. The conflict existed especially on my mother's part. And on my father's, too, because he was worried about my traveling on the subway to Manhattan at the age of fourteen. With my mother, the situation switched because she was the one who had wanted me to have music lessons and all of that, but when the chips were down, she was afraid. Afraid that if I went off into the world of music and art and the theater—not that she would lose me, but I might lead a "bad" life.

Mothers should not be condemned for their choices and positions. It is too easy to say, "Mother was jealous. She did not want me to have a different life." There is too much of that kind of thinking. That is unfair. Maternal opposition is often based on real fear and concern. Like Amanda in *The Glass Menagerie* of Tennessee Williams. If you really look at that woman, she is *not* an evil mother. Eventually, my parents did concede and I went to Music and Art. That was the real breakthrough. But I went home every night. If not, I would be thrashed.

At seventeen, just getting out of high school, I left the house. This took place during my transition period. Even in my teens I did a lot of theater in the city and spent less time at home. But leaving was not really official—I was living half the time at home and half in the city. The situation was difficult and touchy. Girls just did not go off and get their own apartment. If you went off to college, that was different. I had a scholarship offer to go to Oberlin College in Ohio. It was a wonderful school and I wanted so much to go. But in my parents' eyes, the whole idea of a girl of eighteen going out of the state was outrageous. My father never got past New Jersey, for God's sake—he was an Italian father, after all. And there was not any money to support me, even with a scholarship.

Instead, I went to a local college, the City College of New York in Manhattan, and while there led a separate life with my friends. But at home, my father was always in a rage if I came home too late. The questions were endless.

"What is she doing?"

"What's going on?"

Of course, I never told him about my doings or my life away from home. It was a hidden yet open secret. My mother was aware that I was a normal young woman with normal sexual appetites, but this was never acknowleged at home. I had to lie. They never really knew that I lived with my first husband for a year before we married. My mother suspected it, but the cover-up was artful and careful. Living half at home and half in the city, I was supposed to be sharing an apartment with my girl friend. My future husband lived across the hall with John Walsh—that was my story. John Walsh himself was from Brooklyn and in the same situation with his parents. Nobody believed our stories. John's parents didn't believe them any more than my parents did. But they did not say anything. As long as it was not talked about or discussed, it was accepted. At nineteen I got married, partly because it was a legitimate way out.

When I was in my early teens, I left the Church, or you might say the Church kicked me out. I went to my local priest to ask a question.

"Can you explain the Holy Trinity to me? I don't understand it."

The priest said, "There is no way I can explain it. You just have to believe it on faith."

"I don't understand what you mean. It just doesn't make sense to me."

"Well," he said, "if you don't believe it on faith, you are not going to be a Catholic for very long." And that was the end of *that*. I accepted that. As far as the Church was concerned, I wrote it off.

Many years later, at the age of thirty, that question was still in my mind, and others like it. And the writer in me, the poet, began to assess things on a more metaphorical level. Today, the history of Christianity and Judaism fascinates me and is a study of mine. I have reached a point now where I feel a strong connection to the Roman Catholic mass. However, I can walk into *any* church and experience the same religious feeling. If I am in the Midwest doing a show and a Roman Catholic Church is not available, I will go into another church. You carry the church with you.

As a child, about five or six years old, I had very fervent beliefs, almost like Saint Teresa. I was drawn into Catholic rites—the music, the incense, the Latin. These are theatrical, and they influenced me. Their imprint is still felt. Everything I write—my plays, especially —is very Catholic in that sense, Roman Catholic. The plays have that same kind of feeling.

World travel is not for me—I have never been to Italy. I travel in my head and in my plays to places that have not yet been discovered. When I *do* travel, it is mostly in the United States for theater work.

This country never ends in its mystery and fascination. When I first discovered America—oh, my God!—the things that were opened up were unbelievable. I traveled a good deal in the Midwest, and suddenly my connections with Europe here in the East took on meaning. Most of our backgrounds in the Northeast are European, so we grow up as *Europeans in America*. Then suddenly, you are in middle America, the core, and you begin to discover that you are an *American*, and what that is, and that was incredible. For me, travel to Middle America is more mystical, I am sure, than going to the Vatican.

Someday, I would like to go to Europe, but so far there has been no time.

At my age, being Italian comes into my life less and less, just as being a woman is less and less important. I do not like the idea of groups banding together for a purpose, and I do not like joining them—women's groups or Italian-American groups or societies of women playwrights. Why do we have to be polarized? I avoid the woman's caucus at the Dramatists Guild. I avoid it like the plague. What *is* the woman's caucus really? An opportunity to push the ladies into a corner so they can write their own little plays, you know. Then, if the plays are really good, they can join the big guys. It is ridiculous; it is absurd. And the women themselves are doing this.

What grouping together really means is less political and more psychological. In a funny sort of inverted way, it is an attempt *not* to lose your identity, *not* to be assimilated to the point where you lose that special identity, which may be being black or being Italian. My new play, *Angelo's Wedding*, is my first work with an Italian theme, but it is not a play about gravy on the cuffs. If anything, the play is a lucid statement of the Italian as a non-cliché. After all, we do claim people like Michelangelo and Fra Angelico and Dante. The inferiority complex that exists among us in this country is something that has to do *with this country*. That is the thing we are breaking out of.

Perhaps the only period of my life that I experienced feelings of inferiority was the time I first went into the theater. Whether this had to do with being Italian so much as with being poor or lower class, I do not know. It may have been more of a class thing rather than racial or religious. I was deeply aware of the incredible sophistication of these Broadway producers. They were all WASP. They were like the rulers of the world. The feelings had mainly to do with my reaction, like, "You're from Brooklyn, how can you compete?" That was something that had to be overcome, and I knew that. I did overcome it. Those old-guard producers, like Alfred de Liagre and Guthrie McClintock, were real aristocrats. Some are still around. *Now* I have an appreciation of these men. For one thing, they are the last of the gentlemen of the theater. They are dying out and I appreciate them now, have a rapport now that was lacking then.

On second thought, part of the inferiority I felt did have something to do with being Italian. How can you separate it, anyway? You can't really. Jewish kids from Coney Island probably experienced similar feelings.

When I started out in the professional theater, I was dealing with a vanguard kind of theater. Strange types of people flocked to it because we had to make *our own place*. We had to establish a bulwark against the Establishment, against the accepted ones—actresses like Colleen Dewhurst, for example, who were pretty much all Anglo-Saxon. Among the successful members of the vanguard, or non-Broadway, theater, there is Joe Papp, the Jewish boy from the Lower East Side, who punched away there, carving out his place. He was not going to be stopped or intimidated, and he is one of the biggest theater names today.

My problem was I was uncastable. All the roles for young women were for the Anglo-Saxon types. If you did not look a certain way, you just were not cast. And that is something that still exists. Plays for the WASP kind of woman were all that were being performed. There weren't any roles for women who were not blue-eyed with blond hair—I had blue eyes and blond hair, but everything else about me is ethnic. And the roles were unavailable even though as an actress I had done Shakespeare. But I had to go out of the city to do Shakespeare. I had to go into the regions to realize myself as a classical actress and did a lot of regional theater—the American Shakespeare Festival, all of that. That is where I really learned to act and to come into my own. To be able to do classical acting—that is the thing. You do not have to be Greek to play Medea. You have to be a damn good strong actress, you know.

In recent years, after changing my hair from blond to brunette, I have been able to play Italian women in the movies and on television. In *Saturday Night Fever*, I played Mrs. Manero, John Travolta's mother. She was second-generation Italian, and her son was third. The movie was fun to make. All I had to do to prepare for the role was turn around and look at my Aunt Marie. [Laughs.] And *there* was Mrs. Manero. I did not have to research very far. And every time I play a role like that, there is Aunt Marie or Aunt Katie or Mrs. Falsicchio, our landlady in Brooklyn, who was a real old-type Italian woman. In a Paul Mazursky movie, *Willie and Phil*, I also played an Italian woman, a real cliché role and very funny.

In *Saturday Night Fever*, there was one scene that I, as an Italian-American, took exception to. The scene shows the Manero family sitting around the dinner table, and Tony, the son, says something his father doesn't like and he slaps Tony. Mrs. Manero slaps her husband for slapping Tony, and the slap goes crazily all around the table as one person slaps the next. It is very funny, but what Italian behaves like that, for goodness' sake? Who does that? I saw something like it in the Broadway play *Gemini*, by Albert Innaurato. Danny Aiello, who played one of the roles, picked up the spaghetti with his hands and ate it.

When I saw Danny after that, I said, "Danny, what were you doing picking up the spaghetti with your hands? Where did you ever see anyone do that?"

"Come on, Julie. That's what they want. That's what they expect."

To me, such a scene is as objectionable as when we saw Stepin Fetchit, the black actor, in old Hollywood movies, looking owl-eyed and acting slow as molasses and talking gibberish.

Another kind of caricature in American life is the fat, short Italian mamma of the 1930s, '40s and '50s—often uneducated, with an immigrant mentality. She is *not* a comical figure. This little lady performed her function in terms of her time extremely well. She was involved in the process of evolution, and the fact that she devoted all her energies and talents to the house and family does in no way detract from her stature or importance. My own mother has some of the characteristics of this Italian mamma. In her frame of reference, what is most important to her is that she raised two intelligent children, an artist and a playwright and actress. To her this is accomplishment, an extraordinary one. I am not going to burst her bubble and say, "Yes, but look what you might have done if you had been *educated*." That is evil. We exist in time and space. Let's face it. If she had not done what she had to do, I would not be here today in my present form.

I claim the distinction of being the first ethnic heroine on television soap opera. The soap was the series *From These Roots*, in the 1950s. *Variety*, the theater magazine, was stunned by Rose, the ethnic heroine. The Anglo-Saxon woman had always had the lead. I was an Italian Mary Worth, you know, solving life's problems as a good wife and mother. The role was an Italian woman who married into a WASP family, the first time that anyone in that family had married an ethnic person. I did not play Rose in a cliché way; I played her as a person and put aside the fact that she was Italian. In a funny way, this helped to change the image of Italians because the fan mail that came in from around the country was unbelievable. I would get mail from Tennessee and other places, saying they loved Rose, that she was a nice Eye-talian. I could just read the written word that way. It was a breakthrough. I broke through, and broke out, of that. For four years I stayed with the role and left in 1959, after a fight with the director. I walked out in the middle of a telecast and left television and soap opera behind me.

The Italian theater has always attracted me, but there is not much theater coming out of Italy now. Ugo Betti, who is dead, was the last of the modern playwrights from Italy of any stature. His plays came to the States in the 1950s, but he was not well received here. The last American production of a play of his, *The Queen and the Rebels*, which I directed, was blasted by some critic, who called it a ridiculous play. Of course, that was simply a ridiculous critic—it is a great play. Betti is beyond us, as beyond us as Beckett is. And when was the last time you had Beckett on Broadway for a continuous run? Betti was a judge—and a Sicilian, like Pirandello. His plays are wonderful. I'm not sure they are still in print, but you can probably get them at the library. There is a book of his plays—about six, in one volume. I produced *Island of Goats* and *The Queen and the Rebels*, but did them out in Middle America. They were appreciated there. Isn't that wild? I did them at the Cincinnati Playhouse and in Baltimore, Boston, and other regional theaters all over the country. The regional theaters are a little classier. At least they were when I was last on the scene. Now they have been taken over by the universities to a large extent, and I don't know what has happened as far as quality is concerned.

Assimilation certainly has taken place in America, and it is inevitable. But in the process, people cut off a certain part of their instinctual behavior that reminds them that they are of this issue, of this stock. If we do not remember our heritage, we start to feel that something is missing and we begin to search for it. It is like cutting off your tail and trying to find it again. And we might just, within ourselves, stumble on that thing we have cut off.

The best of all possible worlds is to get beyond being Italian or being black or being Chinese and arrive at the point where we are simply people, individuals, beyond the ethnic, beyond male-female, in order to realize our individual quality as persons. In other words, we are now *in transition*. We have to get beyond national characteristics that keep us tied and bound and go through the process of assimilation *in order to get back to them*, with greater maturity and selfhood.

Does that sound odd? To come full circle, we have to make the trip, the journey, and come back to our natures with a different understanding. The same thing is true of being a woman. I understand this differently now, and feel today, for the first time in my life, that yes, women *did* have it much harder. [Laughs.] I am finally, at the age of fifty-four, admitting that there is a difference in equality between men and women. I was one of the holdouts, you know, against the feminists. They were much too militant for me, much too shallow. Again, there is always something more. And I never wanted to jump on bandwagons.

Now I understand the feminists from my own depths, not from a political standpoint. Politics have nothing to do with it. Really. But we have to go through the politics in order to arrive at the other. If women achieve equality via legislation before they are emotionally ready to deal with it, there is something tragic about it. There is something wrong. But of course, we have to have the legislation. But *not* at the expense of denying the feminine, *not* at the expense of denying the whole feminine principle, for God's sake.

I know myself as an Italian now differently than ten years ago, far differently. My theater writing illustrates this. As a playwright, I have never treated or taken up an Italian-American theme until my most recent play, *Angelo's Wedding*. My concern was never with the personal, as it was with the transpersonal. Contrary to what most people do, I come about things backward, you might say. By transpersonal, I mean people as symbols or allegory, representing an idea. Then in midlife, I began to investigate the personal, and that is when *Angelo's Wedding* emerged. Generally in my work, I started with the idea, with the myth, and then came to the personal via the myth. Now it is a question of bringing both together, which I attempted in *Angelo*. The characters are very real; they are flesh-and-blood people interacting with one another. Two brothers and a mother are the central figures in a conflict that goes way back to another generation.

As a writer, and as an Italian-American, I have come full circle.

Rudolph Giuliani

RUDOLPH GIULIANI
Battler of the Mafia

The name of Rudolph Giuliani, United States Attorney for the Southern District of New York, receives top billing in almost all the incredible crimebusting cases that are taking place in the 1980s, not only against the Mafia but in the political-corruption scandal in New York City government.

With a clean-cut profile that helps belie the stereotype, Rudolph Giuliani is typical of a new breed of Italian-American —young, well-educated, aggressive. Along with the tough-minded image is a sensitive, artistic man whose love of family and love of music are bulwarks of his life.

◇

"It's more important to go to a funeral than a wedding because everybody wants to go to a wedding," my father would say, always concerned with what was really the right thing to do.

For years, I would look at Ellis Island and think, That's where my grandparents landed. Then I gave a speech down in the Battery and in doing some research found out that they had come in instead at Clinton Castle in New York Harbor. It looks like a circular fort and was used as a receiving center for immigrants until the turn of the century. Ellis Island only began to operate in 1900 or thereabouts. My family came here in the 1880s. So that now when I think about my grandparents coming to the United States, I have to switch the locale to Clinton Castle, which is something I didn't know.

My mother's mother was a terrific storyteller. She was born in 1882 in Avellino, near Naples, and came here in 1884. Her husband was a barber who died in 1925, long before I was born. She stayed with us from the time I was born. She lived through the Coney Island fire and would tell you, for example, how the fire started and how she saved her little sister. She remembered people talking about the Civil War who had actually fought in the Civil War and could tell you what they said and the stories they told. She lived through the First World War and used to be able to tell you about the Kaiser as if they were contemporary events. The Second World War was for her a recent memory.

She died in 1976, at the age of ninety-four. She was living at home and my mother took care of her. She was not an invalid, though, until the very end. About six years before she died, she got very sick and it looked as if she was going to become an invalid. She became disoriented, but then she recovered. And for a few years she was fine. By that I mean she got around the house and read the newspapers every day and watched television and cooked. At ninety she could tell you everything that was going on. It was only in the last two years of her life that she began to deteriorate somewhat.

My first suit was the one my father's father made for me. He was a tailor and made men's clothes, working at home mostly and sewing on order. In other words, he made custom-made clothes. He and his wife came from Montecatini, thirty or forty miles outside of Florence. He died in 1948, when I was four years old. Both my grandmothers lived long lives. My father's mother died at eighty-two. She had five children and was a seamstress. She was a member of the Garment Workers Union and worked until she was sixty-five. I knew her quite well, since I spent holidays and summers with her at her beach house out in the Island.

My mother's mother, who lived with us, did not speak Italian. She spoke English and had no accent. She understood Italian but had really almost forgotten how to speak it. My mother knew more of it than she did. Occasionally, I heard the language spoken, words here and there, but not full conversations. My great-grandmother, who also lived into her nineties, spoke Italian. My father would take me to visit her. I must have been three or four and can remember her speaking Italian to him. I speak very, very little of it, *un poco*.

Rudolph was my paternal grandfather's name, and I was named after him. His family, being from northern Italy, had names that were more Austrian in origin. He had a daughter named Olga and a son named Arraldo (my father, Harold). Rudolph is not a common Italian name, but it is not an uncommon one, either. And of course, there's the famous Rodolfo of *La Bohème*. The name was well-known enough so that Puccini used it in the opera.

Before I was born, my mother worked, but after she gave birth didn't work again until I was about fifteen. I was an only child. When she returned to work, she became secretary to a doctor. For a long time, my father owned a restaurant and bar in Brooklyn. He had been a plumber and a whole bunch of different things. The restaurant was in Flatbush, which has never been a single ethnic neighborhood, like Bensonhurst is now an Italian section. I really grew up in the suburbs. After spending my first seven years in Brooklyn, we moved to Garden City and then North Bellmore, on Long Island. The two neighborhoods were very similar. They were mixed in the sense that most of my friends were Jewish. But since I went to parochial school, most of the kids in school were Italian or Irish. I went to a parochial high school in Garden City and to Manhattan College in New York City, which is also Catholic.

The Catholic religion was a very important part of my life. For a good deal of my childhood—actually until I was about twenty—I wanted to be a priest. My parents were not fanatically religious, although my father was more religious than most Italian men. The usual stereotype of the Italian family is the religious mother and the father who doesn't go to church. Actually, my father was probably more religious than my mother. He had his own version of Catholicism, but he was a very strong believer in God and Jesus and prayed every day. He didn't go to church every Sunday, but went almost every week. He and his mother liked to go when the church wasn't crowded, so he would substitute going on a Saturday, which now is allowed, or on a Monday. If he went on Sunday, he would go to an early mass, when there were few people. He thought you could go to church anytime you wanted. Neither my mother nor father wanted me to be a priest or encouraged me in that. I think it was partly because I was an only child and they wanted grandchildren.

I was very close to my parents, probably a little closer to my mother. But going into my teens and in attempts to be independent, I had the normal number of fights and discussions. My father was a very strong person, a domineering person, who wanted things to be done the way he thought they should be done. So did my mother. Both had strong personalities. I appreciated a lot of the lessons and things my father taught me *after* I moved out of the house. Actually, my father had a tremendous amount of courage and a terrific outlook on life. He knew how to look at problems and not get down about them and how to be optimistic about things. He also had physical courage—and emotional and mental courage.

When you're living with someone, you don't understand or realize all that. I mean, I knew it, but since I was stopped from doing exactly what I wanted to do—you see, I also have a strong personality and want things my way—I resented it. But when I was *out* of the house and could recall all that and remember the lessons he taught me, it was a bit different. I actually didn't understand how close I was to him until some friends of mine told me. I remember being in law school and talking to my roommate, who said, "You must really love your father a lot." It was other people telling me things, like how I repeated what my father taught me, and their saying, "You really must love your father a lot," that made me recognize the quality of our relationship.

My parents got along real well and had a good open relationship. They fought, but mostly they argued about things like politics and not about substantial matters. My mother would never undercut my father with me in any way. She explained why he required me to do certain things and why he disciplined me rather than create situations where I might resent him. When I became an adult, he was the same about her. He'd call me and say, "You really should call your mother more and go see her. She needs to talk to you."

For my father, loyalty was one of the three or four most important characteristics of a good person. If his friends were in trouble, he would do anything for them. He was constantly saying how important it was to have good friends in life and to be loyal and help them when they were in trouble. The same thing with your family. He was like that with his mother, mother-in-law, and aunts. A good person, in my father's book, was also good to older people, respectful of them, caring of them, and always aware of what they had done for him and what he owed them in return. This kind of thinking becomes part of you after a while.

"It's more important to go to a funeral than a wedding because everybody wants to go to a wedding," he would say, always concerned with what was really the right thing to do. "There will always be enough guests at a wedding to make it a happy occasion, and unless you're very close, people don't need you at a wedding. Going to a funeral or wake is when people *really* need you." Yet my father hated wakes, and he never liked to be in the same room with a dead body. It was an effort for him to go to them, but I don't think there was ever a wake of anybody he vaguely knew that he didn't go to. [Laughs.] I don't know why he avoided dead bodies like that. He should have been used to them, being Italian and going to so many wakes. He must have gone to a thousand. He would go in, pay his respects, say a prayer, and then go out to the next room. Before he left, he would go back in, pay his respects, and leave.

Being brought up in an Italian family, you're taught a lot of things about living that are enormously helpful. Love is an important part of the family, and it becomes an essential part of your own personality and outlook on life. Relationships with people, handling yourself well in those relationships, caring about people. The parents were usually self-sacrificing. They put aside things in order to help their children. That is also something you learn, though it's unspoken. You learn it in the most effective way possible—through example. My mother would *never, ever* buy things for herself. Instead, she used whatever money she put aside to buy things for me or for my father. That's something she never told us about. I realize it now when I look back. You learn to judge yourself by these things. Even if you can't quite be that way, you say to yourself, That's the way I ought to be. I wish I could be as good to my mother as my mother was to her mother or my father to his. The most important element is the family, the way it grows up, the emphasis being on love, caring, loyalty, and self-sacrifice.

In high school, I became a very big opera fan. When I was about thirteen, I bought an opera record, Handel's *Julius Caesar*, because I liked the play. It sold for sixty-nine cents. I'm not even sure I knew it was opera and thought maybe that it was an excerpt from the play.

I followed it in Italian, loved it, and from then on I was an opera fanatic. Every Friday evening, I would go to the old Metropolitan and stand in line. I was there when Leontyne Price and Franco Corelli made their debuts in *Il Trovatore* in 1959. I began buying opera records and listening, following the librettos. I had no musical training—it was just something I took to. Today, music is a very important part of my life. I keep records in the office. Although I still love opera, probably baroque music is my real love. I like Bach and Corelli and Vivaldi and enjoy going to concerts to hear baroque music played on authentic instruments.

There has to be something genetic about my love for music. I did not acquire it environmentally. My parents were not opera buffs, I never heard opera in my house, and they were not classical-music lovers. My two grandfathers liked opera, but one died twenty-five years before I was born and the other grandfather never talked about opera, and most of the things I remember about him was seeing him while he was dying. So I didn't grow up with opera. But somehow when I first listened to it, from the first moment, it was like love at first sight. And this is true not only of opera but baroque music and music in general. That has to be inherited. It just wasn't learned. It has to be something in my genes somewhere that makes me react to music in a certain way and makes it a very pleasant part of my life, particularly Italian music.

After I reached my teens and became more independent-minded, there was one thing my father and I used to fight about all the time. Even my mother would fight with him about it. He was an Italophile, and I couldn't see it. Without being able to speak Italian, he loved everything Italian. Even things you shouldn't love. Now that I've gotten older—maybe it's romanticizing one's past—I find myself thinking more like him. Even in the last years of his life, I would agree with him more about things Italian.

All during my childhood, even before I knew what history was, my mother, who was a lover of history, would tell me stories about the past and my father would talk about Italian history and the contributions the Italians have made. This, combined later with my own interest in opera, which independently got me into a world in which Italians have made, oh, tremendous contributions, shaped me slowly into an Italophile. About ten years ago, I started reading books about Italian history and became very interested in what it means to be Italian and what it means to be an Italian-American. I think it is a unique heritage.

There is a certain way of looking at life and looking at the world that Italians bring to America which is very helpful, a kind of mature attitude about people and a tremendous emphasis on the beautiful parts of life, on living life and enjoying it. You just have to spend a little while in Italy to realize that Italians have a heightened and very mature sense of beauty of all kinds. Music, art, clothes. And all this stems simply out of *an enjoyment of being alive*. I don't think it is accidental that the Renaissance, and the humanism of the Renaissance, sprang from Italy and the Italian city states. The tremendous love of being human that Italians have isn't necessarily true of all people. There have been too many movements, whether political, philosophical, or artistic, stemming from Italy and revolving around enjoying the human being, and loving the human being, to make it just accidental that these humanistic directions occurred in that little portion of the world. I'm referring to the Roman Empire, to the development of the Catholic Church, which was really an extension of the Roman Empire with much more humanistic and loving principles, the Renaissance, and the present reemergence of Italy as one of the cultural centers of the world for art and for fashion. Too many people go to Italy and say, *"I love it there, the people are wonderful,"* to make it just a kind of accidental thing.

Now, you could get carried away with that. Not all Italians are wonderful; not all Italians are artistic. Like in other groups, there are those who commit crimes, who are mean to their mothers, who have no feeling for the family. I just think *when* they are good, they have a special outlook on life that makes life a happier thing to live and a wonderful, full experience.

One of the things my parents instilled in me is a healthy appreciation of who I am and being comfortable with that. And being proud of it, but not unrealistically proud in the sense that you look down on other people or feel you're better than they are. My parents shared a real pride at being Italian. It was a very important thing to both of them and continues to be for my mother. My father is now dead. You said before that this book will be about the joyful and good things about being Italian *and* some of the bad, difficult things. To me, it has been about ninety-five percent a very joyous, terrific thing and about five percent a set of problems. My parents told me there were people who didn't like Italians and would treat you differently. And I saw some of that in Catholic school, because within the Catholic Church, particularly back in the late '40s and '50s, there was a tension between Irish Catholics and Italian Catholics, particularly among the priests and nuns. I think there was a sense and an attitude that Irish Catholics were better than Italian Catholics. I certainly felt that. In the past ten years or so, a lot of this has passed away.

At home, the way I was taught to deal with that was to realize that everybody has these problems—people discriminate against Jews and people discriminate against the Irish and people discriminate against blacks (though it was a little early for that). So I didn't feel it was unique to have people make fun of my name and give me problems because I was Italian. Yet my father imbued me with a kind of aggressive attitude about it.

"Don't let anybody make fun of you because you're Italian," he'd say. "If they call you a name, make sure they take it back. Or if you have to, punch them in the nose." I was called a guinea and wop. They made fun of my name. When I was seven and eight and nine and ten, I had fights.

My father was a boxer and taught me how to box when I was two and three. He had been an amateur boxer and was very good but couldn't box professionally because he had very bad eyesight. He wore glasses but not only wore glasses, he had such bad eyes that he *needed* the glasses. He had the terrible problem in the ring of not being able to find his opponent too easily. But he had a terrific punch and was a good boxer and strategist of boxing, and he taught me. I never felt real worried about defending myself. He was very good, though, about training me from early on that just because I knew how to box, I shouldn't pick fights with anybody.

"If ever I hear that you started a fight with someone, you're going to have to fight with me. It's fine to defend yourself, but someone else has to start the fight and even then, you should try to walk away from it if you can."

He was very good about that. I got into a certain number of fights as a kid, but I really don't think I ever started one. Defending yourself—that is something I would want my son to know how to do. It gives you a certain amount of confidence and eliminates some of the fears that children have. I also think that if you train a child the right way, if you teach him karate or some method of defending himself, he will learn how to control his temper. And because he feels confident about himself, he's not going to bully somebody else.

Some of the fights I got into were caused by people who made fun of my name or made fun of my parents because they were Italian. Not even knowing who they were, they would make fun of them because of their nationality. Strange thing—that happened more in Catholic school. In fact, it happened almost exclusively in Catholic school rather than at home, where most of my friends were Jewish. I don't remember a Jewish friend ever making fun of me because I was Italian. Up until the time I was in law school, all the situations where someone ridiculed me or said something prejudicial occurred in school.

My attitude toward the Mafia stems not only from my father, who hated it, but from my grandmother, my mother's mother, who had experiences with organized crime, then known as the Black Hand, or *La Mano Nera*, that go back to the turn of the century. And her father did, too! She would tell me stories about the way the Black Hand and the *Camorra*, another crime gang, acted. It took a while for organized crime to form itself in the United States and then, when Sicilian immigration took place and when the Neapolitan immigration took place, street gangs were formed, and the Sicilian street gangs were known as the Black Hand and the Neapolitan street gangs as the *Camorra*. They merged together in the 1930s and formed what we now know as the American Mafia or the Cosa Nostra, whatever name you want to give it.

My father's attitude about the Mafia probably had to do with his growing up. He saw them essentially as bullies—in other words, as people who had to band together in groups in order to have the courage to do things, rather than stand on their own. He would say to me that when he was a child growing up in New York, some of the kids that went on into the Mafia or crime gangs were really the cowards, the ones who needed three or four others to help battle their way out of situations. Banding together into gangs was a sign of being a coward rather than of a real man, who could handle himself on his own.

According to my father, the Mafia hurt Italians deeply. How? First of all, when they were an immigrant community, by being bullies,

banding together, and threatening to break up their stores. By prey-
ing on them, taking what little money they could accumulate, acting
as parasites. In a more general way, they hurt Italians and gave them
a bad name by creating stereotypes that other people used to poke
fun at. It was a complicated situation, and saying, "Oh well, the
stereotype doesn't exist," did not help. In fact, there *were* people like
the stereotype—they did exist; he knew about them; he grew up
with some of them. All the movements that tried to wipe out the
Mafia found big support with my father—the Kefauver committee,
the things Bobby Kennedy was doing, Valachi's appearances in court.
Whereas a lot of Italian-Americans looked at this activity as somewhat embarrassing, he saw it as an opportunity to destroy the Mafia
and hoped that "Maybe, now, we'll get rid of them." By the way,
as a restaurant owner, my father was never approached for protection
by the Mafia.

I did not deliberately plan some kind of crusade against the Mafia,
and I don't quite know how it has focused on me as much as it has.
In my former job as an assistant United States attorney, most of the
cases I did were white-collar criminal cases, involving only one or
two Mafia cases. For a long time, I was in private practice. Then,
when I was an associate attorney general in the Justice Department,
the Mafia was only one of twenty or thirty criminal problems that
I dealt with. And in my present job as federal prosecutor, it happens
to be true here, too—the Mafia is one out of twenty or thirty criminal
problems that I deal with.

Then why does it seem that the Mafia cases have taken over? I
think two things combine to make it appear as if that's all I do, or
most of what I do. One is that the Mafia has been romanticized
beyond its real importance because of the movie *The Godfather*, which
as a movie I think is one of the greatest ever made. *The Godfather* has
placed the Mafia image from whatever it was before to celebrity
status, so that if you are investigating or prosecuting the Mafia, it
becomes something that people pay much more attention to than if
you were investigating and prosecuting Cuban organized criminals
or Columbian organized criminals or the Israeli organized crime
groups, all of which we prosecute, or the white-collar crime that we
do or the drug-related crime that we do. The Mafia cases get more
attention not only because of the celebrity status, but also because
they have been around longer. I mean, the Mafia is a historical phe-

nomenon that has been going on for a long time and has acquired more power and developed more tentacles than these other groups, more infiltration into legitimate business, legitimate labor unions, illegitimate labor unions, some infiltration into politics. These other groups have not had that kind of infiltration, although they may be more violent. That, I think, makes it more important or more focused on.

The fact that I have an Italian name, I hope, will help to dispel, to some extent at least, the unfair prejudice and the unfair stereotype. When I first got into this area of crime and became more aware of how the Italian-American community feels about this, how hurt they are by it, I thought that there would be some value to my being an Italian-American, because as people read revelations about what the Mafia has done, they will see a couple of Italian names involved in investigating and prosecuting. This will present a different image of Italian-Americans to them and will tell the community and the world that they can do a pretty effective job of cleaning up these problems.

It has also helped that the Italian government has been as aggressive as it is now in combating the Mafia. When I went to Italy in July 1984, I told the Justice Minister that as an Italian-American, I was very proud of the fact Italy has in the last three or four years been so effective in wiping out the Mafia. I explained that these actions would accomplish something that he probably would not understand unless he came to the United States. And that is that it would help wipe out unfair prejudice and stereotyping, since it would be impossible for Americans to read all about that and still think there was any kind of affinity with the Mafia, either in Italy or among Italians anywhere. It would graphically demonstrate the vast majority of Italians have no connection with them and don't want them around any longer.

I agree with Governor Cuomo when he says that the word *Mafia* should not be used as a generic term and should not be used to describe *all* of organized crime or other organized crime groups except the group that is actually the Mafia or Cosa Nostra. For example, you should not say the Chinese mafia or Israeli mafia, or Cuban mafia. They are not the Mafia. When you use the term *Mafia* connected with another crime group, it makes it sound as if the Mafia has more influence, more control, more power than is, in fact, the case. It's dishonest to do that and, I think, very harmful to Italians.

However, it is just as harmful to lie in the other direction and try to hide our heads in the sand and say, "There is no such thing as the Mafia," "There is no such thing as the Cosa Nostra." We don't serve anyone's interests by saying that, because we make it appear as if Italian-American public figures and groups practice the big lie, which is to say, "There is no Mafia—it doesn't exist" when everyone knows that it does. Think of what it's like for the businessman in the garment center or in any other enterprise who is being extorted by the Mafia. He's not Italian. They're taking money from him every week or every month. He knows that they are part of the Gambino family or the Genovese family or whatever family they are. Maybe they've beaten up his drivers or done other things to him. He *knows* that this organization exists, and he has been paying them off for fifteen or twenty years.

It is counterproductive for Italian-Americans to try to approach this problem by banning the use of a word or by censoring other people in what they say or do. The most effective thing for Italian-Americans to do is deal with the truth. And eventually the truth will prevail. I mean, you are operating from a tremendous amount of strength when you're dealing with the truth. You are operating from a position of weakness when you try to vary the truth or ban words or play semantic games. Also, it is very important to stop isolating groups in our society *by stressing discrimination.* When you say to people, to a group that has a tendency to isolate itself—all groups in America do, the blacks tend to isolate themselves, the Jews tend to isolate themselves, the Italian-Americans tend to isolate themselves—that they are being discriminated against, they isolate themselves even more. That often removes them from society rather than draws them in.

Prejudice is never isolated on one group. There is no person I have ever met who is prejudiced only against Italian-Americans. The person who walks around saying, "All Italians are gangsters," "All Italians are part of the Mafia," "All Italian politicians are involved in the Mafia," the person who throws around that kind of thing is saying precisely the same kind of stereotypical remark in different terms about Jews, blacks, Hispanics, and every other group but his own. The kids who used to make fun of me for having an Italian name were exactly the same ones who were poking fun at the Jewish and black kids. Prejudice is a sickness and an evil way of thinking that focuses *on groups*. Prejudiced individuals see people as identified with groups. When I get the opportunity to talk to an Italian-American audience, I try to use it as a way to break them out of their *own* prejudice. I use the occasion to get them to look at blacks and Jews and others as having the same kind of problem they have and to impress on them that the only way we're going to end this thing is if we end group thinking and group bigotry. If all we do is attack a prejudice against Italians, we're not going to solve the problem. That's not the way to win. You've got to get people *to stop identifying someone with a group* and think he must follow the evil pattern that, in their own sick minds, they have applied to that group.

Now, I should make the record clear that I don't think I can break the back of the Mafia *alone*. I don't think even my office can, which is a lot bigger than just me. But I think we have a chance to break *a lot of their power now*, a chance we never had before.

First of all, there is a nationwide effort in the United States to deal with the problem of the Mafia that is far broader than just my office. My office is an important part of it, but we are only a part of it. The FBI, the Department of Justice, and the President of the United States have involved themselves in this effort and have put the resources into it to get it done. There are cases against the Mafia in New York, Boston, Kansas City, Cleveland, all over the country. You *have* to do it that way. If you work against them in just one city, you might for a while eliminate them from that city, but they'd be back again. You have to attack them nationwide, and we've got to keep up this effort for another four, five, six, seven years. We're on the right road, we've won some battles, but the war is a long one, and there are a lot more battles to be won.

The worst thing that can happen to us is if we start to think that we're too successful. Then we might decide, Well, we've done enough. If we stop, they'd be back in business in a year or two, exactly the same way they were in business before. But if we can continue our pursuit in the United States, we can put a tremendous amount of pressure on them and, I think, break their power here, particularly because of the second reason. That is, the Italian government is as committed as it has ever been to breaking them. And I think they are doing an even more effective job than was done under Mussolini, who had the backing of totalitarian power. Italy doesn't have that today, and she is dealing with it in a lawful, decent way. I would say that her effort against the Mafia is at least as successful, if not more successful, than ours. Thousands of Mafiosi are in prison, many of them convicted already, and many more cases are coming up. So this is a perfect time to try to break their power on both sides of the Atlantic.

The most important reason the Mafia can be broken now is that it no longer has any kind of refuge in the Italian-American community, nor does it have the ability in that community to recruit itself in large numbers. In any battle, you have a real good chance of winning if enemy resources are being strained, that is, if you're fighting the enemy's last five thousand troops and they're going to have difficulty recruiting another five thousand. Maybe they can recruit another thousand, but they can't recruit another five thousand. The Mafia is in that position today in the United States. They cannot recruit in large numbers. That is not to say they cannot recruit at all, but they can't replace themselves one for one, or one for two, as they were able to do in the 1930s and 1940s. And that is a tremendous credit to the Italian-American community because that community is not what it was in the 1930s. The people they would have recruited in the '30s are now in college, law school, medical school, working hard as part of the American way of life, whereas in the '30s they were isolated from that way of life. So that today the demographics are against the Mafia's being able to continue itself the way it has existed in the past. For this reason also, this is a perfect time to attack it very, very heavily. That's why I think we have a chance to break their power.

However, it is unrealistic for any government or any law-enforcement agency to think they are going to wipe out crime. We've had crime with us since we've had human beings, so that the goal here has to be to eliminate Mafia power, to try to reduce it as much as possible. Having broken that power, what you would have eliminated is an influence that goes beyond the influence that a crime group should have—an influence over labor unions, an influence over industries, an influence over politics. These are things that you just cannot tolerate, because when that happens, you let them operate their own kind of government.

We must not fool ourselves into thinking that even if we wipe them out, that twenty years from now either that group or some other group will not form itself. It's a never-ending battle rather than one that you can win all at once and have the problem go away. There will always be people who will try to prey on other people. And law enforcement and government, when they are operating correctly, should be trying to reduce crime to the minimum, knowing that it can never remove it completely.

How do you become totally American when you are a hyphenated American? I think the Italians have provided a wonderful lesson for dealing with the so-called hyphenated American. They became *totally American* a long time ago, and it is something that we pass over too quickly. They became totally American during the Second World War, when older Americans of Italian origin, born in Italy, had to face a situation in which the country of their citizenship was going to war against the country of their birth. And they faced that magnificently, without the slightest question of their loyalty to the United States. My grandfather, who was born in Italy, had three sons—they all engaged in the war. Luckily, none of them had to go to battle against Italians. They were in the Pacific War, but many of my relatives did. My cousins went to war against Italy. Most of them weren't born there, because we were second and third generation. But their fathers were born there, and their fathers were alive, and I can remember my father telling me that my grandfather had no reservation about that. Some of his old Italian friends would sit around talking Italian and say things like, "It's awful that America is going to war against Italy," and my grandfather, who was very Italian and loved Italy, said that Italy made a mistake. *She was wrong, and we must fight her. This is our country now. We decided to come here. This is where we live.* I don't think there has ever been a real problem for Italians with divided loyalty. They became complete Americans, at the same time valuing and cherishing the tradition of being Italian.

America is going to continue to have immigration—it should and will—and there will be many hyphenated Americans in the future. I think the Italian experience is a good model for all newcomers on how to integrate, become American, learn the language, grow up in our society—with total loyalty. But at the same time that people are totally loyal to the United States, they can still love their heritage without that becoming political.

But Italians have been laggard. They lost a generation in their development because they did not educate their children fast enough.

For example, my mother was a good student, smart and bright. Her mother was also extraordinarily intelligent. But my mother couldn't go to college, though she graduated from high school and went to teacher's-training school. She couldn't go to college because in her family the boys went to school, not the girls. She is someone who could have done anything—could have accomplished anything with the right kind of education. In the 1920s and '30s and '40s, too often the Italian family experience was that the children should go out to support the mother and father. To some extent the children were seen as assets, financial assets, and, particularly for females, there was no need to be educated. Girls were only going to become mothers, after all, and so I think we held ourselves back a generation by not having at that stage the same attitude that Irish immigrants and Jewish immigrants had earlier—which is: *The key to success in America is education.* The key to success is not necessarily going out to work at thirteen because you're going to be doing the same job at fifty that you were doing at thirteen—but sacrificing, saving up money, and sending the kids to school, getting them a college education so they can enter the professions—and when they are in business, they can become leaders like Lee Iacocca is today.

For all the pluses of the Italian family, there was something stifling about it as well. It was all-encompassing and dictatorial. There's a wonderful movie with Richard Gere—I forget the name—about two Italian-American brothers who are construction workers. In the depiction of the family, it's like a serious version of *Saturday Night Fever.* This stifling, this suffocation, is also part of the Italian-American experience. And in that experience there has also been child abuse, wife beating, and so on.

Beginning in the 1950s, the Italian-Americans reversed the education lag in just tremendous numbers. In the last ten years, they have become among the highest groups represented in colleges and professional schools, law schools and elsewhere. It is a phenomenon we don't write about. But I can remember seeing statistics about ten years ago showing that they were among the largest numbers in colleges. Just from my own experience here in the U.S. Attorney's office, where we pretty much get the cream of the crop in terms of law graduates, Italian-American lawyers of this calibre are available in large numbers, graduating from the best law schools, at the top of their class. They are among the best students and people with the highest academic qualifications. That is something that could have happened in the 1930s and '40s. The talent was there, the family background was there, even the resources were there to send them to school. We were a little late, but they are all arriving now, and I think in the next ten to twenty years, you're going to continue to see that in even larger numbers.

The emergence of Italians in American government is valuable because they have their own special thing to contribute, as most of us with an ethnic background do. They can bring a certain kind of maturity to our government, which it needs. We are a very young nation, a relatively new one, and this has both its advantages and disadvantages. The Italian-American comes from a culture that is very old. Its traditions and attitudes have become an intrinsic part of his own nature, and he can temper American brashness with a more loving way of going about what we are as a country and what we do as a country. Certain family qualities are terrific qualities for a government to acquire.

I hope that the lessons the Italian has learned from his journey in America will be used for the benefit of others, of the next group of newcomers, so that they don't have to go through the same problems. In other words, we lost a generation in not assimilating fast enough by not understanding the value of education. To new groups, we should be among the first to speak and advise:

Get those kids through school right away. Get them to learn English. The quickest way to success in this country is through a good education— and working hard. You'll be surprised how fast things can happen. If you get those kids in school, working hard in school, understanding the value of education, we're not talking about success in thirty or forty years, but in five or ten years. In just a short time, an immigrant group can turn around and become a leadership group.

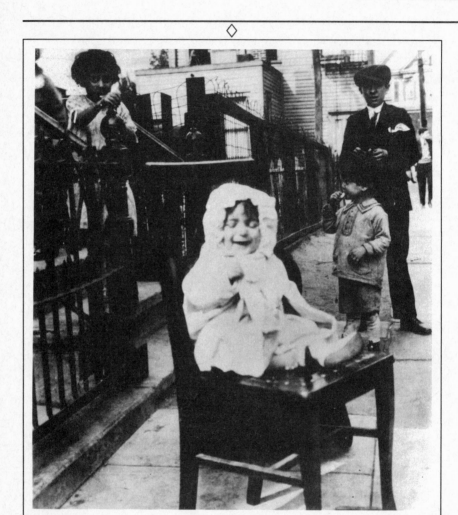

Tony Bennett

TONY BENNETT
Mama Knew Best

◇

Throughout his life, Tony Bennett has maintained the values and ties he had as a child growing up in Queens, New York; he still finds strength within an intimate family circle. His two sons are now his managers. A thoughtful man, he has traveled widely and formed opinions about many things. His singing career began after World War II, and he is today one of the most respected and admired troubadours of American popular song.

In the living room of his apartment in New York City (a few blocks from where his father opened a grocery store in the 1920s), Tony interrupted his painting of a still life to be interviewed. Some apples, grapes, and flowers were arranged on a windowsill. Painting is his second love. This day, he was elated because a publisher had decided to bring out a book of his oil paintings.

Americans overwork. That is why so many of us fall over from stress, from worry.

My singing abilities come from my father. He had a beautiful singing voice. We were very oriented to music. The whole family—my mother, father, aunts, uncles—got together on the weekends and sang and played music. It was during the Depression, and the big entertainment was gathering the children and having them entertain the grown-ups. My brother and I sang, and together with my sister, we put on shows with singing and acting for the aunts and uncles. I remember them very well. I don't have total recall, but I remember the good vibrations, the warm feeling that we got from one another, and the fun we had.

My brother was a tremendous singer in those days. His name was Giovanni Benedetto, and he was called the little Caruso. He sang at the Metropolitan Opera and did solo spots; he also went on radio. He became the hero of the family. When he came out of the service at the end of World War II, he did not continue in music. He had a large family of children and had to find steady work to support them. He lives in Florida now. He is very happy.

My dad was born in Calabria, which is at the southern tip of Italy. He was a very intelligent guy. He came over here, an immigrant, and chose Fifty-second Street and Sixth Avenue in Manhattan, right down the street here from where I live now, as his first grocery store. It was right in the heart of town. He picked the right address. That was about 1922 or '23. I was born in 1926. But then he took ill and the doctor said that he should get away from city life. So we moved to Astoria, in the borough of Queens, which was really country in those days. There were sheep and goats where people walk now; it was farm country. Imagine! But he was a sickly man and died when I was nine years old.

Many guys say this about their mothers, but my mother was really quite exceptional. She was a fantastic lady who raised my brother, sister, and myself all by herself after my father died. My older sister helped; she took over a motherly role. My mom was born in Little Italy in Manhattan, on Mott and Hester Streets. After my father died, she worked in the garment center as a seamstress and then came home to look after the house and kids. Looking back at her life— she died about seven years ago—I realize she was a tremendous motivator and *very, very* clever about life.

She had an artistic way of handling people, and this included us kids. It was subtle. She never spoke about music or art and yet . . . something about her led us in those directions. I'll give you a good example. There was a Czechoslovakian boy in my neighborhood called Rudolph DeHarak. His mother died when he was very young, and my mother felt compassionate toward him. She took him in and he became more or less like a brother to me and my brother. Now, as I have said, she never spoke about music and art. Yet my brother got to sing at the Metropolitan Opera House, I sing and paint, my sister has spent her working life with books as a librarian, and Rudy DeHarak is now considered one of New York's finest graphic designers. He has worked on the American wing of the Metropolitan Museum of Art and the United Nations Plaza Hotel and does graphic design for IBM and *The New York Times*. Do you know those wonderful diagonal posters that are displayed on *New York Times* trucks? He designed them.

When I was a kid, I always wanted to travel and have adventures, like Huck Finn. Now I look back and realize I was around something regal right in my own house and that I had a tremendous upbringing. Even with my mom working, she had a way of making it all come out right. During her final illness, I stayed by her side and tried to ease her suffering. Once I said, "Do you know how well Rudy is doing?" And I described all the things he was accomplishing.

She said, "Didn't you know that he was always good?" To this day, Rudy and I are very close. He is the one who got me thinking about painting and being an artist.

Judy Garland and my mother got along beautifully. By the way, did you know Judy was from Queens? Duke Ellington and my mother were good friends. There is a book right on my shelf [he takes it from the shelf] called *Music is My Mistress*. It is the Duke's autobiography. In it, he mentions my mom. He wrote about everybody that he knew, but he told me of all the people he met, he was more impressed with her than anyone else. In the book he says, "Tony's beautiful mother is there [at all her son's openings] to give support to Tony. [She and his family] are wonderful optimists, and you must know by now what I think of optimists."

I learned many things from her without her teaching me. As a seamstress, she never worked on a cheap or badly conceived dress. The only time I ever saw her get angry was the day she had a bad dress to work on. Later on, I found myself subconsciously turning down all bad songs and realizing only until much later that I learned about refusing the second-rate from her. If I am going to do a song, I want to sing the very best song and not compromise. That is what she taught us: Work with the best. Not to compromise is a marvelous thing to learn. In our kind of materialistic society, our only concern is making money, but you know, you have to keep your integrity to have some peace within yourself. Just to make money is not enough; that is greedy. Keeping your integrity, you *can* produce and make money. It gives you a quiet dignity and substance. Otherwise, you feel unhappy.

When she died, the church was filled with people. She had gathered so many friends. People have asked me, "Why did you choose show business?" I think it was because my mom loved people. And that communicated itself to me. She loved having everybody come over the house. It was nothing for her to cook for eighteen or more people a week, aside from working. Singing for people is a way of expressing my own love.

I have never been to Calabria, where my father was born. My two sons have gone there. And that was quite fascinating. When they visited their cousins, it was almost like they met their clones. They all looked so much like the family here! And the boys were treated beautifully by people. My sons did not know exactly where my father's family lived, so when they arrived at the outskirts of the town, they asked some villagers, "Do you know where the Benedettos live?"

Even though the boys were complete strangers, the villagers said to them, "We think we know where they are, but stay and rest with us tonight." They fed them and put fresh linens on their bed. The next day they took the boys to the Benedettos.

I had my first experience of Italy in the fall of 1984. I did some concerts in Milan, Viareggio, and Rome—God, what a reception! The critics reviewed the concerts by saying mine was the best voice they ever heard. Can you imagine? Coming from Italians, that is a big compliment. The fans were very warm and enthusiastic. I still get bottles of wine from them. It was just a short time I stayed there.

Not being able to speak Italian was a nuisance. One of the pressures of being an Italian-American child is that you are told, *"Hey! Speak English."* Now, that is absolutely wrong. It is good to know as many languages as possible. But in those days, in order to make a living, you had to speak English, so we were told, *"Don't worry about speaking Italian."* My father spoke it, but since he died when I was nine, we never really had it around the house. My mom spoke a little, but she was basically *American*, in *Italian-American*. She was trying to make a living and so spoke English, and trained us to do the same.

* * *

Just like the British excel in theater, the French in fashion, and the Germans in science, Italians have it in their genes to excel in music and art. When someone raves to me about an opera singer, I can be a tough critic because I have this kind of accurate ear that tells me whether that singer is *really* singing well. And I am a *popular* singer, not trained in opera. Still, I can tell whether someone has a really magnificent voice, not because of volume or anything, but because of the true spirit of the singing—and know when it is absolutely authentic. That came from my upbringing. Italians have an understanding of singers that is inherent.

And they have a particular feeling for art. When it comes to the creative eye, the creative feeling, *the soul of things*, they surpass others. Maybe it is the spirituality of Christianity behind Italian life, but whatever it is, there is an extra something in the sauce that makes a piece of art great. I remember in Milano seeing a statue of Garibaldi in the center of a piazza. It was not a famous statue, yet I never saw anything quite like it. It was beautiful, and you could almost feel the life underneath the stone. The spirituality in Italian art gives a tremendous lift to people. It has a life-expanding quality that surpasses most other art.

My Catholic upbringing made me into a Christian, not a Catholic. Duke Ellington referred to my kind of Christianity in his autobiography. [He reaches for the book and reads.] "Tony is a Christian, and he lives as one. He is the most unselfish performer/artist today. He gives credit to everybody with him, including the fourth triangle player."

Both my wives were not Italian. I look for the human being. I like Italian girls, but can't generalize. I cannot say all Italians are good. There are a lot of them who are pretty strange. I look for the human being—that is what I have learned to do. But I like Oriental ladies. There is something very romantic about them—they don't get in your way and yet are a strong influence. They work *with* the man . . . I like that system. This sounds like a blow to woman's lib [laughs], but I really like that. Well, three-quarters of the world lives that way. This great experiment of woman's lib! You know, America is the only place where everybody makes such a big thing of it. I don't know. The ordinary man-woman relationship seems to work everywhere else. I really have not figured it out. You have to be very lucky—to find a proper mate.

Italian-Americans are the most misunderstood people in our society. We have a lot to offer, but we need love and understanding, like everyone else. When encouraged, we can offer so much to any community, any city. But we have an unfair stigma to cope with. It came up again with that terrible, terrible movie *The Godfather*. That film should have been banned. Despite the marvelous directorial techniques, *The Godfather* was pernicious. In graphic detail, it describes the sins of the Mafia and leads the audience to believe that the Mafia is all-Italian when in fact it includes every nationality. The film has made Italians lose their dignity and feel embarrassed.

One book that I think would make a wonderful film is *Blood of My Blood* by Richard Gambino. A filmmaker could do a kind of *Roots* documentary on Italian-Americans with that book, which describes our beginnings here and what we had to go through. It would present a much more realistic view than *The Godfather*.

It is so important that we do not walk away from our heritage. Being Italian-American is not a hindrance. As a singer, I have always been encouraged by fellow artists and by my peers way beyond anything I ever dreamed of. There are a lot of wonderful people out there who go along *with what you contribute*. That is the important thing. We should look at the positive side of our heritage. I am not speaking only of the past. I am speaking of today, of writers like Arrigo Benedetti, of filmmakers like Vittorio DeSica, and musicians like Manuel DeSica. These are the kinds of artists and human beings who should be pointed out and hailed and put in focus, because they are really saying something and they are contributing to society. They uplift the human spirit and make you feel like there is a great deal to live for.

It's a known fact that Italian-Americans have made good pop singers. It goes back to what I was saying about singing being in our genes. Vic Damone's voice gets better every year. Everybody loves Perry Como. He has a magnificent Christian philosophy and attitude that you can hear in his music. Dean Martin is a great all-round entertainer/singer who communicates so well with the public. And of course, there is Frank Sinatra, the king of the entertainment world, who has contributed so much to modern music. He is a magnificent musician.

People get sidetracked from Sinatra's contribution to music when they read about his personal life and his battles with reporters. We all know that. Let's get to the heart of the matter. I look at Sinatra as a musicologist would look at Mozart or Bach or Beethoven. In our lifetime, he and Crosby were the pioneers of a new form of art called intimate singing. Before them, there were no microphones. They invented a psychological way of singing, a kind of getting inside someone's brain, intimately. Nat King Cole also had this quality. Their kind of singing was not meant to say, "Listen, how glorious this voice is." It was a matter of what the singer was thinking and an ability to syncopate and to bring to it a jazz-improvised attitude that developed into a style which is truly American. No other country has this quality. It is a new form of music. Everything Sinatra has ever done musically—with artists like Nelson Riddle, Axel Stordahl, and Bill Miller—is a tremendous contribution to popular music because it has a timelessness to it. It will never be dated, and it will never sound dated. That is the test of art, and his music is art. Everybody in the world knows Sinatra, and everybody responds to him. Many authorities and musicologists throughout the world look at him as a musician of great importance. I have met them in England, France, and Japan, and they have already categorized him like that. His work will become classical as years go by.

There is so much opportunity in the United States for everyone. That is what is so great about it. You have no idea how stifled people are in the rest of the world. There are *no names* outside the United States. Analyze it: Do you know a Chinese star? a Russian star? Over here, we have thousands of stars—all kinds. Each is an institution in his or her own right. We have all kinds of names and celebrities: sports figures, movie and TV stars, baseball stars, recording artists, ballet and Broadway artists—and they are all famous. That happens only here. In other countries, it is a miracle if you get one or two names that the world hears of. Some, like Julio Iglesias, come to the United States to make it really big. Once you make it here—it's like the Sinatra song: *If you make it in New York, you can make it anywhere.*

When one makes it here, the name splashes out throughout the world. This will not happen anywhere else.

Many Americans are inclined to think that immigrants are ignorant, that we Americans have all the know-how and expertise and that they should give up their ways and adopt ours. I take issue with this. They should *not* relinquish their ways and what they know, and should instead show *us* alternative ways of doing things. I saw my doctor today and he told me that people are going back to using herbs of primitive societies in the cure of disease, which help more than some modern chemicals. Certain cultures—the Chinese, the Italian—are thousands of years old and the accumulated wisdom of these cultures should not be cast aside. Modern medicine does not have all the answers. We can learn from the immigrants. We may be powerful and rich, but they have ancient knowledge. And not only in medicine.

From the Orient, we can learn Eastern philosophy, meditation, yoga. Yoga is a great thing for the body. There is no running, no jogging, that can work better than yoga. And for peace of mind, meditation is fantastic, a center where you know where you are at. These are systems that took generations of thinking to evolve, and they are magical. We should learn these things, we should learn from the world, instead of acting as if we know everything and *will teach the world*. From all the nationalities in America, we have the opportunity to take the best that each has to offer and apply it to our American style. We are a relatively new nation, and we have some growing up to do. We do not have to teach *them* to grow up. They grew up a long time ago.

From the Spanish and Italians, we can learn how to take time out and simply live. We call these people lazy because they sleep in the afternoon. Actually, they are sane and we are insane because we never stop working. They know how to stop. They close their shops at one o'clock, go home, spend time with their family, take a siesta. Whatever kind of shop they own, they know that if someone needs a certain item, he will come in at four o'clock—when the shop reopens—to buy it. They do *not* have to stay open all day and waste lots of precious hours. It took centuries of experience for them to realize this. Americans are just beginning to take time for leisure. Old countries have done this for centuries, *and they know when to walk away from their business*. They know about the art of living.

Americans overwork. That is why so many of us fall over from stress, from worry. We should not preach to the world; we should listen. We are brand new and other countries are ancient. There are guys in India who are known to walk through walls. We don't know how to do that yet.

From the Italians, we can learn how to give of ourselves and not to hold back. There have been many film actresses, but I've never seen anyone like Anna Magnani. To me, she typifies the Italian spirit: feeling, directness, openness, simplicity. That is why she was so loved by her own people—and the world. The world understood that she was what Italians are like. The way my sons were accommodated by Calabrian villagers who invited them, complete strangers. *Come sleep in our house before you go see your family.* That kind of warmth. When I was in Rome, Manuel DeSica, the musician, got angry when he found I was staying in a hotel, regardless of how good it was.

"You can't stay in a hotel. This is ridiculous," he said.

"I am very comfortable. I live in hotels all the time."

"No, no. I know someone down south. You can stay in his villa or you can stay in my house, but you can't stay in a hotel."

That is how they are. They are givers. You can learn from that.

And we can learn from them how to express ourselves. They are not frozen and frightened about every little thing or stiff-upper-lipped and reticent. They express what they feel. If they are angry, they say it. If they are happy, they express their joy. One way or the other, they are definite. Expression is very good in the creative arts where you cannot hold back. They are givers and that is very important in communicating. In art and acting classes, students are told to give more, exaggerate, whereas the Italian is told the opposite. *That is a little too much. Tone it down.* He can *feel* it.

I am not waving the flag. Special abilities occur in all nationalities and peoples. I believe it is in the genes. Aborigines in Australia have fantastic traits. They can tell what the others are thinking, like ESP. They can actually read one another without speaking. A whole tribe can feel it at one time. Not many of us can do that.

The average Italian-American male is made up of four characteristics: He's proud, shy, positive, and humble. That describes me pretty much. They may sound conflicting, but they are like a good meal. You put in a little salt, a little pepper, a little sweet, a little sour—and a dash of basil—and before you know it, you have a good meal. There is a balance in these four traits because you have opposites—four different qualities that balance one another out, *and you are in touch*. You don't get bored. And you are never so proud that you are overbearing: You are proud, and then you become humble. You retreat from the pride, and you look at the pride and say, "Well, now, what was *that* about?"

You look at these different aspects of yourself, and ask, in another instance, "Now, why was I that shy? Why did I have to be that shy?"

Or, again, "Why did I have to be that proud?"

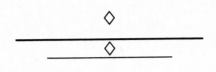

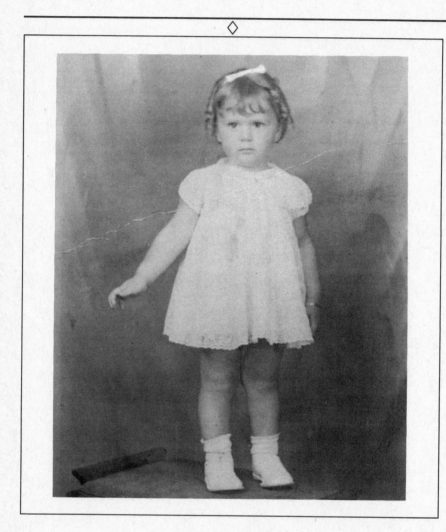

Geraldine Ferraro

GERALDINE FERRARO
Why Can't Italians Catch Up?

Geraldine Ferraro's place in history is assured as the first woman, and the first Italian-American, to run for national office in the United States. Her press coverage has been phenomenal—more than for any other woman of recent years.

Shown here are rarely touched aspects of the woman behind the politics—in her roles as mother, daughter, and child. Also included are her reflections on why Italian-Americans abandoned her during her campaign for the vice-presidency.

Because I am Italian, I or my family is suspected of being gangsters. And I must say, that while we were heavily involved in a grueling presidential race, many of the leaders in our [Italian-American] community . . . seemed ready to remain silent and let others shape events.

I don't speak Italian well, but have two children who speak fluent Italian, and I am thrilled that they do. They both took it in school. Donna is fluent in French and took Italian as a third language After the campaign, my son, John, Jr., went to Florence and spent six months in Italy, and he is totally fluent. My younger daughter is going to take Italian next year in college.

During the days of the campaign, they became aware to a greater degree of their heritage, but I don't think that's all positive. The fact that we were hit as far as we were by various allegations of organized-crime connections put my children into a position of recognizing that being Italian-American has certain disadvantages. I don't think they were aware before, but I think that they're fully cognizant of it now.

When my candidacy for the vice-presidency was announced, my ninety-one year-old aunt and her son, Carlo Andrusani, a pharmacist, who both live in Marcianise, a town north of Naples, appeared on American television as part of the news coverage. They were my father's family—my father's sister and her son, my first cousin. My father was born in Marcianise and came here when he was in his early twenties. I've visited his birthplace several times. I went there in 1957 and saw the family for the first time. On my honeymoon in Italy, I stopped and met with them again and introduced my husband. In 1978, on a trip with my children, they came up to visit us in Rome. Since the campaign, I've gone back to Marcianise and visited my aunt's grave—the aunt who was on television. She died the following January. I also visited my grandparents' graves and spent time with my family.

On my mother's side, my grandfather, I think, came from Sorrento, my grandmother from Salerno. My grandmother was fifteen years of age when she came here. My grandfather was already in America. They married, and my mother was born on the Lower East Side in Manhattan.

I did not grow up in an Italian community or with immigrants—that's not the way I grew up. My mother and father lived in Newburgh and my father died when I was eight years old. I don't really remember very much of my early years. In Newburgh, my best friend was an Italian-American girl, but her parents were both born in the United States. When my father died, I went away to boarding school. I would be away at school from September until May and then at camp in the summer. My mother worked, you see. Yes, my mother worked. So I didn't know people who focused on being Italian.

In the South Bronx, where we moved to after my father died, we never lived in an Italian neighborhood. Our neighbors were mostly Irish, some Italians. My mother's sisters and my cousins lived across the street. But the majority of my friends were Irish and Jewish, and then after a while, the blacks and Puerto Ricans started moving in. I did not grow up in an Italian community that separated me from the world at large, not at all. As a matter of fact, in the boarding schools where I went, there were very few Italian-American kids. There were lots of Irish-American kids—the larger community was the Irish-American one, and you did not separate yourself out as an Italian-American.

My brother Carl (I had no sisters; there was just the two of us) was older than me. But even though I was the only girl in an Italian family I don't think I was treated any differently from him or coddled because I was a girl. My mother is a very affectionate woman, and I think I am with my children. I give my son a hug as often as I give my girls a hug, which is often. I mean, I love having them around. We're demonstrative people, so I don't think there is any difference in the way a little girl or a little boy is treated. My mother didn't show me more affection—I'm sure she didn't.

I'll tell you where the differences were in our bringing up. They were not in education obviously. If I wanted it, I got it and my mother would never, ever deny me and not only that, she *pushed* for an education because she realized how important that was. Very unusual for an Italian-American mother. When I was sixteen and graduating from high school, my uncle said to my mother, "Don't bother, Annie. She's pretty. She'll get married."

My mother said, "Forget it. She's going to have an education."

So my mother pushed for that, and she pushed certainly with my brother. In this, we were both treated equally. Where Carl had it a little easier, got a little more, was—not in love, not in affection—it was in that *he was allowed to go out*. I wasn't allowed to date until I was seventeen. He was allowed to go out, date, whatever. He was allowed to travel, to go to college weekends, to go to dances. When I wanted to go away for a college weekend, my mother would say to me, "You can't."

"How come he can go and I can't?"

The response was, "He's a boy."

Her concern was how people would view her daughter—what my aunts would say if I went away for a weekend at a college, what they would think was going on. In that way, I was treated differently. I was really restricted socially. And that was fine. I knew what was expected of me. And I think I performed. So in that way, it was different. And also he was allowed more money, more spending money. She was always afraid of what might happen if he didn't have it, what he might do, this kid without a father, and therefore, she wanted to reassure herself on that.

Carl was young when my father died. He had just turned fifteen on March 28, and my father died on May 29. I think Carl would have liked to assume a disciplinary role toward me, as happens in some families when the oldest son takes on a head-of-the-house role after a father dies. He used to boss me around when I was a kid and continued to do that through college. But my mother wouldn't allow him to take over. And I wouldn't allow that to happen.

I used to say to him, "You're not my father." And it was as simple as that.

We had a good deal of sibling rivalry. Perhaps it was because he wanted to boss me around. I don't know whether that was because we were Italian-American and he being the male, or because our father was dead. I look at my own three kids—my son was in military school, and he'll try to be a little more bossy. Maybe there's a little bit of macho. But I don't permit it at all in our house. It's absolutely understood that we are equals. Remember, I was brought up by a mother who was an American.

Carl now works for the city. He was in business for himself. He has three children, three boys, and lives with his family in Queens.

I dated Irish boys. I dated Jewish boys. My mother had no problem with that. However, back in the 1950s, when I was dating, had I wanted to marry outside my religion, I think that would have been a real problem for my mother. In fact, I know it would have. When Carl was seriously dating a Jewish girl, both my mother and uncle went totally berserk when they started talking about marriage. That was in 1950, 1952. There was a totally different outlook. My mother would have been upset if I had married outside my religion, but it wasn't necessary that I marry an Italian-American boy. She just wanted me to marry someone that was good.

My mother's attitude about Catholicism was very strict. I don't know how other Italians felt about their religion. I went to Catholic schools and to a Catholic college. Today, if I were to choose a college, the choice might not be so automatic. When I was a kid, Catholic parents were expected to send their children to Catholic schools. And if they didn't, they weren't fulfilling their job as Catholic parents. Not so today. It's just not so. If I were to choose a college now, my attitude would be a little different. It's not that I simply would not choose a Catholic college. I would do what the kids today are doing—that is, look at the universities to see which have the most to offer in the quality of professors and courses. That's how I would pick. That's what my kids are doing. Competition among the schools is great. Catholic universities are up there, but . . . I mean, I have a daughter who's working on her MBA at Harvard. I think that's important. What they have available to them is tremendous.

The Catholic schools I went to—that's thirty years ago—don't exist today. Religion is not being taught the same way. When I went to Marymount, it was a semi-cloistered institution. The religion was part of our lives—we went to mass every day, we had retreats, many girls entered the convent. It's a different school now, and there's a different attitude both on the part of the school and the parents. When my kids were little, I felt the obligation to give them a Catholic education. I don't think that sense of duty even exists now, ten or fifteen years later.

My mother lives alone because she wants to. She doesn't want to live with us. She is very independent. Again, you have to understand my mother is not an Italian stereotype, and neither was her mother. My grandmother never walked around in a black dress. And she also lived alone and did not want to live with any of her children. In fact, when my father died, my mother asked my grandmother to come live with us and take care of me so she would not have to send me to boarding school. My grandmother refused. She was very independent; she would not do that. My mother has that same quality. She loves watching soap operas anytime she wants. Loves having her friends in if she wants to, loves the idea of having her grandchildren in if she wants to. And if she doesn't want to have them, she locks the door and nobody comes in. And she's great. She does, though, live five minutes away from here, as does my mother-in-law. They both live by themselves, the're both widows, and they maintain themselves. I can walk to their homes from my office, and it's a three- or four-minute ride from my house to their houses.

And so what happens is that we see them regularly. They're at my house or we take them out to dinner—we aim for once a week, and we try to do that. Since they were small, my children were taught to stop in and see their grandmothers. My brother's children do that. My nephew works right up here and he stops in to see his grandmother. This past Monday morning, my mother had an attack of appendicitis. We went out to dinner Sunday night and she was fine. We asked if she wanted to come to the movies with us, and she said, "No, I'm too tired." But she called me up at five-thirty next morning and said, "I've got pains in my stomach." I was over there in ten minutes and got her to the hospital. When she comes out, she will come home with me, as she did when she was sick in August. My mother-in-law has also gone into the hospital. I want her to come home with me, but she won't come. We'll get someone in to spend the night with her until I'm sure she's all right. We are physically there, we are still an extended family—though they are not physically living in our house—because if they need us, we're there. By choice they want to remain apart, but they're close to us. They are very independent little ladies. Thank God, we're able to allow that. Again, remember that they are both Americans. Italian-American they may be, but the stress is on the American.

The Italian women who brought up a whole family of children and never went to school are fast disappearing. Today, the younger women are getting all the education they want and I think that's fine, though I don't think we should put down the role of wife and mother. My uncle's advice of thirty-three years ago would never be offered today. But with all our education, I think that, fortunately, we're still transferring to our children the attitudes that were transferred to us—the tradition of motherhood and fatherhood and family. I have pointed out to my children they can be whatever they want to be and that's great, but you know, being a wife and mother is a good profession, too, and I'd like that to be part of their lives. And I point out to my son that I think being a father and husband is important, and I'd like to see that part of his life.

In my acceptance speech to run for vice-president, I said to my children that my mother had not broken faith with me and that I would not break faith with them. By that I meant that we all have an obligation to our children. And the obligation is to provide them with the means to make a better life and also, within our capacity, to help create a world for them which will be a better place than we found it. My mother felt an obligation to me by working hard, providing me with an education, providing other things and trying to make it a better world for me, and I want to do the same thing for my children.

[At this point, when asked several questions on why Italian-American groups did not come forward to defend her during the campaign when she was hit with rumors about Mafia connections, she provided a copy of a talk she had recently given to the Coalition of Italo-American Associations.]

The answers to your questions are in this talk. Use whatever sections that are appropriate. [The sections in italics that follow are from that talk.]

When I was nominated, nobody was more aware than I was that we were creating history. I was not just the first woman on a national ticket, I was also the first Italian-American. In my mind, that was also an important step in American history, and I was proud of it.

Immediately upon my receiving the nomination, investigative reporters started swarming all over us. Now, that was fine—to a point. I believed then, and I believe now, that people are entitled to know about the person who is running for vice-president of the United States. But as the campaign wore on, it went beyond the bounds of reason. You all know what happened. I don't have to tell you about the stories with innuendoes about our "crime connections." You read them first in New York *magazine, then, more boldly, in the* New York Post, *then more boldly still in* The Wall Street Journal. *Again and again, they bore on the same theme: Because I am Italian, I or my family is suspected of being gangsters. And I must say, that while we were heavily involved in a grueling presidential race, many of the leaders in our [Italian-American] community were acting less like leaders . . . They seemed ready to remain silent and let others shape events.*

I admit, I was surprised. I had expected unequivocal support from a community I have always considered my own. For years, during my terms in Congress and in my professional life before, I have supported our causes. I had helped form the National Organization of Italian-American Women. I had spoken at fundraisers, addressed groups on our heritage, supported Italian education and cultural organizations. In Congress, I worked with the American Committee on Italian Migration and in Queens with the Italian federations. Whenever I could, I worked to strengthen the Italian-American political voice and spoke out against discrimination and stereotyping by the media.

So when my nomination came, it seemed just one more step in that battle. At the time, I thought, What better way to break down discrimination than by having an Italian-American on the national ticket? I saw it as a step for all of us to celebrate.

Of course, going into the race, I knew there would be attempts to smear me. But I wasn't worried. First, the charges of organized-crime connections were not true, and no matter what the media might try to do to fabricate a story, they would not find evidence to support a connection, because there was nothing to find.

But there was a second reason I was not concerned. I knew that leaders in our community have a long and honorable record of standing up against slander.

But I was wrong about the second part. In fact, for those four months, most of our community rolled over and played dead. When the New York Post *published story after story suggesting that the Zaccaro family was connected with organized crime, with no data to support the claim, our community was silent. When the Philadelphia* Inquirer *made baseless charges about my family history, about events that happened to people I never met, before I was born, and used them to imply that my family and my candidacy were tied to the Mafia, our community held its tongue. When* The Wall Street Journal, *in one of the most irresponsible articles of the campaign, tried to link my father-in-law to the mob, never did our community rise up and say: Enough!*

Halfway through the campaign, analysts began to notice this fact. An editor from The New York Times *was quoted in Richard Reeves's column, saying, "For 20 years, whenever we have used an Italian man's name in the same story with the words 'organized crime,' we've been hit by an Italian-American organization, but with Ferraro, not a peep." He went on to say, "The stoning of Geraldine Ferraro in the public square goes on and on, and nobody steps forward to help or protest—not even one of her kind." There we were, several months into the campaign, and it took a non-Italian to point that out.*

Others agreed. Jonathan Aulter, writing in Newsweek, *asked the question we ourselves had not: "Short of hard evidence that Ferraro and Zaccaro associated regularly with mobsters—which the press has not come close to finding—was there anything worth printing at all?" Others, like Ken*

Auletta in the Daily News, *also took note of this community's silence. Behind all the comment, one question loomed large: Where were my people when they brought out a string of such baseless and prejudiced allegations? Why were they silent?*

I don't want to paint a one-sided picture. There were some who spoke up. Aileen Riotto Sirey, president of the National Organization of Italian-American Women, wrote a letter to Italian-American organizations across the country, including this one. In that letter, she called the reporting for what it was: ethnic slander. She said, "Every Italian-American leader in this country is vulnerable to the innuendoes of organized crime. We must stop this irresponsible media smear." But of all the leaders she contacted, only two, Fred Rotandaro of the National Italian-American Foundation in Washington, and Bill Armanino, an Italian-American leader from California, did anything.

Of course, what was heartening was how so many individuals spoke out. I received hundreds of letters from Italian-Americans who had felt in their own lives the damage that such hearsay and slander do. Again and again, they told me to stay strong, fight back, and stand up against those who would use our surnames to discredit us. But there were others who believed what the press had written and told us so unequivocally, "Dagos, why don't you go back to Italy?"

Those who did not speak up accomplished several things. In the most immediate way, that silence helped deflect the focus of our campaign from issues to innuendo. Second, they allowed the image of Italian-Americans to remain stained by unfounded suspicion and rumor. From the coverage that I received, there will be people who are encouraged to think that all Italian-Americans drive fancy black cars, attend midnight meetings, and plot to murder each other.

The third effect was political. The silence of our community reinforced the legitimacy of bringing up the magic word Mafia *as a tool to undermine any Italian-American candidate who runs for office.*

As commentator Richard Reeves wrote: "If Geraldine Ferraro is stoned without defenders, she will be only the first to fall. The stones will always be there, piled high, ready for the next Italian, the next Catholic, the next woman."

So why did it happen? Some have suggested that Italian-Americans took a low profile because they opposed the candidacy of a woman. Some have said that the political principles the Mondale-Ferraro ticket stood for conflicted with the beliefs of some leaders in our community. Either or both of those may be true.

But then why did those people not stand up and say just that? I don't think everybody had a responsibility to support our ticket. But I do think they had a responsibility to draw a line between Geraldine Ferraro the Democratic candidate and Geraldine Ferraro the Italian-American. If they want to put politics before their ethnic heritage, that's fine. I can certainly accept that. In a free system, that is their prerogative, and I would have it no other way.

But instead of standing up and disagreeing on the issues, they let others take the lead, and those others went ahead and raised all the same tired charges against Italians that they always have.

This time, our community let them do it with impunity. This time, the charges were not answered. Nobody stood up and called the issue for what it was: dirty ethnic stereotyping.

Shortly after the election, we found our voice. I have to tell you, Bill [addressing William D. Fugazy, president of the Coalition of Italo-American Associations, who was in the audience.] I chuckled when I saw you defend Frank Sinatra because Doonesbury had printed a cartoon showing him having dinner with an organized-crime figure. And just last month, when White House spokesman Larry Speakes made his comment disparaging Nobel Prize-winning economist Modigliani and the Sistine Chapel ceiling, Mario Biaggi came out to demand an apology. Am I wrong to ask where you and he were last year when those same anti-Italian comments, and worse, were aimed at me?

What is important is not what the events of last fall meant for Gerry Ferraro—that is history. The question is what we have allowed to happen. This time those bombshells were aimed at me. But you know, and I know, that the resulting fallout affects every Italian-American.

I am not talking just about politicians here or just about public figures. Discrimination is a real issue for millions of Italian-Americans every day of their lives. For too long, our families and our parents' families have felt its sting. And unless we are vigilant in our own lives, our children's families will as well . . . What will make you speak up? Suppose it was decided all Italian-Americans should be denied an education or a job or the right to live, as was done to the Jews by Hitler. Will you still remain silent? If you continue to allow bigots to intimidate you, you will always be second-class in a country which is great and strong enough for us to be equal.

After that speech, Bill Fugazy came up to me and said, "Gerry, you're right. Maybe we should have done more. But we'll be there in the future." A short time later there was a terrible article in the

New Republic, which was ostensibly a review of my book *Ferraro: My Story*. The article was full of innuendo, a rehash of all that had gone on during the campaign. I was distressed by it. I called Bill Fugazy and said, "Bill, now's the time." And the coalition wrote a very strong letter to the *New Republic* on my behalf and called the article what it was. With this promising beginning, I hope the Italian-American community continues to come forward.

I have been brought up to like people and have a facility in dealing with people. Whether it's because I'm a woman or an Italian, I have no idea. But it works well.

My inspiration has always been Eleanor Roosevelt. It has never been another Italian-American.

Do Italian political leaders have any camaraderie among themselves? That's almost laughable. Down in Washington, there's a group called the Italian-American Caucus, or something like that, that goes out to dinner once every couple of months. Or they get invited to the Italian Embassy for dinner. That's better.

In the early 1900s, melting-pot values were essential. When my grandparents came here and began to have children, it was essential that their sons and daughters be Americans, become accepted, and lose telltale traces of being Italian. My mother doesn't speak Italian. She spoke a dialect when she was a kid with her parents and spoke it up until the time my grandmother died. The kids never spoke the language outside the home. It wasn't chic to be Italian-American.

My uncles and aunts all had these strange names and diminutives that my grandparents had given them. They changed them when they went to school. My mother's name was Antonetta. She changed it to Anita. Now it's back to Antonetta, and has been for a number of years. But when she was a little girl, it was Anita in school. My Uncle Gennaro became Gene. My grandmother used to call him Gennarine. I don't know whether Gennarine was in dialect, but he became Gene. My Uncle Fernando became Freddie, and Uncle Michelangelo became Mikey. My Aunt Giovannina was called Jenny. They anglicized their names. They spoke English. They wore American clothes. They bobbed their hair. They wanted to be American because being Italian was not nice and you weren't treated well. That attitude. Even my father, who was very proud of being Italian and loved his background, became a naturalized American and got more American as time went on.

Now, Italian-Americans have taken root and gained strength and are in a position to go back and discover what is *truly* Italian and not accept what Americans gave us as the image. I mean, my children are discovering the language; my son went to live in Italy for six months. When they go there, they enjoy the art, the architecture, the literature. They see the true components of their roots and are proud of them *here*. What also helps is that we live in a time when the culture, the fashion, the cuisine have become quite "in." And that's fine.

I am not in favor of accepting all the melting-pot values of that earlier period. I don't want to see us become a homogenized society. We're not. Our strength is in our diversity. Mario [Cuomo] calls America a mosaic. I look at it as a tapestry, you know, one with slender gold threads that go through it. If you pull them out, the tapestry loses its beauty. The beauty of the tapestry is in each of those individual strands. I think that's America. We don't have to blend in order to survive—which was necessary during the 1910s, the '20s and '30s. It's not necessary today. I'm delighted that it's not.